HALFWAY UP PARNASSUS

Halfway up Parnassus is a personal account of the University of Toronto with particular emphasis on the period when Dr Bissell was its president, from 1958 to 1971. The first half of that period was the flowering of the old, self-confident university, with its established patterns of government, and its untroubled constituents. The second half saw the slow, powerful emergence of a new university, uncertain of itself and its role, seeking to find a form for democratic aspirations—not, however, without some dramatic confrontations with left-wing students. Nowhere in Canada was the process more sharply defined and more dramatically expressed than at the University of Toronto. This book records that process from the point of view of a major participant. It is also intended as a series of portraits of major academic figures and as an intimate recollection of a society that is passing away.

It is not a philosophical book about education, but a human document—an attempt to render the tone of academic society, and in this account Dr Bissell has combined, to great effect, autobiography, descriptive narration, and historical analysis. The book will be of interest to Canadians concerned about our intellectual and cultural life, and to academic societies everywhere.

CLAUDE BISSELL received his BA and MA from the University of Toronto and his PHD from Cornell University, both graduate degrees in English. He taught at Cornell and the University of Toronto and was professor of Canadian Studies at Harvard for a year, but his primary function between 1948 and 1971 was as university administrator. From 1956 to 1958 he was president of Carleton University and from 1958 to 1971 president of the University of Toronto. During this time he also held a number of national and international positions in the academic world: as chairman of the Canada Council, president of the National Conference of Canadian Universities and Colleges, president of the World University Service of Canada, and chairman of the Carnegie Foundation for the Advancement of Teaching. He has edited a number of books, and is the author of *The Strength of the University*. Dr Bissell is now one of five University Professors at the University of Toronto.

CLAUDE BISSELL

Halfway up Parnassus

A PERSONAL ACCOUNT OF THE
UNIVERSITY OF TORONTO
1932–1971

UNIVERSITY OF TORONTO PRESS

FOR CHRISTINE

Contents

Preface

This book is a personal account of the University of Toronto from 1932 to 1971. It is 'personal' in a number of ways. The dates enclose the years of my active association with the university: I entered the University of Toronto as a student in 1932, and I concluded my term as president in 1971. I have thus written about a university that I knew at first hand (except for four years at Cornell, one year at Harvard, and three years in the Canadian army.) Of course, I knew it far more intimately during the period of my presidency, 1958–1971, and it is these years that are chronicled in some detail.

It is personal, too, in the sense that I have written about the university from my own point of view. I have not sought the comprehensiveness and objectivity of the historian. My account is highly selective, and describes only those events and those areas of the university in which I had a special interest. The book is unapologetically prejudiced and deeply biased; but it is, as far as I could make it, scrupulously accurate in its factual record. I have checked my memory against official documents, letters, and a journal that I kept during most of the period.

Finally, it is personal in the sense that it places great importance on individuals, and strives to present them as human beings and not as political cartoons. Histories of universities are usually dull, because they avoid dealing with what alone can make them interesting – the colourful, unconventional, opinionated men and women who determine policies and create traditions.

My arrangement is broadly chronological, although, since the book deals in major themes, I have ranged back and forth in time in each chapter. But there is a general progression. There is a general theme too – the change that took place in the sixties from the feudalistic, ordered university that still 'whispered from her tower, the last enchantments of the middle ages' to the new university that has rejected much of the past, without as yet fixing upon a distinctive form.

I apologize to the many friends and associates whom I do not mention – as well as to those whom I do. Behind all the events I record lie the loyalty and dedication to the University of Toronto of hundreds of colleagues, both within and outside the university. This is the ultimate grace that no words can encompass.

I am grateful to Professor William Walsh of Leeds University, who read and criticized early drafts of the opening chapters; and to my colleague, Professor Robin Harris, with whom for many years I have discussed the ideas and events in this book.

Toronto, March 1974   CLAUDE BISSELL

HALFWAY UP PARNASSUS

1 / The Great Good Place

When I came to the University of Toronto as a freshman in 1932, it was like all Canadian universities, an elitist institution in the sense that admission was restricted to a few narrowly designated groups. The proportion of college-age young people going to university had not changed greatly since the turn of the century, and in 1932 did not exceed four per cent. One could distinguish three principal groups of undergraduates: the first was made up of the children of families that had an established tradition of university attendance, although never for more than two previous generations; the second was made up of the children of families that had prospered conspicuously in the last twenty or thirty years, often immigrant families that had come to Canada only a short time before; the third group was made up of scholarship winners drawn mainly from middle class families of modest means with no previous university associations. The three groups were not exclusive, and students from either of the first two often held a scholarship, thereby reinforcing the process of social and economic selection.

I belonged to the third group. My parents put education only slightly below religion in their hierarchy of values, but to them education did not encompass the university. It was thought to be a special area reserved for the children of the wealthy and a few unusually brilliant students. I was not free to decide to go to university; the decision was forced upon me, so to speak, by the winning of a provincial scholarship. This eventuality had not been anticipated. My high school – Runnymede Collegiate Institute – was a new one in what was then the suburbs, with no tradition of scholarship, glorying chiefly in a rapid rise to football fame. The school had no special scholarship class, as there often was at the older urban high schools. Indeed, the school authorities had forgotten to submit a scholarship application on my behalf. A late application was accepted, but it seemed to me at the time to be of little significance, since I was sure that I was not a serious competitor. In the school I had a high academic ranking but this, I thought, meant little in the wider provincial context.

The examinations in English and history, where my hopes lay, were that year unusually congenial to me. I was especially pleased by the subjects in the English composition. Some adventurous examiner, no doubt bored by reading masses of simple, cheerful narratives or solemn discussions of minor, moral issues, had set as a topic 'My Idea of Utopia.' That was heaven-sent to a youngster excited by the more accessible ideas of Bertrand Russell, Bernard Shaw, and a host of popular exponents of the enlightenment.

The scholarship I won was a small one – the kind that usually went by reversion from the spoils of a young scholarly pluralist; it was worth only fifty dollars in cash, but like all provincial scholarships carried free tuition throughout the four undergraduate years, subject to my obtaining first class honours each spring. The news of the award came by a telephone call from a newspaper reporter and even today, in retrospect, it is one of the great, dazzling moments of my life. Such moments are no longer possible now that scholarship has become an evil word and, to determine awards, educational bureaucrats scrutinize bank balances and not examination papers. No doubt it is all for the better; a bland non-competitive academic world has advantages over one in which an occasional triumph took place against a background of frustration and injustice.

I had chosen to go to University College. By upbringing and by religious background, I should logically have gone to Victoria, which was affiliated with the United Church; but my family had no firm convictions on such remote questions as the choice of a college, and I was anxious to assert my own freedom. The strongest factor in my decision was the influence of my English teacher at Runnymede Collegiate Institute, K.J. Shaver, who treated his better students as intellectual associates and talked to them arousingly about the great things that lay in store for them at the university. For him that meant University College, and in particular, University College's English department. He took us to public lectures at the college, two of which remain in my memory vividly as happy foretastes of the pleasures that awaited me. One was given by W.J. Alexander, the emeritus professor of English at University College. As far as I know, it was his last public appearance. The lecture was on contemporary poetry; the main point, as I remember, was the sterility of technical experimentation for itself, especially when it abused syntax and destroyed the integrity of the word. He then read a contemporary poem that illustrated to him the perfect fusion of technique and theme, of form and substance. It was D.H. Lawrence's 'The Snake,' familiar to high-school students because it was included in the volume of shorter poems that Alexander had chosen and edited for fifth-form use. I have never heard poetry read more movingly and more sensitively. There were no histrionics, no self-conscious invocation of the muse, simply a sense of complete absorption in and understanding of the words of the poet. When years later Professor Woodhouse, in his moving tribute to his great teacher, wrote about Alexander as expositor and reader, I remembered that lecture and felt myself back again in the hushed and entranced audience.

The second lecture to which we were taken was given in Convocation Hall by Irving Babbitt, professor of French at Harvard and exponent of humanism. It was one of the Alexander Lectures which had recently been established as tribute to the great professor. Most of what Professor Babbitt said passed completely over the head of a fifteen-year-old, but I remember the packed auditorium, the sense of expectation, the frisson that passed through the audience when Babbitt talked freely about Wordsworth's natural son.

The decision to go to University College was a wise one for it meant I would encounter an English department at the height of its powers, and English was to be my main interest. I suspect that rarely on this continent has there been assembled in one place a group of teachers of such diverse and splendid power: Malcolm Wallace, principal of the college, Renaissance scholar and moralist, whose undergraduate teaching was unfortunately confined to an introductory course on Shakespeare for freshmen (these were the days before harassed graduate students took over freshmen sections); W.H. Clawson, meticulous, diffident, benign, student of Anglo-Saxon and Middle English, gentle emissary from the grand Kittredge days at Harvard; R.S. Knox, Aberdeen with an Oxonian gloss, whose lectures were models of lucidity, the work of one completely absorbed in his subject; Herbert Davis, later to be head of the English department at Cornell, then president of Smith College, and finally professor at Oxford, whom we thought of as a finely-tempered critic with particular passions – Blake, Bunyan, Lawrence, and above all, Swift – and not at all as a meticulous textual scholar of later international fame; J.F. Macdonald, a salty non-conformist Grit, in a department that was latitudinarian and ecumenical in its attitudes; E.K. Brown, at the beginning of a career that was to be as brilliant as it was tragically short, already in full possession of his great powers as teacher and critic, urbane, incisive, authoritative; A.S.P. Woodhouse, back in his alma mater after some preliminary years in the west, now fully launched into his studies of Puritan thought, every lecture explosive with enthusiasm, crammed with fresh observation and new material; Mrs M.M. Kirkwood, skilled in arousing in-

terest, tirelessly concerned with her students; Norman Endicott, a bib-
liophile and sceptic, with an immense range and knowledge of literature;
J.R. MacGillivray, reserved and modest, at his best with senior students who
could value his scholarly sureness and his spare witty prose.

These judgments are conditioned no doubt by the years of postgraduate
association and do not reflect at all the occasional acerbities of undergraduate
judgment. We had our favourites and our strange distorted animosities. I
remember hearing, as a graduate student, in shocked unbelief, that Woodhouse had had great difficulties in the classroom during his early years and
had faced undergraduate complaints about his competence.

The history department, which provided instruction in my second major
subject, left less of an impact. In part, this was because I decided to shift more
and more weight to English (one of the few decisions that a student in the
honours course in English and History could make in a carefully constructed
four-year program); in part it was because I found little to arouse me in the
classroom. The first two years, devoted largely to medieval, Renaissance,
and European history, I recall as a dreary succession of constitutional, dynas-
tic, and military complexities (relieved only by some warm, humane lectures
in our first year by the chairman of the department, Chester Martin, which
came like a reviving rain after a long exhausting drought). But in the third
year we had Frank Underhill for lectures in Canadian history, and, more important, in both third and fourth years I had him as a group leader for the entire range of history. Few have rivalled Underhill as a lecturer, either at Toronto or elsewhere – a judgment shared by a wide range of informed observers. The manner was quiet and undemonstrative; the voice, slight but clear,
was never raised – indeed it became almost a mesmerizing monotone; the
structure was carefully articulated, the main theme clearly set forth and then
precisely demonstrated; the attitude was not dogmatic and messianic, but
cool and objective. Underhill was the satirist of human folly, more a Shaw
than a Webb.

On the public platform Underhill was relentless and formidable, uncompromising, tracking down non sequiturs, uncovering platitudes, making full
use of the full arsenal of the controversialist. But at home with his friends, he
knew how to abandon the acerbities of politics for genial reminiscence and
friendly banter, and for the delights of music, literature, and art. After my
graduation in 1936, I saw him only occasionally. When in 1940 he came
under bitter attack by the Board of Governors for uttering what now seems
like a historical commonplace (he had declared that the British Empire was
moving rapidly towards dissolution), I was at Cornell and could only join in a
petition on his behalf. When I rose in the university administrative hierarchy, he became suspicious of my views and once attacked me in public vigor-

ously for showing what he thought was typical administrative softness towards the quality of Canadian culture. But to be attacked by Underhill was to achieve some temporary distinction. Besides, he did not hold grudges; and in the last review I saw under his name, he spoke well of my idea of the reformed university. When the University of Toronto gave him an honorary degree in 1962, I gloried in the opportunity to pay tribute to my old teacher. In the discharge of his official duties, a university president is called upon to paint some faded lilies; in this instance, it was a question only of telling the truth.

In the 1930s Donald Creighton had not yet emerged as a central, dominating figure, the successor to the founder of Canadian historical writing in Toronto, and, indeed, in Canada, George Wrong. He lectured to us briefly in English history, but it was only much later, when we gave a graduate course together on Canadian literature and history, that I realized the splendid range of his interests and the subtlety, akin to that of a great novelist, with which he combined thought and feeling, the general and the particular.

But the dominating figure in the University of Toronto in those days for me, and for most of those who elected to specialize in English literature, was A.S.P. Woodhouse. He was a tall man, inclined to be a little stout, with a strong emphatic voice; he walked with a lurching stride, his body leaning forward slightly as if to keep up with the movement of the legs; the face was severe, at times clouded and forbidding, but it could among congenial company break into a wide, almost radiant grin. He smoked incessantly and joyfully; his desk was ringed about with empty flat fifties of Gold Flake cigarettes. He was immensely pleased when graduate students in his seminar on Milton presented him with an ashtray on which was inscribed this apposite quotation from *Paradise Lost*:

> So spake the Sovran voice, and clouds began
> To darken all the Hill; and smoak to rowl
> In dusky wreathes.

Behind his desk was a reproduction of Reynolds' portrait of Samuel Johnson, presented by Roy Daniells when he left Toronto to continue his academic career in the west. Daniells has written that he departed 'feeling that a symbolic act had been accomplished. ... the resemblance between the archetype and the contemporary scholar has become more and more apparent with the passing years.' Woodhouse was thoroughly aware of the resemblance and relished it – a resemblance that went beyond appearance to manners and opinions. As a graduate student and later as a junior member of the staff, I liked to play a bland Boswell to his great Doctor. On one occasion, we were looking at space in the college used temporarily by the department of psychology. It was space that the English department coveted, more so since it was presumably not used for active instruction. The room was filled with photographic equipment, and as Woodhouse peered in with growing distaste, I said innocently, 'What do you think they use all that stuff for?' Woodhouse's frown disappeared, his face was gradually suffused with a malicious grin, and I waited eagerly for the crushing retort. 'No doubt to photograph their own platitudes' – and then came the prolonged burst of un-restrained laughter.

Sometimes the wit was mordant and irreverent. At the end of my MA year at Toronto, having twice failed to win a Rhodes scholarship, I decided to apply for the available overseas support, a scholarship that was offered by the Imperial Order Daughters of the Empire. All other things being equal, preference was given, so the conditions read, to a student who had a close relative who had served in the world war. I pointed this out to Woodhouse, and remarked that the ideal situation was to have had a parent killed in action. 'Oh yes,' said Woodhouse, immediately spotting the concealed epigram. 'In matters like these, it is desirable to have an edifying corpse in the family.'

On the lecture platform, Woodhouse was a model of comprehensive and deeply informed scholarship. His lectures were meticulously prepared and written out in strong clear handwriting in exercise books (or, sometimes, on stout pieces of cardboard from newly laundered shirts). He delivered them as if from the pulpit at St Paul's, with intense concentration. He brooked no in-attention; any sound, even the faintest whisper, aroused his anger. The lec-tures were always relieved by wit and epigram, always carefully fashioned, the telling phrase at the end repeated triumphantly. Thus, 'Pope's Ariel in *The Rape of the Lock* was Shakespeare's but with a difference: he was Ariel with a periwig' – a pause, then with slightly more emphasis, 'with a periwig.' He did not always remain on the heights. I remember a long series of graduate lectures on neo-classicism, lectures that were dense with ideas and elaborate historical parallels. Woodhouse was like some fearless guide lead-ing a little group of anxious followers through a thick forest, but pausing now and then to gather the band around him for some morale-building banter. The Aristotelian idea of probability, that probable impossibilities were to be preferred in poetry to possible improbabilities, was illuminated by a newspaper headline which I suspect Woodhouse concocted, 'Man Digging Wife's Grave Strikes Oil.'

In his attitude towards his students, his department, and indeed to English studies throughout Canada, he was a benign despot. After he assumed the headship of the department of English in 1945, he had plenty of opportunity to exercise his authority. Indeed it was said, usually with friendly exaggeration, that he acted like an imperial emperor, dispatching his graduate students to serve in the outlying provinces. Henry Kreisel, who became vice-president of the University of Alberta, recalls how as a young graduate student anxious to get a secure job, he appealed to Woodhouse for help. There was a pause, then the great man said, 'Very well, Kreisel, I will send you to Alberta.' The centre of his intellectual firmament was Toronto. In his heart of hearts, observed his successor as chairman, Clifford Leech, he held only three universities in respect: Oxford, Harvard, and Toronto, and of these Toronto was the first. When on the completion of my doctorate in 1940 I was offered a junior appointment at Saskatchewan, which was the only Canadian vacancy in English available that year, Woodhouse wrote advising me to accept it. I record the relevant passage from his letter, for it tells us so much of the man – his shrewdness, his loyalty to Canada, and his complaisant sense of the superiority of the east. 'I think that there is something to be said for taking Saskatchewan. It has three advantages: Canada, permanence, and teaching over the whole undergraduate range. This last is important. It is much more impressive experience for getting another job than is mere freshman instruction. I agree that no one would wish to spend his life in the west, but reputations can be made there. And a good young man isn't likely to be trapped, especially if he publishes and has influential friends in the east.'

Woodhouse was a devoted and skilful administrator, and like all good administrators he devoted a great deal of his time to schemes on behalf of others. He was tireless in the work of maintaining his two main ideals: high standards and productive scholarship. Like all good administrators, too, he did not place too high a value on innocence. 'Calculated indiscretion,' he said, 'is the better part of valour.' Respecting higher authority, he was often critical of those who exercised it. He had no high opinion of university presidents. I suspect that I fell in his esteem when I joined their company. Shortly after I went to Carleton University as president, I sent him a copy of a book that contained the papers presented at a recent national educational conference. There were a number of illustrations in the volume and most of them were of senior administrators. 'It was nice,' wrote Woodhouse, 'to have this presidential portrait gallery which confirms my impression that you are the best looking of them and have an honest face.' In almost the last conversation I had with him he talked sadly of the futilities of a recent meeting of the university's senate, 'Why is it, Bissell,' he enquired, 'that the more exalted the administrative body, the more tedious and worthless its deliberations?'

Woodhouse's whole life was devoted to his work, his college, and his university. To those who knew him only as the austere and serious lecturer he was the academic incarnate, a dedicated bachelor who was not even faintly aware of what lay beyond his little self-contained world. But his own world was far more various and colourful than people imagined. He was a man of immense vitality and joviality, whose affection for his mother, with whom he lived, was beautiful and moving. She was a handsome woman, at once regal and benign; she worked on her son's manuscripts, shared his intellectual interests, and when he became caustic in his comments on colleagues, she would smile and say, 'Now Arthur,' and he would retreat gracefully. Her death came just a year and a half before his own. He was thrown into deep sorrow. 'Work and memories,' he wrote to me, 'are all there are left for the few remaining years.' Although he seemed to recover and regain his old zest, it is doubtful whether he had the will to go on.

Woodhouse's influence sprang out of a combination of character and scholarship. He was a great man and his scholarship was simply one principal strand of his greatness. He had resolute convictions on education, and, in particular, on the place of literary studies; and in subsequent years I would constantly recall his words and examine my ideas in relation to his.

Like Doctor Johnson, Woodhouse had a whole arsenal of prejudices that he would stoutly defend as if they were unassailable truths. The honours course system at Toronto was the best possible model for higher education – the practice of Oxford and Cambridge adapted and, no doubt, in Woodhouse's opinion improved. The honours course was frankly elitist and indeed should be. 'It should be jealously preserved as the best means available for educating the intellectual elite of the country and as preserving that respect for scholarship, without which education, however functional, withers at the centre.' He succumbed too often to the Canadian indulgence for ascribing the cause of cultural deterioration to disturbances 'south of the border,' and he responded instantly and combatively to any proposed reforms that came from progressive educationalists or 'prowling psychologists.' Many people thought that Woodhouse was simply a British elitist in the colonies. This judgment was profoundly wrong. He admired and loved England, but he was often severely critical of English scholarship and education. Although he distrusted much in the United States, he valued the best in American university life. For appointments in the department he was more likely to turn to a Harvard PH D than to a British honours graduate. He valued Canadian studies (although he would have found contemporary Canadian cultural nationalism tedious and destructive), and did a great deal, both as editor of the *University of Toronto Quarterly* and through his sponsorship of graduate work, to help Canadian studies in the university. I recall a dean of a major American university remarking that although he had designs on many Canadian scholars, he never thought of trying to capture the greatest prize of all, namely Woodhouse, because Woodhouse was indestructibly and inalienably a part of the Canadian scene.

Woodhouse accomplished much during sixty-nine years of life, perhaps as much as any Canadian humanist has ever accomplished. Much remained to be done, particularly the great book on Milton, and his sudden death was a brutal shock. Just a week before, his colleagues had gathered to pay tribute to him, and he had been deeply moved. In a letter of thanks to those who had sponsored the dinner, he wrote, 'When I looked around the department and saw the different overlapping groups (old comrades from the beginning, former students, and those whom I had appointed) I felt proud of having been one in such a company.' He was pleased by some lines I had written:

> A man not for one season, nor indeed one age,
> Johnsonian Squire, yet a timeless sage;
> Whose gay halloo proclaims a breathless chase
> Not of the fox, but nature, wit, and grace.

At the memorial service for him, which was held in the West Hall of University College on November 6, 1964, Douglas Bush, Norman Endicott, and I gave brief tributes. There was a feeling that a great era in Canadian scholarship had come to an end.

My second major source of inspiration and instruction as a student in the English department was Herbert Davis. He had come out from England as a young man in 1922, after an honours degree in English at Oxford, two years of service in France in the first world war, and a brief period at Leeds as a lecturer. Like his friend and colleague, Barker Fairley, he rapidly became a part of the Canadian scene; and the renaissance of arts and letters in Canada after the war owed much to these two men – scholars who were both to win great international reputations but who were always deeply interested in the contemporary scene and enthusiastically Canadian, despite the Manchester and Northamptonshire accents. Davis was in many ways a direct contrast to Woodhouse, the two men constituting a lively polarity in the department. The contrast carried through in physical appearance and manners. Davis was slight and spare; through the rimless, thick glasses the eyes sparkled with friendliness and gentle irony. His seminars, unlike those of Woodhouse, which were a little like parliamentary committees presided over by an authoritative minister, were relaxed and informal. Davis acted as a senior member of the seminar, lighting and relighting his pipe, offering a comment or two, occasionally reading an illustrative passage in his deep resonant voice. I remember particularly his reading of the passage from Swift's *A Tale of a Tub* which concludes with the sentence: 'This is the sublime and refined Point of Felicity, called *The Possession of being well deceived*; the serene, peaceful state of being a fool among Knaves.' As Davis read, we felt as if we were walking down a long corridor, with doors suddenly flung open, revealing rooms flooded with intense ironic light.

The contrast in appearance and manner between the two men carried over into their prose styles. Woodhouse wrote with majestic authority and his prose had what Douglas Bush called 'pregnant succinctness'; word and idea clung to each other tenaciously. Davis was the master of the spare colloquial style, a sparkling stream beside Woodhouse's mighty torrent. For students painfully fighting their way towards a style of their own and in the process falling into pomposity and wordiness, Davis was the best of mentors. He would read a particularly congested sentence in a draft chapter of my thesis, then pause, remove his pipe and say, with a gentle smile, 'You sound very much like ————,' mentioning a public figure famous for his swollen rhetoric. The technique of gentle raillery was never used more effectively and more painlessly.

Davis was the director of the master's dissertation which I wrote in Toronto in 1937 and of the doctoral dissertation which I finished at Cornell in 1940, he having gone to Cornell in 1938 as professor and chairman of the department. The subject of both theses was Samuel Butler, and it was Davis who had led me to that subject. His own chief interest was, of course, Swift (at Toronto he had already begun the work of editing Swift's prose), but he had a wide variety of other interests that lay outside his special field, among them William Blake, D.H. Lawrence, and George Bernard Shaw. He was attracted to Butler because he was in the Swift satiric tradition, but also for more personal reasons of shared experience. Like Butler, Davis had been destined for holy orders and, like Butler, had lost his literal faith and turned to other things.

Underhill, Woodhouse, and Davis – Canadian Fabian, Tory radical, urbane sceptic – represented different traditions and as far as I know, had few associations with each other. Woodhouse and Davis worked together in the same department for many years; they had a high respect for each other's scholarship, but differed in most other subjects. In the late thirties, Underhill irritated the Board of Governors by his delight in cutting through orthodox pretence to the truth. Davis's political views were advanced and radical and he would have had no difficulty in accepting Underhill's kind of social comments. Woodhouse, on the other hand, with his respect for authority and his profound distaste for academic involvement in politics, was, no doubt, unsympathetic to Underhill's plight. Yet Woodhouse admired Underhill's power of lucid exposition and his skill in the presentation of ideas: I remember his delight at a famous lecture Underhill gave on Macken-zie King as Canadian national symbol. In spite of their differences, these three men had certain characteristics in common. The greatest of these was a deep concern for moral and social values and for the expression of those val-ues in the written word. They admired and expounded writers who examined fundamental dilemmas. For Underhill it was Hobbes, Goldwin Smith, and Shaw; for Woodhouse it was Milton, Johnson, and Matthew Arnold; for Davis it was Blake, Bunyan, Lawrence, and Swift. They were all concerned too with the question of style, with how to express themselves in a way that would arrest the attention, both of an immediate audience and of audiences yet to come.

As an undergraduate, I knew well only members of the English and his-tory departments. The course I was taking included two other languages – for most of us, French and Latin – and an assortment of less demanding 'pass' courses that provided an obscure back-door entry to the physical and social sciences. French and Latin, although officially part of our honours program, were not studied intensively; and few of us emerged with any deep know-ledge of the language and literature. We knew our instructors only at a dis-tance in the classrooms. Sometimes, however, even remoteness could be electric. The great Gilbert Norwood, one of the best known classical scholars of his time, gave only one class to our year, a lecture on Latin prose 'unseens,' but it remains firmly in my memory – an unending stream of wit, sarcasm (directed not at us, but at the great multitude of philistines without), and banter. Charles Cochrane, then working on his great classic, *Christianity and Classical Culture*, lectured to us in our first year, but he was remote and overpowering for youngsters never before exposed to scholarship. I re-member more fondly meetings of student clubs in his home, one in particu-lar where he argued the merits of Robert Bridges' *The Testament of Beauty* before a group of sceptical undergraduates convinced that *The Wasteland* was the only genuine poetic utterance of our time. In French I remember best from student days Robert Finch and Archile Jeanneret, but I came to know them well only after I had joined the staff. Robert Finch, the supreme artist – in words, in sound, in colour, and also in manner, where warmth and under-standing joined perfectly with form and pattern; Archile Jeanneret, as prin-cipal of University College and chancellor of the university, the wisest of counsellors and the stoutest of allies.

We were closely tied as undergraduates to our major department and to our college, and were ignorant of the wider university. There were plenty of other good teachers and scholars on the campus, but I knew these only at a distance. From friends in the social sciences I heard often of such giants as Harold Innis, W.P.M. Kennedy, and Griffith Taylor. On the other hand, I knew almost nothing about scholars in the sciences, with two exceptions. The university still lived in the glow of the discovery of insulin, in which Frederick Banting and Charles Best had played the predominant roles. Never had science come clothed in more shining robes; no single event did more to give international status to the university. From friends in University College studying philosophy, I heard a good deal of George Brett and Fulton Anderson. Anderson I came to know outside the classroom. Our first meeting was at a debate at which he was a judge and I was a participant. In his summing up he awarded the decision to the opposing team on the grounds that the arguments put forward by my associate and me were 'sophisticated, but completely irrelevant.' In later years as a colleague, Anderson continued the same salty approach, always with humour, elaborate style, and essential kindliness. I deeply regret not having known Brett. From the evidence of hundreds of students and from his published work he had, I should say, the widest range of knowledge and the most powerful mind of any member, at that time, of the staff. Barker Fairley, professor of German, had interests in art and literature that went far beyond his own specialty; eternally youthful in spirit and outlook himself, he attracted the young. Our friendship began after my graduation, but it seems now as if there was never a time when I wasn't aware of his restless, encompassing enthusiasm. In English outside of my own college I knew well only Ned Pratt at Victoria, and then only as an occasional visitor to his class on modern poetry and drama. It was after the war before I got to know him well. Then I was often a member of his famous York Club dinner parties, where he brought together groups from all colleges and all departments, from junior lecturer to senior professor: the common denominator was belief in direct speech, a distaste for pomposity, and a liking for academic and literary gossip. Ned was the kindest and most genial of men, in appearance and manner a little like a benign, rural clergyman; but he had a penetrating eye for the absurd and he loved to collect examples of pretentious speech from colleagues and fellow poets. I remember the delight with which he produced this excerpt from a chapel address at Victoria, in which the speaker had attempted to endow the Christian dogma with intellectual toughness: 'The crucifixion is not an event in our horizontal continuum; it rather impinges perpendicularly on our euclidean consciousness.' But most of his stories were directed at himself; he was the Chaplinesque victim of great hoaxes and absurd reversals; and the stories were told over cigars and whiskey, with epic embroidery.

The academic world of the thirties was not easily aroused by internal issues. It was led by the president, who combined the power of a prime minister with the mystique of a monarch. There was no concerted movement to challenge seriously administrative edicts even when (in the name of propriety and good taste) they clipped freedom of expression. But this passive attitude did not extend to public issues. We were bitterly critical of the provincial premier, Mitchell Hepburn, who had revived the Liberal party by appealing to anti-intellectual populism and who associated higher education with subversion. As the drift towards war became more pronounced, we espoused pacifism; we protested against limitations on the freedom of assembly; and we looked not to a lethargic United Kingdom for our political inspiration, but to the radical America of the New Deal.

I was generally leftist in my political sympathies, but drew back from activism. I took part in political debates in the Parliamentary Club at University College, but never summoned up enough interest, or courage, to take the plunge into the debates at Hart House, which was the federal House as against the colleges' provincial assemblies. This had the incidental effect of cutting me off from the direct influence of Burgon Bickersteth, who, as warden of Hart House, had turned many of the most talented undergraduates at Toronto to a career of public service. The two most brilliant men in my year at University College, Arnold Smith, now secretary-general of the Commonwealth, and Saul Rae, now a Canadian ambassador, came within his sphere of influence. In a way I reacted against the reigning assumption that politics and public service were the highest calling of man. In the preliminary editorial for the 1936 edition of *The Undergraduate*, the University College literary magazine, of which I was the editor, I wrote that 'the mutual suspicion existing between those who write, even those who study imaginative literature, and a world whose thinking is dominated by vague political and economic generalizations, is reflected in an acute form among the student body.' Literary studies are not, I have since reflected, a dead-end street with an ivory tower at the end. Two men of my generation at the University of Toronto – Northrop Frye and Douglas LePan – who have had an influence on national ideas and attitudes came out of the literary tradition.

The University of Toronto that I knew as a student from 1932 to 1937, and as a teacher during a brief period before the war, derived its quality and flavour from individuals – strong minded, unorthodox, concerned with morals without being moralistic, living and working in an environment that they themselves had created. In the classrooms students expected and welcomed the grand manner and the authoritative stance; and if they mimicked or ridiculed their instructors, it was a form of flattery.

There was a strong sense of community, or, more accurately, there was a group of communities, each linked to a subject, a course, a college, or a faculty, but bound together easily by tolerance and respect. The Board of Governors seemed distant, like a deity believed to be powerful and necessary, but having little to do with the important matters of the university. The Senate had a larger and more expanded image. It was a gathering of senior professors; it conducted itself with parliamentary sobriety; and it would rise to important pronouncements or launch dignified protests.

The university was an ivory tower, but with spartan furnishings, and with many observation posts. It reflected the attitude of its most distinguished social scientist, Harold Innis: the university should be disinterested, objective, keeping a wary distance from government and business, dreading subservience to established power, preserving itself as an immaculate source of criticism.

In the modern jargon, it was elitist, in that it made judgments on intellectual grounds. But the judgment once made, there was a bracing democratic tone. For a time I was employed as an instructor in English at Cornell and as such was one of a large group of struggling menials, untenured and unrecognized by my seniors; but when I returned to University College in a similar capacity, I became a full member of the department, and was treated as an equal.

The university accepted students as senior associates. There was no cosseting, no elaborate system of tests and quizzes; and at the end of the first year came a severe separation of the weak from the strong. For the good student it was a bracing climate, and it led to a strong entente between teacher and taught.

In Henry James's short story, 'The Great Good Place,' a famous writer, overwhelmed with the mass and multiplicity of his obligations and interests, escapes briefly to an ideal world. It is not so much a refuge as a place of simple uncluttered intensity: it is both 'calculated and generous' where one does not so much put off one's self as get it back, a place of which one could not say 'if it were the last echo of the old or the sharpest note of the modern.' To me, the University of Toronto was such a great good place. When I returned to Toronto in 1941, E.K. Brown, who had been a Toronto graduate, wrote from Chicago: 'I hope that you will not come to adopt the prevailing Toronto opinion that Toronto is not only the port after stormy seas, but the crown of North American culture.' I had, I fear, adopted the prevailing attitude, and although years and experience gave me a less provincial perspective, I remained resolute in my belief that the university of my youth would always be a model for the academic society, not even then a place 'of simple uncluttered intensity,' but a place where one could discover oneself.

2 / Halfway up Parnassus

The academic tradition in which I was reared, and which I treasured, was not an obvious preparation for administration. Indeed it was in most respects a deterrent rather than a preparation. It stood for the contemplative life as opposed to the world of 'telegram and anger,' that, according to E.M. Forster, dominates the world of affairs. Administration, it seemed to me, meant dehumanization, a separation out of people into groups, using money as a leash to bring enthusiasm and speculation to heel. I had brushed the world of administration and undergraduate clubs in my editorship of the literary magazine at University College: there one had ultimately to respect a budget and rely on non-literary, practical men to work out contracts and secure advertising. At Cornell I made my boldest administrative foray when I became the secretary of a co-operative dining club. It was a brief experience since I found the political climate in the club increasingly oppressive. In 1937 and 1938 the Spanish Civil War was running its tragic course, and the young Trotskyites and socialists at the club would argue endlessly and violently with the Stalinists. At the end of that academic year 1938, I was happy to exchange community living and eating for a private table in one of the cheerless restaurants where graduate students on slim fellowships or subsistence appointments gathered and argued.

By accident I acquired some administrative experience during my army days from 1942 to 1946. It was, in the fullest sense, on-the-job training without preliminary preparation. During the year before the invasion, I had been happy to follow the undemanding routine of the infantry officer which, amid periods of acute discomfort, gave plenty of time for loafing and inviting one's soul. Fortunately, no one thought of sending me on one of the courses where one was forced to memorize great gobbets of detail about weapons and army organization. A few months after we went into action in Normandy and had suffered severe casualties, I suddenly found myself made Intelligence Officer, on the grounds, I presumed, that since I possessed a PH D, I had had some dealings with intelligence. It was an act of faith on the part of the commanding officer, since I was bad at map reading, ill at ease with any communication system, and hazy about organization beyond the battalion level. In action I discovered that professional training was not terribly important provided one had a good rapport with the commanding officer and communicated to one's fellows a general sense of assurance. The commanding officer, during the first crucial months of action in Normandy, and later on in Belgium and Holland, was Dave Stewart, a Prince Edward Islander of Scottish descent, brisk, shrewd, perceptive, with a self-confidence that inspired confidence in others, and a gruff geniality that won and kept loyalty. He did not command in accordance with the book, and he looked among his subordinates for human qualities rather than for technical qualifications. Towards the end of the campaign in northwest Europe, I became adjutant, a more narrowly administrative job than intelligence. I held this post until I left the unit in Holland after the end of hostilities. The adjutant's job I came to dislike thoroughly. It was administration in its purest and dullest form. There was no escape from routine, and an adjutant of imagination and dash was a contradiction in terms.

Shortly after the end of hostilities I applied for a job in England as a rehabilitation adviser to returning veterans. I had no particular interest in the work, but I wanted an excuse to get back to the UK. On my first short weekend leave after arriving overseas in the late summer of 1943, I had met Christine Gray, a slim, beautiful girl, working in a government office in London; she came from Bothwell, a little village near Glasgow, but the low, easy cadence of the voice proclaimed her hebridean roots. We had seen each other as often as possible during my year of training, and during a leave from the front in the late winter of 1944 had decided to get married as soon as the war was over. As a rehabilitation adviser, I would be close to London, and, before going to Canada, we could enjoy the city that was, for us, a place of trysts and sweet, dancing memories. I assumed that our stay in England would be brief. But Canadian Military Headquarters discovered that I had a doctorate (not a common qualification for the infantry), and directed me to join the staff of Khaki College, which had been set up by the government in a former military hospital just north of London to prepare veterans for university entrance. That meant an extended stay in London – not an unmixed blessing. I knew that I should get back to Canada as soon as possible. The scholarly life had receded into a distant past. I would have to begin again, and that would take time and freedom from pressure.

When I returned to civilian life in February 1946, I was immediately plunged into a special teaching job – a spring and summer course for veterans. At the same time I took a half-step towards administration by accepting the post of dean in residence at University College. It was an undemanding post, so I thought, since its initial responsibilities extended only to the selection and supervision of a small group of students living in a residence on St George Street – a grand old Victorian mansion benumbed by institutional use. (Later, with the adaptation of another mansion into a residence for returning veterans, my responsibilities widened and my problems, chiefly disciplinary, expanded.) An attraction of the job to a veteran recently married and returning to a city with almost no new accommodation was the dean's house at the northwest corner of the college, a structure dwarfed on the outside by the mass of the college, but inside, a home with spacious rooms. At the time I did not think that my decision predetermined the future, but there is a simple law in the world of administration of which I was then unaware: that any administrative responsibility gives visibility and automatically makes one a candidate for higher positions. I had become visible at a time when the university world was expanding in extraordinary fashion.

Early in January 1948, I had a call from the president's secretary, Agnes MacGillivray. The president wanted to see me. I was surprised and troubled. This was the first time that I had officially come within the presidential orbit; and, with army experience still pressing on my consciousness, I concluded that 'higher command' had found something in my conduct that was irregular. It was, I concluded, an insufficiently stern attitude towards drinking in the residence. The residence rules forbade the consumption of alcoholic beverages on the premises, although, I was to find out later, there really was no legal prohibition provided that normal regulations about age and place were observed. A number of the residents were veterans and they resented giving up personal privileges now that they had officially ceased to defend their country; and I, as a veteran, saw their point. Clearly my disciplinary wavering had been noted and considered so serious that it had come to the attention of the president himself.

I had met Sidney Smith only briefly on a few social occasions. Some time previously, Christine and I had gone to a reception for new staff at the president's home; and Dr Smith, buoyant, exuberant, face aglow with good feeling, had greeted my bride in his basic Cape Breton gaelic. He had also dropped in at a residence Christmas party and we had chatted briefly. But I had no clear impression of him. He had left the presidency of the University of Manitoba in June 1944 to become principal of University College and assistant to the then president, Dr H.J. Cody, with the right of succession; and had duly become president on July 1, 1945. When I went to see him in his office, he was in the middle of his third year. It was too early yet to assess the place he occupied in the university. Some of the faculty were critical of his public manner, which, in its mixture of homeliness and geniality, violated the academic canons of decorum; his critics talked of 'rotarianism' and suggested that he had a fatal zest for platitudes. He had not escaped from the bitterness among the faculty and alumni that had been aroused by a sudden decision of the board in 1947 to reduce the term of chancellor from four years to three, and, thereby, to enable Vincent Massey, back in Canada from a term as high commissioner in the United Kingdom, immediately to succeed Henry Cody, who had been elected chancellor in 1944 and remained a greatly beloved figure. There was concern, too, about Smith's interest in politics; he had been active in the Conservative party and might well have had the leadership at the convention in 1942 if he had pressed ahead with his candidature. Wasn't his coming to Toronto, then, bound up in some way with the return to power of the provincial Conservatives, and didn't this demonstrate the way in which the university subserved political ends? But these doubts and criticisms, vague, undocumented, characteristic of the academic relish for mysterious complexities and dark prophecies, had been blunted by Smith's administrative vigour and obvious grasp of essentials. He was the type of new university president more versed in men and their ways than in scholarly techniques, more aware of the university as part of society than as a privileged retreat. When he arrived at Manitoba in 1934, the historian, William Morton, has pointed out, that university needed 'not the cloudy benevolence of a scholar President, but the brisk drive and the dapper confidence of an academic man of affairs.' Sidney Smith had met this need at Manitoba, and during his ten years there, a university divided and shattered in morale had regained a sense of purpose and unity.

My interview took place in the president's office in Simcoe Hall. Few members of the staff in a large university ever see the president's office, and as a junior teacher and administrator, I had not been one of them. Indeed I had been inside Simcoe Hall only two or three times in my life, and then only briefly to collect my scholarship cheque (or cheques, in the later years of academic affluence) from an impassive official in a teller-like cage. I had never thought of going upstairs: that was the region of the president, the Board of Governors, and the Senate – all remote and unalluring.

Simcoe Hall was to become my habitat for almost twenty-five years, but I never developed any affection for it as a building, partly, I suppose, because I unconsciously accepted the popular attitude by which it became a symbol of bureaucratic remoteness and stuffiness. It was, indeed, a stuffy building. It had been erected in the twenties, and it draped itself around the northeast side of Convocation Hall, like a formal cape on a large expansive dowager.

The entrance was elaborately Georgian. Immediately within the doors was a rotunda with a series of formal panels, one exhibiting in brilliant colours the arms of Governor Simcoe, the official establishment founder of the university, and the others listing those who had held its principal offices – the presidents, chancellors, chairmen of the board, and, from an earlier time, the vice-chancellors and visitors. The building had been designed essentially to provide dignified quarters for the Board of Governors and the Senate. The Board room was a circular, spacious room with tall windows facing toward the front campus and University College. The Senate chamber jutted out prominently to the northwest, a large rectangular, elegant room with a dais at one end, as if it were designed for royal visitations (and indeed it was graced with royal arms). The administrative offices opened onto a long corridor on both the first and second floors, and they seemed to be second thoughts, hurriedly attached to the official areas. Upstairs, one section of the corridor was lined with pictures of governors-general and their consorts, an uninspiring mélange of formal garb and pallid aristocracy. (When I became president, I began a campaign to substitute pictures of our famous scholars for these irrelevant dignitaries. I was successful in getting rid of the old pictures, but somehow or other no new ones took their place, and I abandoned the project.) The presidential office escaped from the general atmosphere of hurried improvisation. It was tucked in against Convocation Hall at one end of the corridor on the second floor – a handsome, symmetrical room, with two sets of windows looking out on the campus. It had no direct physical communication with the other offices except with the chancellor's office below, which could be reached by a door and staircase accessible only from inside the two offices. This was a convenient escape route from persistent crack-pots.

My first extended talk with Sidney Smith prefigured a great many that were to follow during the next ten years. There was, first of all, the great human sensitivity that lay behind the exuberance, at times even unctuousness, of manner. Dr Smith quickly sensed that I was ill at ease, accurately assessed the cause of it, and threw in a comforting aside: 'You're not on the carpet now.' Then followed an elaborate build up – general reflections on the presidency at the University of Toronto, asides on a variety of questions, comments on the academic life, and the occasional personal question – before it emerged that the purpose of the interview was to ask me to come in as his assistant. This was my first exposure to the technique later described by the chairman of the board as 'complicated simplicity.'

The job was to be a part-time appointment, with which I could retain my teaching and residential duties with some reduction in classroom obligations. The financial advantages, although not great, were a factor in my decision.

We had quickly exhausted my veteran's allowances in the purchase of new furniture; and entertaining, which we liked to do and which, in the dean's job, we considered an obligation, was a heavy drain on the salary of a junior assistant professor with no expense account. I was flattered by the offer. The president, I knew, had thought first of more senior members of the staff, but it was difficult to persuade an established academic to change his pattern of work. I wondered what evidence Sidney Smith had for thinking that I could be helpful to him. There was precious little that one could point to. But if he had confidence in me, I thought, perhaps I shouldn't question his act of faith. Christine's attitude was that it was a decision for me to make in the light of the plans I had for my future. It was an attitude that she would always take. She was never troubled by ambition, nor dazzled by place and position. Once I made up my mind, she would throw all her energies into supporting me.

I joined the office of the president on May 1, 1948. Dr Smith had worked out an elaborate agreement whereby at specific times within the next five years I could return to a full-time academic position without loss of seniority. It was my first exposure to the legal mind, which views human activity as an attempt to outwit a malevolent fate. It was also Sidney Smith's way of expressing his personal concern for the career of a young man about to take a major gamble.

During the first two years, I was several times on the point of taking advantage of my contract and returning to the academic world. I was not convinced that I was doing anything useful or was giving any real assistance to the president. Initially my principal function seemed to be to draft citations for the presentation of honorary degrees. This was an agreeably varied task. The subjects that first spring were a prominent agricultural scientist, whose main work had been in pomology; the retired director of the Royal Ontario Museum of Archaeology; and the heads of Canada's three largest religious donominations. The writing of citations presented a problem distantly related to the writing of verse; one aimed at concentration, allusiveness, and wit. It was not, however, a major task and I did not like the idea of being retained as a literary amanuensis.

Gradually my duties widened. Dr Smith, who had had a great reputation as a teacher at Dalhousie Law School, and later at Osgoode Hall, was using the pedagogic technique of gradual immersion. Early in 1950 he made me chairman of the university's mental health committee, and this turned out to present in microcosm many of the basic administrative problems that I would face in the next twenty years. The grants for mental health – at that time the leading social concern, comparable to pollution today – came from the federal government but were administered by the province. I was thus plunged into the gray, impenetrable seas of federalism. Within the university, mental health covered a spectrum from the most detailed scientific investigation to the most Olympian sociological study (*Crestwood Heights*, an influential study of the Toronto suburb, Forest Hill was a by-product of the mental health committee); this meant an introduction to the polite but implacable fight for power among the various disciplines. The mental health grants embraced full-time appointments, and this brought up a central and difficult academic problem, the gap between research and teaching staff. The programs depended on both 'hard' money (money in the basic budget controlled internally and therefore certain) and 'soft' money (money coming from outside sources on an annual basis and therefore uncertain); this vital distinction provided yet another basic theme in academic administration.

Then followed a number of appointments, each held along with my three basic appointments in the department, the University College residence, and the president's office. For the academic year 1951–2, I was chairman of division one (humanities and social sciences) in the School of Graduate Studies. This gave me a chance to know Harold Innis, a dean of graduate studies who never let administration interfere with his scholarly work. He was then in his philosophical and speculative period, feverishly consuming books and writing, aware that his mortal illness left him only a few more months of life. I suppose that Innis was technically a poor administrator. He presided at meetings as if he regretted being there; most of his communications to the president came in the form of scrawled, handwritten notes; and he could be peremptory and unreasonable in his stands (as when he vetoed the appointment as chairman of the geography department of a distinguished scholar, a man who was clearly a great catch for the university, on the grounds that he was an Englishman and the job should go to a native Canadian). But no academic carried with him more unmistakably the mark of greatness. He was not to be judged by ordinary standards, and it mattered little if he was occasionally inarticulate and inaudible in the classroom, or arbitrary or casual in a committee: he was a man who had gone to the heart of great problems and issues, and his words were as much for posterity as for the present.

For a few months in the spring of 1955, during the illness of Principal Jeanneret, I was acting principal of University College. This appointment took me outside the president's office. University College had its own proud sense of autonomy; it had been, after all, in effect the original university before the sciences and the social sciences engulfed the humanities; and one could not look upon the principal of University College as a staff officer of Simcoe Hall, especially if one's allegiance as student and teacher was to the college. Sidney Smith had not realized the depth of college loyalties, and he was surprised, and I think a little irritated, at the extent of the withdrawal of his assistant, who, on July 1, 1952, had been elevated to the title of vice-president.

The office of vice-president had existed briefly at the turn of the century during the presidential tenure of James Loudon, but I was the first of a new breed – senior staff officers advisory to the president, but with a *de facto* responsibility and authority in prescribed areas. At that time Sidney Smith did not indicate particular areas of responsibility for the vice-president; the new appointment was simply to carry greater authority across the administrative board, but was, under no conditions, to block off direct access to the president.

By the middle fifties, I had become a notable pluralist in the university. I cherish an official letter from the bursar: 'I have pleasure in writing to inform you that you have been appointed acting Principal of University College, in addition to your positions as Vice-President of the University, Dean in Residence of the University College, and Associate Professor of English, on February 1st to June 30th, 1955. There is no change in your salary for that period.'

The number and variety of my administrative 'hats' were familiar subjects for academic raillery. One morning when I was carrying a garbage pail from the dean's residence to the men's residence, adjacent on St George Street, I encountered Arthur Woodhouse, bulging satchel in hand, hurrying to his office just behind our house. We paused to chat. His eyes finally fastened on the garbage pail; his severe face creased with a smile, first faint, then spreading triumphantly, and I waited for the words: 'I see, Bissell, that you have acquired yet another appointment' – and then came the great torrent of guffaws as he turned to go.

My debt to Sidney Smith is great and not easily set down in a ledger of accounts. We were not, in the first instance, sympathetic to each other. He was expansive and extroverted (although it was always wise to remember a comment by a discerning colleague that 'Sid is not nearly so amiable as he appears to be'), and I was distrustful of people who wore their minds on their sleeves; and there were two decades between us, not so important then, but still a barrier.

Sidney Smith had grown up in pre-first world war Nova Scotia, in a small devout community, and he believed that the fundamental virtues were faith, integrity, and loyalty. Such a belief provided a firm bedrock, but like all beliefs strongly held, it could be distorted. It could, for instance, harden into a conviction that current ideas of respectability and good taste must be resolutely defended. His sensitivities could be aroused by student slights to the moral *status quo*. One of the issues that exercised him most was a 'gag' issue of *The Varsity*, on March 5, 1952, which took a passage from the president's annual report just published, and by substituting the word 'sex' for the word 'English' in an analysis of student shortcomings in the basic elements of writing, produced most extraordinary and amusing results. 'The examination was designed to test the student's knowledge of punctuation, range, and ability.' 'The live lecture is, of course, a great strain on the teacher.' Sidney was enormously indignant, his indignation swollen by this playful handling of the most important section of his report, even more by the fact that the editor of *The Varsity* for the year was a woman. She vigorously defended her position, and then resigned, thereby relaxing a tense situation.

A belief in the primacy of personal virtue was not without its complications. The administration of a large university (like the administration of a state) rests upon an elaborate calculus of the general good; and this can often conflict with individual assessments. The administrator must, from time to time, heed the Hamletian injunction, 'I must be cruel, only to be kind.' He must always be attempting to determine what is best for the institution, not necessarily now, but in the future. Sidney Smith had these generalizing and anticipatory qualities, and they often had to take precedence over his convictions of the heart.

He was a modest man, aware of his limitations, and quick to take advice in areas where he felt uncertain, but at the same time he saw himself as a public figure, shaping and directing opinion, and he was extremely sensitive to public criticism. He had been an immensely precocious student – he entered college at the age of 14, and had his first degree at 18; this precocity grew out of an enormous capacity for sustained intense work (he once observed that I didn't have his capacity of hard work, and I readily agreed with him; no man I knew came anywhere near him in this respect). Diligence, however, does not make a good administrator. Sidney's success was based not so much on mastery of detail as on skill in choosing his associates, his emphasis on basic principles, and his driving concern for harmony and strength.

In working closely with Sidney Smith, I acquired a number of his administrative habits and techniques, or sought to acquire them: the tendency to stake out a problem in terms of the precise existing situation – the automatic reflex of a legal training; a habit of keeping a number of problems simultaneously before one and letting solutions emerge gradually rather than approaching problems *seriatim*; above all a meticulous familiarity with the interests and biases of individuals (his power to remember names and details about individuals was unrivalled, and I despaired of ever coming close to him here). I also acquired one of his leading passions – for his native land, Cape Breton, so much so that it was often assumed that I was true to one of the great Canadian myths and had my sustaining roots in the Maritimes.

Sidney did not enjoy city life, Toronto life in particular, and each summer when the Convocation period was over and the final administrative problems of the academic year had either been solved or temporarily subdued, he and his family would set out by car for the Maritimes. His sense of relief and joy was so impressive that Christine and I decided to follow in his trail. (We first saw Cape Breton in the summer of 1954 and conversion was immediate and complete; since 1958, when we bought a small farmhouse, we have looked upon Cape Breton as our second home.) The little village of Port Hood, where he was born, remembers Sidney Smith well.

Cape Bretoners are not, however, easily impressed by the pomp of the great world. One summer in the late 1940s he went to visit an old friend of the family in Port Hood. 'What are you doing now,' asked the old man. 'Well,' said Sidney, 'I am president of a university – of the University of Toronto.' The old man looked Sidney up and down, all solid five-foot-eleven of him, and then dryly observed, 'That's not much of a job for a big man like you.' Sidney, being a devoted Cape Bretoner, relished the story. The Cape Bretoners' disdain for the outside world went along with great pride in their own world – a pride that he shared. When I left the university in 1956 to go to Carleton College, Sidney had several candidates in mind for my successor. He finally chose Murray Ross above candidates senior to him in experience. He confided to me that although there were excellent reasons for choosing Ross, the determining factor was his desire to work with a Cape Bretoner. He seemed to be suggesting that although he had managed to get along with an Upper Canadian, he was relieved to turn to a man who came from the same mould that he did.

The final period of his career, from September 1957 when he entered the federal cabinet as minister of external affairs, to his sudden death in March 1959, was, for the most part, an unhappy, even a tragic, anticlimax. This period was not an object lesson, as some people suggested, in the dangers of moving from the academic world to the political world, for that leap has been made with conspicuous ease and success by a great many people. Rather this was an individual tragedy in which special circumstances and fate worked malignly together.

Sidney had never completely lost touch with the political world since the dramatic incident at the Conservative convention in 1942 when he had torn up his nomination speech and apparently placed politics behind him. In the fifties, with the continuing depression in Tory fortunes and the growing dissatisfaction with George Drew's leadership, he was approached to stand for leader of the party. In 1953, he remarked to me that he might not be returning to the university the following year; he decided however to stay in his job, but was again under pressure to run in the convention that elected John Diefenbaker as leader in December 1956. Strong support for his candidature came from Quebec in those pre-secular, pre-revolutionary days. French Canada liked Sidney Smith's strong emphasis on the humanities and his insistence that education should not omit consideration of moral values and religious faith. Sidney was tempted, but finally turned down these approaches. Eric Phillips, the chairman of the board, no doubt helped to make up his mind. 'I told him,' Eric said to me, 'that it would have been like an elderly man deserting his family for a young and voluptuous blonde. The prospect would be glowing, but afterwards he would have bitterly regretted it.'

When the offer of the External Affairs post came, however, it had the flavour of a summons to high duty, not a descent to the political maelstrom. The public reaction was uniformly favourable. Overnight Sidney Smith established himself as a commanding public figure and the 'image' could not have been more refulgent: he was genial and expansive, yet sharp and quick-witted; diplomatic and amenable to persuasion, yet firm and resolute. There were, however, some less encouraging indications. He didn't have a strong rapport with the major figures in the cabinet or indeed with the prime minister, who seemed, in an initial joint interview with the press, to rebuff his new minister for expressing personal opinions that did not yet have the stamp of party approval. Sidney, moreover, had never had, as far as I knew, any pronounced interest in foreign affairs; his special areas were business law and the financing of higher education. And as minister he assumed he had the same freedom to express ideas that he had had in the academic world. He gained headlines, for instance, and much favourable comment, by saying that we should not automatically say 'nyet' to Russian advances. But the civil servants in his department grumbled at this abrupt departure from ministerial caution. One of them, an ex-academic, said to me, 'Sid should realize that he doesn't make policy – we do.'

The lowest point in Sidney's brief political career came late in 1957 when he appeared before a committee of the House examining departmental budgets. He seemed uncertain and fumbling and gave the impression, according to one newspaper account, of 'infinite lassitude.' He was dealing with complex and confused material, particularly with the question of the extent of national control and the recent defence arrangements with the United States (for which the Liberal government was responsible); but the newspapers showed him no mercy. It was as if all the latent ill-feeling between journalists and academics had suddenly emerged. Here was the great representative of the academic life in Canada, a man showered with honorary degrees and academic honours, failing to pass the simple basic test for public life. It was, I thought at the time, an example of the hypercritical element in Canadian life which rarely tempers justice with mercy.

From that low point, Sidney moved slowly upward. He was grasping new subject matter and gaining confidence. I was sure that his restless drive, his moral energy and idealism, his great personal impact would carry him to a position as high in politics as he had occupied in education. Then came his death in March 1959, suddenly and unexpectedly. I remember how the news came to me as I sat in on a dreary meeting late in the afternoon of a tiring and frustrating day. The news of the sudden death of a friend is always a brutal affront, but about this death there was something deceitful and harshly malicious. Sidney Smith stood for life, and death should have come only after he had faded away and lost his glow and energy.

II

When I joined the president's office, I had no idea of the nature and function of the Board of Governors. In the controversy surrounding Frank Underhill in the early forties, it was generally portrayed among faculty as a menacing force that worked darkly and mysteriously. For the most part, during the normal current of university life, the board did not exist for the academic community, but in the president's office, it had a palpable and pervasive existence even if one never attended its formal deliberations.

My first formal engagement in the president's office was to accompany the president to a meeting of the Board of Governors at the Dufferin Street quarters of the Connaught Laboratories. It had been called by the chairman to acquaint the board with this unusual and complex facility, always of particular interest to businessmen because, along with its research, it manufactured valuable products that had an expanding market, and it operated like a sound profit-making corporation. But on this occasion only a few governors had turned out and the chairman was irritated and made no attempt to hide it. It was my first meeting with Eric Phillips, who was to be, next to Sidney Smith, my chief administrative mentor.

Eric Phillips communicated a sense of concentrated power. He had a large head with a wide, deep forehead, but the general effect was one of symmetry and masculine elegance. When he was disturbed and angry, as he was when I first saw him, the face became a dark cloud. He could also be genially avuncular; but for the most part the face was relaxed, exhibiting a consciousness of mastery and of ironic detachment. He had a clear, light, finely modulated voice and used it with the skill and delight of a highly trained actor – to demolish and humiliate, to cajole, to flatter, to persuade and to win confidence. He had a reputation in the business world for brilliance and ruthlessness, a combination that carried him to the top and made him a subject of fierce partisanship. I saw both of these qualities at work, the effect tempered in the academic world where the goals were less specific and the financial stakes of a less personal nature. But of the two qualities, ruthlessness and brilliance, it was the latter of which I was most aware – the easy mastery of facts and the quick divination of a problem. The brilliance was akin to the qualities found in a great creative artist – the quick intuitive matching of means to ends. And indeed he had, along with his interest in, and extensive knowledge of, science and business organization, a genuine concern for the arts. He owned and delighted in paintings by Augustus John and Salvador Dali (it was characteristic that he should like art that was technically brilliant, representational, yet flamboyantly romantic). He read widely, particularly in history, with a special relish for the literature of Napoleon. In one of the last conversations I had with him, he reminisced about a novel by George Meredith that he had read when he was a young officer in the British Army in the first world war – not a wide favourite in the trenches. All this was part of his private life: he took no interest that I knew of in the public support of the arts and I cannot recall ever seeing him at a theatre or at a concert.

Eric Phillips had become chairman of the board in 1945. His reputation as an astute and decisive businessman had been firmly established in the late thirties; and during the war he had been, as initiator, developer, and executive head of Research Enterprises Limited, one of Canada's most successful and creative dollar-a-year-men – that hardy group of enterprising patriots who were to direct and profit from such a major part of the post-war boom. Like all appointments to the Board of Governors, Phillips' appointment as chairman had been by the government. George Drew had come to power as premier of Ontario precariously in 1943; had consolidated his position decisively in the election of 1945; and was now in 1948 about to move into federal politics as the new leader of the Conservative party. Phillips was a close associate and supporter, as he was with George Drew's successor, Leslie Frost. He thus felt a keen sense of responsibility to the government, and this meant seeing to it that the affairs of the university were conducted peacefully and economically.

His appointment was a reversion to a strong early tradition of business involvement in leadership. Sir Edmund Walker, president of the Bank of Commerce, and the most remarkable Maecenas that the Canadian business world had produced – his interests, personal, as well as public and financial, embraced almost every major cultural activity – was chairman of the board from 1910 to 1923. Then followed two chairmen who were clerics with a good deal of experience in education, Dr H.J. Cody and Dr Bruce Mac-Donald. Phillips was another Walker, even more dominant than Walker in the business world, although certainly far less active in community affairs. He brought with him to the university his business habits and attitudes. The university was to him, so to speak, a special, slightly eccentric operation in the expanding empire over which he presided. He remarked to me once that his experience with research scientists during the war had given him the key to the role of the businessman in the university – his job was to surround the academic chaos (which could be creative) with a wall of economic restraint. The great virtue was to fasten on specific objectives and to distribute responsibility precisely. The chairman was there to see that the university did a good job of instruction, in the process carrying out research that was an adornment and could even be useful.

With Eric Phillips as chairman, the university followed a dual system of administration. The chairman took charge of financial and property matters with a senior official, first called the comptroller and later vice-president, directly responsible to him. The president was supreme in academic matters – in academic appointments, curricula, general academic policy. It was a system with which Sidney Smith was familiar. At the University of Manitoba in 1936, following a major financial scandal, a 'two-headed administration' had been established, with the bursar elevated to a position of independent authority as controller and secretary of the board. There was no such occasion for the establishment of the dual system at Toronto; but no doubt an expanding budget and casual habits of administration demanded better financial control. The system was the logical extension of the division between the academic, which was the responsibility of the academically constituted Senate, and the financial, which was the responsibility of the lay Board of Governors. It posed a difficult and delicate problem for the president who was thereby stripped of a good deal of authority (although in the eyes of the public that authority was undiminished) and was always under the threat of a veto from an administrative colleague who was junior to him. The system could work only if the chairman and the president kept in close touch with each other and reached agreement on all matters of policy. Sidney Smith and Eric Phillips maintained their close partnership; when I came back to the University of Toronto as president in 1958, I was aware of this unwritten but crucial administrative rule and I was prepared to accept it. Other universities viewed the pattern of dual government suspiciously, as a serious surrender of academic authority; my acceptance of it was based on my knowledge of Eric Phillips and my belief that I could work easily and harmoniously with him.

III

In January 1956, James Coyne, the chairman of the board of Carleton College in Ottawa, invited me to go to Carleton as its president. I knew nothing about the college except that it existed and a few years earlier finally had been incorporated as an institution of higher education after operating for ten years in a vague educational limbo under the Companies Act. It seemed on the face of it absurd to leave the vice-presidency of Canada's leading university to go to an institution with obscure origins and uncertain future. A number of my senior colleagues at Toronto made this point strongly. There was one variant in the chorus of advice. That came from Joe McCulley, the warden of Hart House, who knew and understood the frontier egalitarianism of Canadian intellectual life, and pointed out that small and undeveloped as Carleton was, it was still one of the Canadian universities, and its president would have a voice in the national councils. He would, as it were, become a member of the general staff in higher education. The point appealed greatly to me because I had, for some time now, been interested in national problems and had had a few chances to take part in national discussion. But the greatest personal attraction was that at Carleton I would have a freedom of action not possible at the older universities. At Toronto, I was part of three administrative structures, each with its own complex tradition – the university, the college, and the academic department – and the shadow of a veto, or at least a polite admonition, lay behind every act I took.

After I had visited Carleton and had talked to friends and future colleagues, I saw that the attractions and prospects were far greater than I had thought. Going to Carleton might be a release and could be an adventure. Carleton was a personal creation – the last in a remarkable series that came from the fertile brain of Henry Marshall Tory. An archetypal Carleton story had Dr Tory moving from one small office to another, as on registration day he performed the office of president, full of inspirational heartiness, then of registrar, bustling with forms and importance, and finally of bursar, briskly taking the first instalment of a student's fees. Carleton was a new university in the days before newness was to become an instant guarantee of affluence, before new foundations clambered out of the cradle as adults, and vast campuses arose overnight like movie sets created for a lavish spectacle. In Carleton's early years, from its beginning in 1942 to its incorporation in 1952, few believed that new universities in Ontario were really necessary. By 1956, however, the mood had changed and governments were becoming conscious of the need to find places for great new armies of students. Awareness of the problem had not yet been translated into adequate action, however, and Carleton had still to act as a private foundation dependent upon the community. Thus much of my time there was spent in the community, trying to rally interest and support.

I knew nothing about Ottawa, outside of the rooms and conference halls in the Chateau Laurier and a few government and civil service offices. My most vivid memory was of a delegation to the prime minister's office in the winter of 1949 which, in the absence of Sidney Smith, I had been asked to join. We moved – a little group of nervous and uncertain university administrators – from the Chateau to the East Block, where we were received by Mr St. Laurent and his finance minister, Douglas Abbott. The prime minister was warm and avuncular, but after listening to us, he told us in so many words that the guns for defence were terribly important and terribly expensive and that he was not yet aware of any great public demand for assistance to the universities. The finance minister seemed to me to be ironically withdrawn from the whole issue. I concluded from this experience that universities had no place in the national capital. But by 1956 there were some indications of change; and Ottawa at any rate, I concluded, had its own sense of civic pride apart from its role as a capital.

As soon as one left the Chateau and Parliament Hill, Ottawa became in those days a small town, the old Bytown with a patina of occasional private wealth and a thin sense of tradition. After Toronto it was a relaxed and friendly society, not nearly so rigid and materialistic as the one I had left. As a head of an academic institution I was in a neutral position sheltered from the complicated class divisions of the civil service and the heavy social obligations of official life. Everywhere we met a warm and enthusiastic welcome. Carleton University might be more an idea than a reality but it was assumed in Ottawa that the reality would come quickly. I could not have found a more engaging environment in which to gain my experience in the organization of community support.

I had brought with me little experience of this nature. The University of Toronto, for all its size and international prominence, was self-contained and introverted. Civic politics and the university rarely intersected. To the newspapers, the university was not news except in so far as it produced a winning football team, a student riot (or more likely, the threat of a student riot), or a faculty squabble. The composition of Toronto's Board of Governors emphasized this aloofness. It was made up mainly of prominent business executives – men who were accustomed to command in powerful private worlds, who had no need to be concerned about public approval. At Carleton, the atmosphere was different. The college had grown out of discussions in a YMCA committee, and for the first decade of its existence it had survived only through community interest and support. Municipal politicians, the newspapers, the churches, the schools, the service clubs – all had a great interest in the institution that they had helped nourish, and were eager to hear about it. One simple result for Carleton's president was an automatic commitment to speak to local organizations, and within a few months of my arrival I had completed my stint in the church basement league of oratory and was moving on to school auditoria and hotel ballrooms.

One of the basic facts of public life in Ottawa in the fifties was Mayor Charlotte Whitton, opinionated, articulate, invincible, in appearance and manner a little like a female version of Lord Beaverbrook. I was warned gloomily that Mayor Whitton was a major problem because she had expressed strong opposition to Carleton's proposed move from an old residential area in the city to a new site along the Rideau River. The opposition was ill-conceived if not frivolous, I was told, and presumably grew out of her personal dislike of the chairman of the board. But at our first interview she took high scientific ground for her stand. The site, she assured me, was a bad one. It was marshy and low-lying. 'Why,' she said, 'the Irish labourers working there on the Rideau Canal in the last century died like flies' (and Charlotte left a vague vision in my mind of students and staff collapsing in laboratories and classroom from a deadly miasma rising from the marshes). 'Under any conditions,' she continued, 'it would be ruinously expensive to extend the sewage system to the new campus.' I told the mayor that I had not come to Ottawa to preside over the sewer system, that I preferred to leave these matters to the engineers in whose competence I had faith, and that they had given the college assurance that the site was a perfectly good one and that the sewer system would have to be extended in that direction whether or not Carleton went ahead with its plans. This was my first and last conflict with Charlotte Whitton, and even it was buried under academic gossip about her alma mater, Queen's, and about the writing of local Canadian history. From that time on she was, as far as I knew, a loyal supporter of Carleton, attending ceremonies in the full regalia of her office, and writing me when I left two years later a warm farewell letter of thanks and good wishes.

The Carleton board was far more representative of the community than was the Toronto board. With the exception of Senator Norman Paterson, there were no businessmen on it whose financial interests looked far beyond the local community. The dominating element was drawn from the ranks of senior civil service. The chairman, James Coyne, was governor of the Bank of Canada. He had lively ideas about the development of Carleton, but was too much involved in affairs of state, particularly after the unexpected defeat of the Liberal government in June 1957, to give more than sporadic attention to the university. The real initiative lay with E.W.R. Steacie, the president of the National Research Council, and C.J. Mackenzie, Steacie's predecessor at NRC, and still, as president of the Atomic Energy Control Board, a powerful advisory voice in government scientific circles. Steacie had been a chemical engineer at McGill, and Mackenzie had come to Ottawa from the University of Saskatchewan, where he had been dean of engineering. Both were strong university men, whose policy at NRC had been to develop in the universities a sound tradition of research in the basic sciences (a policy that later came under sharp attack). Both knew that a new university can acquire genuine strength only by appointing good scholars in the basic disciplines. Both were instinctive humanists, responding swiftly to human qualities, knowing and illustrating in their own lives that the most serious matters in life are always ringed about with laughter.

Almost the first matter on the Carleton agenda was the raising of funds. This had to be a substantial sum because the new institution needed the money dearly, and had to have some way of demonstrating to the provincial government that it could command wide public support. The financial campaign, which dominated my first year at Carleton and raised about $1.5 million, a large sum in those days especially for a small institution, was conducted in a cheerfully amateurish way without any professional advice. In November 1956, Jack Mackenzie, Senator Paterson, and I set out in the senator's sturdy but aging Rolls Royce for Montreal. The senator was determined to consult J.W. McConnell, wealthy businessman and philanthropist, about the secrets of money-raising. McConnell, a genial man with the elegance of a matinee idol, who still retained the aura of his great days, talked discursively about money-raising, and then without any overt prompting volunteered a contribution of $25,000. We were all so elated by this, even the senator, who had privately pledged $500,000, that we retired in high spirits to a neighbouring hotel, and, martinis in hand, hailed the certain success of the campaign.

Most of the money was raised in trips to Toronto and Montreal in which I would be joined by Mackenzie, the senator, and Kenneth Greene, an Ottawa businessman who had held a number of diplomatic posts. We wandered up and down St James and Bay Streets like collectors for some unassailable charity, and we were uniformly successful. The senator, a man not without credentials in the financial world, would in a tight corner substitute pressure for persuasion. At the Royal Bank of Canada, for instance, its chairman, James Muir, had fixed in his tough, Scottish mind that Carleton was a religious foundation and 'we have never given a damn cent to religious schools.' The senator was irate and reminded the chairman of his financial interests. Mr Muir relented. Meanwhile, on the home front, Brooke Claxton, his active political career behind him, was addressing himself with unrelenting energy and drive to the Canadian cultural scene – not only to the Canada Council, the creation of which had just been announced by the prime minister, and of which he would be the first chairman, but also to Carleton, whose board of governors he had just joined. To our fund-raising Brooke summoned his former senior associates in the Defence Department, and they planned and conducted a widespread campaign among the civil service.

Carleton thus gave me a splendid introduction to the way in which institutions become part of the community. It also gave me much of that freedom from constraint, from the checks and balances that develop in an older institution, that I had longed for. I enjoyed the advantage of having been a senior officer in a university from which many of the Carleton staff had graduated, and for a time, at least, I carried with me an aura of external authority. My program was a simple one; it was to bring Carleton as quickly as possible into the mainstream; to raise salaries so that they were comparable with other institutions; to emphasize the basic disciplines (in my installation address, I spelled out the main group as literature, philosophy, history, politics, mathematics, and the physical and natural sciences); and to develop Carleton's responsibilities in the national capital. I was aware of the fact that capital cities, unless they were Paris, London, Vienna, Berlin, and Moscow – great cities in their own right – had never fostered universities of general strength, and that, accordingly, Carleton should select areas for particular attention. One such area was almost predetermined. It was the bringing together of the humanities and the social sciences, in association from time to time with our sister institution, the University of Ottawa, to study the Canadian fact and experience. We launched a series of evening lectures in which leading scholars explored the essential legacy of writers and politicians, lectures that were collected in a series of volumes called *Our Living Tradition*. From an endowment given by Mrs H.A. Dyde in honour of her first husband, we began the Plaunt Lectures, in the first of which the economic historian, Jacob Viner, a graduate of McGill who had spent most of his academic career at American universities, explored the nature of the relationship between the United States and Canada. All of this activity culminated in the setting up of an Institute of Canadian Studies a decade or so before the nationalist revival of recent years made the setting up of programs of Canadian studies almost a weekly occurrence on Canadian campuses. The institute, in addition to its teaching and research, developed the Carleton Library, a series of documents and new collections of source material relating to Canada, and an indispensable basis for any course in Canadian studies as I discovered when I taught in this field at Harvard many years later.

IV

Just two weeks after Sidney Smith left academic life to join the government, Eric Phillips phoned me at Carleton and, after a few introductory flourishes, asked if I would accept the presidency of the University of Toronto if it were offered to me. A selection committee, he said, had been set up, drawn entirely from the Board of Governors, and it was now systematically going over a great host of names, most of whom Phillips dismissed with contemptuous amusement (one of the board members, he dryly reported, had suggested 'some damned Methodist parson'). 'But at the proper time,' said Eric, 'I shall take your name to the committee. I will get unanimous support and discussion will end.' He was, I think, a little taken aback that I did not reply immediately that I would accept the appointment if it were offered to me. In a day or so he called again, obviously displeased by my silence. 'What,' he asked in a cool, ironic tone, 'is going on in that vast mind of yours?' What was going on was a balancing of reasons for going and reasons for staying, and as yet the balance did not tip clearly in one direction. I had every reason to be happy with my work at Carleton and sanguine about the future. A return to Toronto had never occurred to me and it had taken two unexpected events to create even the possibility – the Conservative victory at the polls and Sidney Smith's decision to go into public life.

Gradually, as I weighed the reasons for staying at Carleton and for returning to Toronto, the latter began to tip the scale. The University of Toronto was still, in my mind, the great good place. It had given me some idea of what a civilized, humane society could be. It was certainly the strongest Canadian university by the only criterion that mattered – the international distinction of the academic staff. With a number of changes it could easily become a great university: better laboratories and a major research library; a strengthening of staff both in number and quality; a sharpened awareness of its own traditions and powers and a willingness to talk about them openly and proudly.

The city of Toronto, too, was a magnet, particularly to Christine. Shortly after we arrived in Carleton, we had been the subject of one program in a TV series. The script followed a basic formula – a long, serious interview with the husband, succeeded by a brief domestic scherzo. For a parting shot, the interviewer asked my daughter Deirdre, then aged ten, if she liked Ottawa. The answer was swift. 'I like Toronto better.' She was, I suspect, reflecting her mother's views. Christine's views of Toronto had changed dramatically from the time she arrived as a war bride in the spring of 1946. After London, Toronto had seemed to her an urban disaster – a congeries of dull, small towns, dangling from a dark entanglement of overhead wires. And in those days, the official social life in the university was stiff with protocol and inhibitions, a trial to a girl who had known the gaiety that was always erupting amid the grimness of the wartime British capital. By the fifties, the Toronto environment had begun to change: a genuine city was beginning to emerge with some sense of style and a growing pride and confidence in itself. Such change had not yet come to Ottawa: one felt that the city still had only a fragile hold on the wilderness. The official Ottawa attitude acknowledged that. 'It is so easy to get out of,' the Ottavian would say innocently; and it was indeed a fine base for swimming and boating in the summer, and skiing in the winter. In the late fifties, Toronto seemed to us – especially from a distance – to be a place of alluring variations, and Ottawa, a pleasant but dowdy town.

There was appeal, too, in the wider scope that a bigger university could give. The president of the University of Toronto has a number of *ex officio* advantages. The one of most interest to me was membership in the American Association of Universities, in reality no association but an informal club made up of the presidents of the major American universities. I had a natural North American orientation developed by my years of graduate work at Cornell and subsequently reinforced by generous support from the Carnegie Foundation that enabled me to study the structure of universities in the United States, the United Kingdom, and Australia. (In the fifties there was no Canadian source of such support.) In higher education, the boundary between the two countries was far less distinct than it was in many other areas. It was important for the Canadian university to be aware of American developments, if only to protect itself against calamities that had already struck the bigger and more complex society.

Another argument for return was the chance we would have to bring together the academic world and the world of affairs and the arts, never, as far as we knew, seriously attempted at Toronto. The presidential house acquired a year before Sidney Smith left for Ottawa promised to be a great help here. The previous one, a solid square structure, right on the campus, and built in the tradition of Toronto upper-middle-class-lugubrious, by this time had fortunately been designated for demolition. The new house, in Rosedale, was not architecturally a notable advance. Externally it gave an impression of sprawling size; the style was indecipherable, perhaps an attempt to imitate an English country-house; but inside it was ideal for entertaining large groups. It had a large drawing room with doors opening onto a balustraded terrace commanding a view of the Rosedale valley, with downtown Toronto obscured in the summer by trees; on one side, a picture window revealed the conservatory, which in the winter was a reviving blaze of colour. It was not a house upon which one could easily place a personal stamp – the basic furnishings were formal and muted – but at least no incubus from the past remained, such as existed in the presidential homes in heavily endowed American universities: homes that were stiff with antique furniture, ponderous silver, and sombre oil paintings of the departed great. Over the years, Christine was able to work a change. The entrance hall, dark, massively curtained, was transformed. The hardwood floor became an expanse of black and white tiles; the curtains disappeared to be replaced by white walls. The hall was now a place of welcome, a combination of a gathering place and art gallery; and gradually the other rooms downstairs were also lightened and brightened.

The house proved in fact to be a splendid background for entertaining – as a television producer once remarked enviously, like a setting for a particularly stylish production of Anouilh's *Ring Around the Moon*. Christine and I liked parties cleansed of academic constraint, with no official close or ceremonial leave-taking, with the party not so much ending as gradually fading away in little bursts of gaiety. Some were carefully planned, like the one in 1968 in honour of Marshall McLuhan's return from the United States, after a year's teaching at Fordham University. For days before, Peter Prangnell, the chairman of the department of architecture, and a corps of young architectural students swarmed over the house, fashioning a décor for the event: a sawed-off TV cabinet displaying a picture of the youthful McLuhan; a screen for a continuous slide show – Marshall in his youth, interspersed with pictures of triumphal returns of ancient generals; large buttons bearing his picture; and, at the entrance, an illuminated arch with the words 'God Bless You, Marshall,' like a Victorian construction for a state visit of the Prince of Wales. Other parties erupted suddenly, like the reception after the production on campus of *The Heart's a Wonder* (a musical version of *The Playboy of the Western World*, part of the program of an Irish seminar), when it seemed as if a good part of the Toronto Irish community came to the house, and a fair number stayed on until first light, as if they were attending an enormous wake. We shall always remember gentle Seán Ó Riada, composer of austere, Schönbergian serialist music, fervent Irish nationalist, sitting at the battered piano in the recreation room, playing Irish folk tunes while the hours rolled away and a mound of cigarette butts formed at his feet.

But that was a decade later. In 1958, there was only the promise of such occasions. The potential was there, however, and this and the other considerations gradually coalesced into a 'yes' to Eric Phillips. I talked beforehand to those who had made the Carleton days pleasant and productive, climactically to Jack Mackenzie. 'You must go,' he said. 'You cannot turn this down, but make sure that Carleton is well on its way before you leave.'

When we left Ottawa in the late May of 1958 and drove slowly past the Rideau River site, I could see the basic quadrangle of the new university. On one side stood the Henry Marshall Tory Building for Science, almost completed, on the other, the MacOdrum Library rising in formal elegance, and between them, the beginnings of Norman Paterson Hall for the Humanities and Social Sciences. A strong successor, Davidson Dunton, was to take over. If there was cause for regrets and for some self-accusation, there was cause also for satisfaction.

V

On my return to Toronto, I became unreservedly and unapologetically an administrator. Up until then, I had always managed to teach part of the time and I had retained one major academic responsibility, the writing of an annual survey of Canadian fiction for the *University of Toronto Quarterly*. But administration was now to be full-time and intensive. I was to be a dedicated professional and not an enthusiastic amateur. My preparation had been unusually wide and diverse, but certainly not intensive. On one occasion, I had attended a senior management seminar given by a leading authority, but I was a poor student, inclined to be sceptical of the whole process. We were told that in scientific management one must scrupulously eliminate political factors in reaching a decision. My experience had taught me that the exact opposite was true; that almost all important decisions are political in that they bring about a change in relationship between people.

I was not inclined to place too high a value on administration and I thought that administrative arrogance was peculiarly repellant. I recalled H.G. Wells's comment: 'It is a universal weakness of mankind that what we are given to administer, we presently imagine we own.' But although administrative talents do not belong to the highest order, they are nevertheless valuable and often completely absent from the intellectual armoury of the scholar and the artist. 'Every one,' wrote Thomas Fuller in *The Holy State and the Profane State*, 'who can play well on Apollo's harp, cannot skilfully drive his chariot, there being a peculiar mystery of government. Yea, as a little alloy makes gold to work the better so perchance some dulness in a man makes him fitter to manage secular affairs; and those who have climbed up Parnassus but half way better behold worldly business, as lying low and nearer to their sight, than such as have climbed up to the top of the mount.'

The view from halfway up Parnassus is often the only comprehensive view it is possible to have of a university. The view from the top may be bracing and inspiring but it can ignore essential detail or fasten too exclusively on distant objects. The expositions of the middle view need not be dull and prosaic. Administration at Toronto, as at Canadian universities in general, was in the hands of teachers and scholars who had accepted, usually at an advanced stage in their careers, appointments as deans and principals. They retained some teaching responsibilities; all were close to the classroom and scholarship. They were intermediates between, on the one hand, staff and students and, on the other, the full-time professional administrators who worked out methods and procedures. The heads of the colleges had a special role to play here. They were, first of all, spokesmen for the college traditions, concerned more with ideas and assumptions than with administrative machinery. The heads of the federated colleges during my years – Arthur Moore at Victoria,

John Kelly at St Michael's, Derwyn Owen at Trinity – were philosophers and theologians, and they gave a humane and liberal bias to university discussions. Moffat Woodside, who was principal of University College from 1959 to 1963, was more closely attached to the administrative world. He had been successively registrar of Victoria College, dean of the Faculty of Arts and Science, acting president of the university, and was later to be provost of the university. But, for him, administration was a scholarly field, and not an engine for control and power. He turned his fine and subtle mind and his classical education at Toronto and Oxford to the study of the university; and his memoranda on a variety of subjects, written with economy and clarity, demonstrated that administrative prose need not be a pastiche of jargon and flat bloodless diction, that university administration could be a scholarly pursuit.

University administration could be also, despite the popular image, a warm and exhilarating activity. The life of the scholar is often intensely lonely. The administrator, by comparison, leads a gregarious existence; he is surrounded by associates and he can flee from his own self-questionings and doubts to a committee meeting. It is appropriate for academic administrators to deplore committees, but they are secretly enchanted by them. They glory in verbal exchanges; they love to unpack their hearts in words. Even if no decisions are reached in committees, the problem has been exposed in all its complications, and by being exposed, has been subdued.

Administration and ceremony are alike in that they attempt to impose a process of order on human activity. This is ultimately, of course, an impossible task and administrative and ceremonial procedures often end up in a tangle of absurd words or meaningless gestures. University administration is fatal to those who are inclined to be solemn and self-important. That is the reason why most student activists whom I have known would have been disasters if given power. They were consumed with a sense of their own overweening self-importance; of the centrality of what they were doing and saying; always teetering on the edge of absurdity, but convinced that they were marching steadily up the central path of truth. The revolution made by humourless ideologues always end up in violence and a worse repression than existed before. Humour is not a preservative of the status quo; it is a means of compelling examination, of dissipating tensions, of revealing new problems.

Certainly in the later years of my tenure of office at Toronto, there were few opportunities for humour. In the long succession of confrontations, I was constantly urged to root out all evidence of humour from my remarks, all ironic glints, all colourful anecdotes, because in the Red Guard atmosphere that prevailed, such an approach would have been thought frivolous and contemptuous of the higher faith. The undergraduate newspaper, *The Varsity*, became steadily more solemn and more turgid, or in response more shrill and more hysterical; and the style of debate in the council of the Faculty of Arts and Science, over which I presided, lost its political urbanity. This was no time for comedy. The only release came in the convocation period that stretched over the last week in May and the first two weeks in June. By dividing the graduating class into small groups and giving each its own convocation, we tried at great expense of time and administrative labour to preserve the atmosphere of intimate concern for the individual within the large university. I enjoyed the ceremony, but the succession of presentation of candidates to the chancellor brought on inevitable waves of monotony, which I tried to overcome by exchanging light verses with the organist who sat immediately behind me. Both the university organists in my time, Healey Willan and Charles Peaker, were men of letters as well as music, who took Bach, Palestrina, and university ceremonies with a mixture of gaiety and seriousness. At a Dental convocation, Healey Willan sent the following note: '"Change and Decay in All Around I See" – an appropriate hymn for dentists.' I replied with the following elaboration:

> The strains arose and filled the noble hall
> 'Change and decay in all around I see'
> The dentist, laureated, turned and said,
> 'Sad sentiments, but a damn good thing for me!'

On one occasion, Dr Willan attempted a higher flight. He wrote me a note saying that on Sunday his choir would be singing 'Lauda, Sion, Salvatorem,' and that, inspired by St Thomas Aquinas, he had written the following verses:

> On this day of jubilation
> In the Hall of Convocation
> Boys and girls in glad array.
> After weeks of perturbation
> Now proceed to graduation
> Hear with joy 'Admitto te.'

> Some in happy contemplation
> Some in nervous trepidation
> On their Graduation Day
> Kneel in ill-disguised elation
> Hear the Chancellor's citation
> 'Now you're through! Admitto te!'

Charles Peaker's verses tended to have a sharper edge. At one ceremony devoted to the professional faculties, he wrote the following lines:

> The Mus. Bach. is a dreadful thing
> He does not play, he does not sing
> Well paid, he will talk baroque and such.
> He does not care for music much.

I replied with the following verses:

> Nurses exude bedside grace
> Engineers bespeak both pelf and place;
> But teachers with worries fraught
> Behold with gloom their tangled lot.

At another convocation, I noticed that the girls graduating from Victoria College, besides being unusually attractive, had non-Victorian leanings in dress. The following lines resulted:

> John Wesley, whom may the Lord bless
> Deplored all sin and wantonness;
> Surely he would banish hence
> Victorian mini and hot pants.

But in the early days, one did not need the protection of humour or raillery. I returned to the university that I loved and to colleagues that I knew and admired. There was expectation of great changes to come quickly, but there was also a feeling that changes would be chiefly physical, that the university would carry its cultural inheritance into the period of expansion. As Donald Creighton said, in his welcoming speech – a small masterpiece, dancing with wit and shrewdness, 'We shall have to try to maintain our old character in the new empire, just as we will have to attempt to preserve the university tradition in a modern world which presses clamorously in upon us with its insistent needs and demands.' We believed that this was so. Our job was, amid outward change, to preserve what had been developed through the years – humane scholarship, a disinterested critical approach, the sense of a community free to go its own way behind a strong protective barrier. We believed that the administrative structure was well suited to our goals. It is true that the structure demanded of the president great diplomatic and political skills: agility in moving between two worlds, symbolized by the Board of Governors and the University Senate, without being entirely identified with either; a sense of when strong opposition had been withdrawn and action was possible; contentment with living constantly in a world of tensions that were rarely, however, harsh and abrasive. But I had confidence that I could play the role, since I knew and respected the men who could make it possible – the chairman of the board, the principals of the colleges, the deans and directors of the faculties and schools, and the senior officers in Simcoe Hall.

In those days, one did not think of separate estates within the university, or of grievances that came with birth. Students were, one knew, the principal beneficiaries of the university. If they found the classes occasionally dull and few teachers capable of inspiring, they could find plenty of compensations elsewhere: in the libraries, theatres, collections of paintings, debating societies, concert halls, bookstores, playing fields, and gymnasia. This the university of the future would provide in ever-increasing measure. Toronto had never been a paternalistic university. The individual student was expected to make his own decisions and to work without constant exhortation and direction. The new university, we believed, would provide an even more bracing climate for self-development.

3 / The Expansive Mood

During my apprenticeship days in administration, from 1948 to 1958, the universities had lived in an atmosphere of genteel poverty – at first resigned in the self-sacrificing spirit of the depression and the war, then cautiously hopeful as the veterans began to swarm into the halls and it became more and more evident that the campus occupied a place in the plan of post-war re-habilitation. This atmosphere of genteel poverty pervaded all parts of the university. By any criterion, professors were abominably paid. (Toronto, under the prodding of Walter Gordon, a member of the Board of Governors, had launched a program of annual increases that by 1958 had given the uni-versity primacy in Canada: it had moved the average university teacher from a position at the bottom of the middle class to one close to the centre.) There was little money for building, either for rehabilitating old buildings or erect-ing new ones. University College, for instance, remained much as it was when it was rebuilt after a disastrous fire in 1890; an undergraduate of that day suddenly transported to the present would have experienced no en-vironmental shock. The university had its cherished cluster of building needs, with residences and a new Arts building among the top priorities, but we regarded them as the devout regarded the second coming: inevitable but not likely to occur in our time. Most of the buildings erected in the forties and early fifties had been made possible by private gifts, but this method of financing was erratic and unpredictable, and obviously provided no firm basis for the systematic needs of the future.

The atmosphere of frugality and cheerful self-sacrifice had persisted through the veteran period of 1945 to 1951. The universities were the princi-pal instrument by which a grateful country had discharged its obligations to those who fought for it, and they tacitly assumed that in the discharge of such a noble task it was indelicate to complain too loudly about financial stringencies. During this period, the federal government gave a special grant to the universities for each veteran enrolled, but this was more a charitable handout than realistic support; and the amount of money actually available for each student increased only slightly. As the post-war spirit of heroic self-sacrifice and disinterested generosity waned, the universities began to take a cold look at their future. The forecast of student enrolment was not speculative; the children from whom the undergraduates of the future would come were there, in far greater numbers than the country had ever known before. Edward Sheffield of the Dominion Bureau of Statistics set forth the projections in a famous paper at the Conference of Canadian Universities in 1955. 'At the very least,' he said, 'there will be a doubling of enrolment in Canada from the present total of approximately 67,000 within ten years' time.' The Sheffield predictions were reinforced the following year by the provincial government's submission to the Royal Commission on Canada's Economic Prospects. It forecast that by 1975 student enrolment in Ontario would be 92,000, which would be more than four times the number in 1955 – a prediction, as it turned out, almost absurdly below the reality.

The universities now had a simple, unshakeable basis for an appeal for help. A plea of poverty aroused little interest and only an occasional declaration of sympathy; the universities belonged to the top stratum of the intellectual and cultural life, and Canadians had never given much thought, or care, to this fragment, beyond accepting it as a theoretical adornment. Now the statistics demonstrated that the fragment was to become a substantial portion – still, it is true, only a small minority, but a minority that could no longer be easily ignored. Besides, it was a minority that more and more people wanted to join. Recognition of these two factors – a growing need that could not be met by the available resources – determined the simple strategy of the universities throughout the fifties. I was chairman of a special publicity committee appointed by the National Conference of Universities and Colleges; our most effective device proved to be a simple one-page letter to the editors of all the newspapers in Canada, giving the statistical core of the Sheffield report, underlining the fact that in ten years' time we would have a doubling of our university population. This, we found, was far more productive than a national program of speech-making to Canadian Club audiences undertaken chiefly by university presidents, travelling knights who daily slew the dragon of ignorance and indifference to polite but desultory applause.

The climax to our publicity campaign was a national conference in Ottawa in November 1956 under the title, 'Canada's Crisis in Higher Education.' At it we made a polite bow to some of the general problems of education with particular emphasis on technological and scientific education; but the beginning and the conclusion were stark and statistical. I began by presenting a digest of data on student enrolment, staff needs, and building needs, which reinforced the Sheffield report and showed, in what now seems pointedly modest terms, what the implications were in men and mortar. Cyril James, the principal of McGill, concluded with a paper on 'Comparisons and Contrasts in University Financing: Canada, the United Kingdom, and the United States.' Principal James was the official chronicler of our depressed condition: he was an economist with a talent for lucid and persuasive exposition, and his English background and American experience gave him an authoritative position. His paper moved simply and, we thought, irrefutably to two major points: that government in Canada, at all levels, did far less for the universities than did government in Great Britain and the United States; and that the burden on the individual for paying the cost of his education was far higher in Canada than in the United States or Great Britain.

Statistics, however, would not have brought about a change in attitude. We had other powerful forces working on our behalf. By the late fifties, Canada was beginning to turn inwards for resources of strength. The period of easy ascendancy in a war-shattered world was over. The country could no longer drift and improvise, confident that nature and the vigour of her people would keep it on an upward course. It needed a national policy, and one that took cognizance of intellectual and cultural, as well as economic, resources. The Royal Commission on National Development in the Arts, Letters, and Sciences (popularly known as the Massey Commission) had laid the broad foundations for this policy in its report published in 1951. Wherever it had turned in its examination of the whole range of intellectual and cultural life – science, literature, art, music, drama, the films, broadcasting – the commission had found a strong interrelationship with universities and often a dependence. 'There is probably no civilized country in the world,' said the report, 'where dependence on the university in the cultural field is so great as in Canada.' The federal government had immediately implemented one of the commission's recommendations, namely, the setting up of a system of federal grants to the universities. But the major recommendation of a Council for the Arts, Letters, Humanities, and the Social Sciences had not been acted on; and for some years there had been rumours, denials, cynical predictions of inaction, and cumulating pressures. Finally the government had moved. At the concluding dinner of the 1956 conference, Mr St. Laurent announced the establishment of the Canada Council. Speaking in his most patriarchal, and self-confident manner, he began with an elaborate legal defence for federal action in the cultural field and closed rhetorically with a suggestion that the government was extending its concern beyond man as an economic force to man as a spiritual force. He announced at the same time a doubling of direct university grants. The delegates had the feeling that a new age had dawned, that the days of poverty and self-justification were now over.

When the Canada Council was established in March 1957 it had a strong university bias, certainly stronger than had been envisaged in the recommendations of the Massey Report. Half of the total sum set aside for its use, $50 million, was designated as the University Capital Grants Fund. This money was to be used up as rapidly as possible in support of university building projects that came within the general area of concern of the Canada Council, and, in the event, went chiefly for libraries and for instructional facilities in the humanities and fine arts. The other $50 million was a permanent endowment of the Canada Council. By far the major part of the income went to scholarships and fellowships; and certainly at the beginning it was easier to deal with the needs of the university community – documented, with an accepted system of awards, ready and eager for expansion – than with the needs of the arts – unorganized, suspicious of any award mechanism. The government, no doubt, believed that giving the council a strong university bias was a good way to establish its respectability; Canadians had a natural suspicion of the artist but they believed that, in some way, the university teacher strengthened the national fabric. During my chairmanship of the Canada Council, 1960–2, I quickly discovered in appearances before parliamentary committees that criticism could best be met and silenced by pointing out how the council supported research and scholarships in the universities.

The federal government's decision to support the arts, humanities, and social sciences, for both operational and capital purposes, thus brought significant additional support to some parts of the universities. The case for remedial action on behalf of the sciences was not so obvious. Since the founding of the National Research Council in 1916, science in the universities had been nourished by grants and fellowships; as a result, the level of scholarship in the scientific departments was generally higher than it was in the humanities and social sciences, and strength was far more evenly spread across the country. The National Research Council had always been university-oriented. The current president, Ned Steacie, was an uncompromising purist, and he had expressed his point of view at the 1956 national conference with bluntness. 'Pure science is concerned with the investigation of natural phenomena with the purpose of advancing knowledge for its own sake. It thrives only in an atmosphere of academic seclusion ... The University is, therefore, by far the most appropriate place for free and objective investigation.' Applied science, he had continued, was concerned with the development of pure science for practical purposes and it therefore 'rests on the foundation of pure science,' and 'employs the same techniques and requires the same training, imagination, and ability as are required for pure science.' But the public concern at the time was not with pure science, or with applied science as Steacie defined it, but rather with what Steacie would have called technology – those 'who wish to be trained not to do research but to participate in the design and operation of technological processes, in other words, the engineers.' In this area, Canada was thought to be gravely deficient and deficiency meant, so it was increasingly believed, national weakness and vulnerability.

The first phase of the cold war, with its grim confrontation, had yielded to a second phase; emphasis now was on a global competition, in which all the prizes went to the most prosperous economy and the most sophisticated weapon system. The USSR was open for foreign travel and businessmen returned, bursting with statistics and information, impressed in a gloomily cheerful way with the Soviet achievements in education and science. Unless we – and this meant the United States and Canada primarily – revised our timetable for the production of engineers, we would lose the race with the Russians and, without a single button being pressed, we would be crushed and humiliated by the superiority of their weapons. At a national conference on engineering, scientific and technical manpower held at St Andrews-by-the-Sea in September 1956, Canadian business, represented by the executive heads of many of the largest enterprises, had gravely marked the crisis. A preliminary brief declared that 'the economic war was now being waged and must be accepted as a national emergency, and we must thus be prepared to accept a wartime solution to the financial aspects of this emergency.' The concluding action, the establishment of an 'industrial foundation on education as a permanent fact-finding and executive organization, to be financed entirely by industry, performing broad functions on behalf of industry in the field of education, as related specifically to the needs and acknowledged responsibility of industry,' was perhaps anticlimactic, as indeed all actions at the end of conferences are. But the conference, carefully prepared and plotted, and given wide publicity, had a profound effect on the public temper. If this was war, we would do what was necessary to win.

The crisis atmosphere at St Andrews was sustained and deepened when, in October 1957, the Russians launched the first satellite – Sputnik – and an American attempt failed disastrously. Clearly, all the warnings about North American intellectual flabbiness and educational inadequacies were true. To the arguments of poverty and expanding demands and shabby treatment of the arts and cultural life in general, the universities now could add the threat of national humiliation. I attempted, in a speech I gave to the Humanities

Association in June 1958, fashionably entitled 'Sputnik and the Humanities,' to extract some bracing moral lessons from the current concern. With the launching of Sputnik 'it became clear, even to the layman, that great technological triumphs like earth satellites could not be produced by technological society alone but depended on the work of pure scientists, seeking to uncover fundamental laws of nature. The university, then, both as a manufacturer of technologists and engineers, and as a centre of research, could, some argue, have a direct and powerful effect on the international race to produce the ultimate gadget, and it should therefore be given greater support than ever before.' I went on to suggest that the new atmosphere could mean a wider intellectual awakening throughout all parts of society. 'Now that the destructive power of arms is absolute, there exists, according to some commentators, a power vacuum which will be filled increasingly by the struggle for men's minds. Canada, as an important power with no pretensions to be leader in the armament race, may well play a key role in the civilized struggle.'

There had been a hysterical cold war note about the St Andrews conference; productivity was a means of insuring the world domination of thought, ideas, and attitudes, and universities, as the great producers of scientists, engineers, and technologists, were the crack, front-line troops. The preliminary report of the Royal Commission on Canada's Economic Prospects, which appeared a few months later in December, took a more sober look at the economy. In the final section, it advanced the now familiar ideas that 'the pace of growth and development depends largely on the ability to use the fruits of scientific reserve, technological improvements, and advanced mechanization' and that 'in such a world the abilities of scientists, engineers, administrators, and skilled people of all kinds are being called increasingly into play.' The universities were again seen as the key to progress; but a strong teaching staff is the best assurance of university strength, and such a staff could be secured only by greatly improved salaries. In the concluding chapter, the report elevated the strengthening of the university to the first priority in any scheme of national betterment.

The popular economic literature of the day gave an uncharacteristically heavy emphasis to higher education, and drew some cheerful conclusions about its importance. The universities were endorsed both from the right and from the left. Peter Drucker, a popular exponent of business ideology, found them a vital part of the capitalist economy. In his book, *Landmarks of Tomorrow* (1957), he declared that 'The development of educated people is the most important capital formation; their number, quality and utilization the most meaningful index of the wealth-producing capacity of a country.' He argued that education is not an overhead cost, but a capital investment, and that the prevailing attitude toward investment in education must be revised. 'Whereas the economic approach to an overhead cost always implies the question: "Isn't it too much?" – the economic approach to a capital investment always asks: "Is it enough?"' Kenneth Galbraith, writing from an advanced liberal viewpoint in his immensely influential *The Affluent Society* (1958), came to equally bracing conclusions. If we are to strengthen the public sector of our economy, he said, then we must channel more and more economic resources into education, particularly higher education. From the universities will come the 'new class' upon which our very survival depends – the class that will possess the knowledge and the technical resources that can never be supplanted by automation. 'This being so, there is every reason to conclude that the further and rapid expansion of this class should be a major goal and, perhaps next to peaceful survival itself, the major social goal of the society. Since education is the operative factor in expanding the class, investment in education, assessed qualitatively as well as quantitatively, becomes very close to being the basic index of social progress.'

I thus came to the presidency at an opportune time: the need was manifestly great and conclusively documented; endorsement and encouragement came from all sectors of society; the resources were there waiting to be marshalled by energetic leadership. I thought of the installation exercises as a public declaration of the new expansive era, and they were, accordingly, conceived on an ample scale.

II

The installation exercises encompassed two whole days. They were designed to display the scope and strength of academic life, and to bring all sections of the university together. There were three public lectures, one by an English scholar on the physical and natural sciences, one by an American on the social sciences, and one by a Canadian (my friend and colleague, Northrop Frye) on the humanities. There were also a number of occasions, no less dear to the academic than to the business heart, for combining food with oratory: luncheons for visiting delegates where the stereotyped speeches were made, full of polite praise and academic jocularity; a luncheon for staff at which Donald Creighton eulogized, with humour and scholarship, the mediaeval and monarchical traditions of the university; and a breakfast in the Great Hall of Hart House for a cross-section of students presided over by the president of the Students' Administrative Council, Vincent Kelly, now a lawyer active in the defence of civil liberties; his vice-president, also present, was Adrienne Poy, now, as Adrienne Clarkson, a television interviewer, novelist, and lively opinion-maker.

The installation ceremony itself was held in Convocation Hall and concluded with the awarding of honorary degrees. This had been a matter that aroused considerable heat. The choice of honorary graduands was the responsibility of a committee of the Senate, but the Board of Governors, by tradition and through its representatives on the committee, took a keen interest in the choice. Some members of the board were known to favour strongly the granting of an honorary degree to John Diefenbaker, the prime minister. It had been a long time since the board, always strongly Conservative in its political sympathies, had had the chance to propose a Conservative prime minister for a degree. Mr Diefenbaker's popularity and influence were at their highest; his erratic populism had not yet begun to bring sober second thoughts to old-time Tory supporters. I was not opposed to a degree for Mr Diefenbaker, and supported the proposal when it came before the Senate later on; but at this particular time it seemed to me to be completely wrong. It would have had the effect of turning an academic celebration into a political event, given Mr Diefenbaker's skill in self-dramatization. My attitude did not please the chairman. Although Eric Phillips was not a strong Diefenbaker supporter, and, like so many Canadian business leaders, eventually deserted him, he was anxious to please his colleagues on the board. It was an unwritten law of the board that no serious request from one of its senior members should be ignored. Sidney Smith, now in the Diefenbaker cabinet, reported a telephone conversation in which Phillips expressed regret at having invited me to return to Toronto. But Sidney saw my point, and spoke to Phillips; the idea of giving Mr Diefenbaker a degree was quietly withdrawn and the Senate committee proceeded to bring forward a severely academic trio: Gerhard Herzberg, a physicist at the National Research Council, whose designation as the most distinguished Canadian physicist was to be reinforced fifteen years later when he was awarded the Nobel prize; Monsignor Irénée Lussier, rector of the University of Montreal, who personified the grace and the eloquence of the French-Canadian academic tradition; William Lewis Morton, professor of history at the University of Manitoba, a scrupulous research scholar, an accomplished stylist, and a man of strong convictions.

I had a theory that installation speeches should resist theorizing on the grand scale and should concentrate on the particular problems of the institution concerned. Thus, my Carleton installation speech had tried to sketch out a role for the new university – a middle power with special concern for national Canadian problems. In the Toronto speech I was saying, not directly, but not too obliquely either, that the University of Toronto was the great Canadian university, 'the successful fusion in an institution of the intellectual trends of the last century', 'the custodian of the excellent', a public university with a 'tradition of vigorous individualism.' I emphasized the virtues of federation and of the honours course system, and dwelt at length on

Toronto's record of achievement in scholarship. If there was an overriding
moral, it was that a university of such strength and diversity could respond
to the forces of change and growth, and not only survive but grow stronger.

In addition to the main argument of the speech, there were of course the
ritual flourishes, pious roll calls of the mighty dead, and a rhetorical confrontation of the future. It was too long, as my colleagues and my daughter, then
aged eleven, pointed out. During its delivery, those of us on the platform
were under the full glare of TV lights (then powerful, merciless devices) – as it
turned out, an empty martyrdom since, to my knowledge, not one shot
reached the television screen.

But despite the protocol, the tensions, and inevitable tedium, the installation ceremony was a happy event. My favourite academic picture was taken
just after I had finished speaking. A group of students in the top balcony rose
and sang the Varsity Alma Mater. An alert photographer caught the reaction
on the platform: I am looking up, still nervously clasping my notes, an expression of mingled relief and delight on my face; the chairman and the
chancellor are smiling broadly; behind me on the platform, colleagues, many
of them old associates, are caught up joyfully in the excitement of the moment. This is a picture that seems now to belong to another age. Some years
later, in the midst of student upheavals, I ventured in an opening address to
students to quote some lines from Yeats:

> How but in custom and in ceremony
> Are innocence and beauty born?
> Ceremony's a name for the rich horn,
> And custom for the spreading laurel tree.

I had in mind, among other things, my own installation ceremonies. In
1968, the quotation seemed to the student journalists a reactionary imperti-
nence.

Such elaborate installation procedures are now in eclipse. Harvard, always
a sure indicator, installed its new president with conspicuous casualness, as if
to suggest that this was only an incident in the great flow of events. The installation of my successor, John Evans, in 1972, was a single occasion in the
open air with a minimum of formalities and a complete absence of attendant
events. The orderly, ritualistic, yet relaxed solemnities of my installation in
1958 belonged to an age that has passed.

I had returned to Toronto in the knowledge that a high priority would be
the financial campaign. Sidney Smith and the board had already prepared the
way: they had determined the general scope of a private appeal and, what
was most important, had worked out a co-operative agreement with the fed-

erated colleges whereby there would be a unified approach, a proportionate distribution of contributions, and a proportionate sharing of expenses. This required delicate diplomacy, for federated college autonomy was intense, and at times the government-subsidized university seemed to them like a flighty woman divorced from the church and now married to an affluent and amoral lover. The agreement thus represented a considerable achievement. With a firm base within the university and a climate of opinion without that grew more favourable every day, there could not have been a better time for seeking money.

The University of Toronto needed such ideal conditions, for it had had an indifferent record of institutional fund raising. On two occasions, long since passed, the alumni themselves had raised considerable sums: early in the century for Convocation Hall; and in the early twenties, for the Memorial Tower. But the major gifts that had come to the university had been providential, like the sudden, unheralded bequest that enabled the Wallberg Building to be erected; or the family philanthropies of the Masseys directed towards specific interests – a residence at Victoria, a building for Household Science, and, above all, Hart House. No concerted campaign had ever been launched. There had been one hesitant, ill-prepared, and ill-fated attempt shortly after I joined the president's office; but it had been discreetly abandoned. Now, all was different; the board was prepared for action.

As the professional fund raisers monotonously reiterated, a financial campaign was completely dependent on its leadership. And the board had acquired two ideal leaders, who had joined it in full knowledge of the time-consuming role they were expected to play. Wallace McCutcheon was an honours graduate of the university in mathematics and physics, who had then taken a law degree and had subsequently risen quickly in the world of finance. He was a close associate of Eric Phillips, and he had an easy command over the entire Canadian network of big business. He was devoted to the university, where he had done brilliantly and had laid the foundations of his career; and he was prepared for a period to make the campaign his chief concern. McCutcheon had a quick, powerful mind that could be ruthlessly harnessed to a given purpose; but the mind was balanced by an engaging, ironic wit. His associate and co-chairman was Neil McKinnon, recently appointed president of the Canadian Bank of Commerce; a central, institutional figure to match McCutcheon's entrepreneurial eminence. In the traditional bank style, McKinnon had risen by native wit and industry, without having a university imprint; but he had a strong intellectual bias and was more sympathetic to liberal education than were many of his fellow board members who had professional university degrees. In manner, he was a sharp contrast to McCutcheon. He was quiet-spoken and undemonstrative, with a banker's assurance that large sums of money contain their own eloquence.

Below the co-chairmen, there was built an elaborate network of committees drawn from prominent graduates and from advertising and public relations officers who were relieved of their duties to work for the university. At Carleton, we had not used fund raisers. There were few alumni to organize, and since Carleton was a young and unknown university, it was difficult for fund raisers to conduct their preliminary exercises in probable expectations. Toronto was another story: the alumni were an army of over 100,000, apparently at the time on permanent leave but prepared, one hoped, for a call to the colours. Through the Board of Governors and through her graduates, the university reached into every corporate boardroom in the country. The task of the fund raisers was to provide the rear echelons for the forward troops.

The professionals also liked to set the tone and write the major releases, in particular the campaign brochure. At this time, hundreds of universities were asking for money and the mail brought with it every day another florid example of the fund raiser's art. The brochures had certain predictable characteristics: on the first page, there would be little jewels of quotations about the glory of the university; this would be followed by a 'think' piece densely written, loosely suggesting that national affluence and security depended upon the success of this particular campaign; then there would be a few comments on the peculiar virtues of the given institution with a great many illustrations – white-smocked students in laboratories, peering into microscopes, or gravely contemplating labyrinths of glass tubes; students gathered around the table before an expounding professor, or sitting in thoughtful rows in lectures. Our brochure belonged to the general type but we did the writing ourselves, controlling the verbal inflation, and insisting that the institution should not be thrown in as an example but should be put squarely and fully at the centre. What picture could be used, we speculated, to symbolize the University of Toronto and to bring it vividly and warmly to the attention of graduates? The answer was clear: an undergraduate kneeling before the chancellor to receive his degree. Samuel Beatty, the chancellor of the time, a great teacher of mathematics, fondly remembered by thousands of undergraduates, and an undergraduate, John Roberts, who later became a Liberal member of Parliament, posed for the photograph. Throughout the brochure, we emphasized Toronto history and tradition. The model for our brochure was an earlier one produced by Harvard, and subsequent publicity underlined the association – we were the Harvard of Canada in national eminence, and in the variety and toughness of our cultural and social traditions.

The campaign was a great success. When the official launching took place on May 23, 1959, we had already collected substantial sums and by the following October, when 5,000 alumni canvassers moved into action, the sum had reached $5 million. At the close of the campaign in May 1960, the total had passed $15 million, exclusive of the contribution of $2 million for social work and business that McCutcheon had coaxed from the Metropolitan Toronto council. This was, in Canadian terms, a triumph – the largest sum ever raised by public appeal.

The money had been raised in an atmosphere of ebullient goodwill. The mass circulation magazines wrote pieces on the university, sprinkled with cheerful anecdotes and lists of achievements – notably, pablum, insulin, and the works of Harold Innis. In suggesting that the campaign had a national urgency, the newspapers were almost fulsomely co-operative. The only small cloud on the horizon was the complaint of one Toronto paper that a substantial portion of the money flowing into Toronto's coffers should be directed to the university's latest child, York College, as yet unformed but already sensing its imperial destiny.

In the campaign literature we estimated that the total expansion program would cost $52 million. The money from the campaign would thus make up almost one-third of our needs. In the event the $52 million doubled, then more than doubled again; and over the years the campaign steadily shrank in absolute importance. But it nevertheless had a lasting impact. It proclaimed the university's commitment to growth and established the psychology of expansion. After the campaign, I continued to give a high priority to fund raising, shifting the emphasis to specific academic projects. Despite the increasing turbulence within the university world, the alumni gave their untroubled support. Graduates living in the United States, through an association incorporated in 1957, responded with conspicuous generosity, as if they sensed in the University of Toronto a star to every wandering bark.

Until about 1965, I spent the largest share of my time on problems associated with the physical expansion of the university; in helping to work out, often over long periods, the delicate accommodations and compromises that finally brought the wishes of users, builders, and governors into alignment. We had begun with a plan for the new area of campus that was to rise west of St George – not much more than a rough scheme that incorporated academic priorities and conveniences – but it was not until early in 1964 that the board established a permanent planning division. This division was an expansion of a three-man team led by a young architect, John Andrews, that had been given the task of planning the new campus at Scarborough, in the suburbs some 20 miles to the east of the original university. In his enthusiasm, Andrews had gone beyond his terms of reference, and had designed the actual building for the college. Carl Williams, then in charge of academic development at Scarborough, and I were delighted by his concept, bold and imaginative, yet a reasoned growth from the facts of the environment and the character of the college; and I was happy at the prospect of breaking free from the style of the central campus, constrained by the pattern of city streets and the conventional approach of established architects. John Andrews was an Australian who had left the University of Sydney to do graduate work at Harvard. He had moved here after his design had been the runner-up in the competition for Toronto's new city hall. He was the kind of architect that the board so far had scrupulously avoided: young and inexperienced, and the board valued age and experience; contemptuous of the approach to a building in terms of a specific style, and the board had a collective preference for homogenized Georgian; abrupt and unapologetic in his presentation of a scheme, and the board valued a smooth sales pitch. But at the same time they were impressed by Andrews: by his self-confidence and his unruffled boyish arrogance, by his easy grasp of detail and his swift response to practical needs.

Scarborough College became one of the most famous buildings of the decade, the subject of long and rhapsodic studies in both national and international architectural magazines – stark, almost brutal in appearance, but on the inside affording great vistas, cunning corridors, and the skilful integration of many functions. It aroused violent reactions. When it was close to completion, I took a group of visiting Ontario university presidents through it, and they moved as in a daze, stunned by the building's total repudiation of every collegiate sanctity. But whatever one might think of the building, it worked; and the initial protests died down and disappeared. In architecture, artistic judgment is a carnival of relativism. One man's horror is another man's Taj Mahal.

Scarborough did not, however, compensate, in the eyes of critics, for the general level of dullness of the new buildings that rose on the St George campus and the absence there of any strong coherent plan. With much of this criticism, coming from both without and within the university, I was in agreement, although there were, I thought, good individual buildings – the Edward Johnson Building for the Faculty of Music, the extension for the Law Building, New College, Massey College (although Massey was not of university doing), and, later on, the Robarts Library (subjected to as much elephantine banter as Scarborough, although with more cause).

As the years passed, I became less sure of the virtue of a single dominating plan. New campuses that had been planned in this way often look like the work of a mechanically-minded deity more concerned with scale and proportion than with human values. Besides, the architectural mark of the Toronto campus had long been bold heterogeneity. The university believed in mirroring taste, not in trying to arrest it.

One essential condition for the integration of the original part of the campus and the new section to the west of St George Street had been denied us – the closing or sinking of that main thoroughfare, which cut through the university like a polluted commercial canal. At least we had kept inviolate the ample green areas of the old campus, now ringed about visually by the glowering sentinels of skyscrapers.

The pace of physical expansion decreased rapidly after 1965, and by 1970 had almost come to a complete stop. It was a period not likely to come again in the century – a prospect not without charms. I was impatient of those who summarized a period by the number of buildings that had been erected, and calculated presidential success in gross cubic feet. For me, physical expansion of a university was healthy only if it were the visible outline of an academic plan.

4 / College Ties

The general plan of expansion, already formulated by a committee of the Board of Governors, called for a concentration of effort in the two faculties that anticipated a doubling of enrolment – Arts and Science, and Applied Science and Engineering; and the campaign brochure, which presented a simplified picture of the proposed expansion, reflected these priorities. I insisted also on a clear recognition of library needs, for I was convinced that Toronto would always remain a good, solid second-class university until library resources were tripled and placed on a footing comparable with those of a few major universities in the United States. The sum arbitrarily set aside for library development in the brochure was $2 million. That amount was ridiculously inadequate, but at this stage the important point was to attach a dollar sign to pious declaration of intent. Medicine did not appear in the original list of capital needs, because that faculty was content with the size of its educational commitment and had made no request for physical expansion. But Wallace McCutcheon, who had a deep interest in medical affairs, argued strongly against going to the public without any reference to the part of the university that most concerned the average person, and so we put in a sum for facilities for medical research.

In one area the plan served the university badly. Additional residential accommodation, conservatively estimated at 1,600 places, was to be provided in a vast high-rise development that was to stretch along Spadina Avenue, the new western boundary of the campus. The buildings were, so I was informed, to constitute, along with parking lots, a great wall against the noise and dreariness of the city. The proposals had a brisk, reasonable quality about them. They were buttressed by statistics and coloured diagrams. And –

this was the clinching argument – they followed the directions of the Board of Governors about economy.

The board's general theory of university expansion was simple and direct. The University of Toronto, as the largest university in the principal city in the province, with direct provincial responsibilities, was to expand as quickly and as economically as possible. Business practice was to be the model: buildings must be factory-like in design and materials; residences must be designed so as to contain as many bodies as possible in as little space as possible. The University of Toronto, it was then believed, could contain the major part of the provincial growth in enrolment; with its strong basis, it could achieve economy of scale, and at the same time receive the blessings of the government.

None of these ideas was explicitly drawn out and expounded in public, but they were sharply enunciated in private. They could be defended in some areas – say, in the provision of laboratory space; but, for the sake of relatively small savings, the proposed concentration and extreme economy in residence building would have undermined the traditional university. Residences had always been considered part of the academic life of the colleges. I was determined to fight the proposals for faceless dormitories. Our scientific planning had completely ignored history and tradition.

History and tradition were bound up with the principle of federation. That principle was embodied in the Act of 1887 and implemented by the federation between the University of Toronto – secular and public – and three other universities – Victoria, Trinity, and St Michael's – religious and private. It was the most distinctive characteristic of the University of Toronto. Indeed, it was a major national characteristic, in sharp distinction to the American approach of segregating the secular and the religious, the public and the private. Victoria, Trinity, and St Michael's all brought with them strong residential traditions. The residence was thought of as an important educational agency, a means of creating a healthy moral and religious environment. With the passage of years the motive lost its paternalistic and doctrinaire character, and became social and intellectual. Residence life was thus woven into the life of the university: it was associated with the preservation of the small decentralized group, and with education conceived of as unspecialized and liberating.

Fortunately I had strong forces working on my side. Before I went to Carleton, the university had established an academic 'plateau committee' (presciently so-called by Sidney Smith because he believed we were dealing not with a sudden bulge, but with a new and higher plateau that stretched out endlessly in the future). This committee, under the chairmanship of Gilbert

Robinson of the mathematics department, recommended 'that in order to keep the "unit" small, two small colleges should be established.' But a division of the university into small 'units' out of concern for the individual would strike the board as extravagant. I needed a wider and more compulsive argument. I therefore emphasized the divisive nature of the proposal; the apartment-residences would split the university in two. On the old campus, east of St George, we would have a university based upon a federated college principle, and on the new campus, west of St George, we would have a big unitary structure. This would be like trying to graft Michigan State onto Oxford.

It was important for my case that University College and the professional faculties should take a sympathetic attitude toward further development of the college and residential system. The federated colleges had their own residential plans and they would not have any natural enthusiasm for the founding of additional colleges under the control of the university. But the problem at University College was different. Given the prospect of a Faculty of Arts of some 12,000 by 1968, and the reluctance of the federated colleges to let themselves become too big, University College could eventually find itself with 4,000 students – in short, no college at all, a faceless holding unit and not a regiment. We could on the other hand establish a maximum enrolment for University College of, say, about 2,000. Then, given the university's policy that all Arts students must enrol in a college, there would be a clear argument for the establishment of new colleges and the consequent division of residence accommodation among them. At my request, the board established a committee on the future of University College with college representation, and it brought in, as I had anticipated, a recommendation that the college enrolment should not, under any circumstances, exceed 2,000.

So far so good. Now I needed the support of the professional faculties – particularly the large ones, Applied Science and Engineering, Medicine, and Dentistry. They were completely outside the college system, and except for Devonshire House, which was the least attractive and the most neglected of the residences, their students could obtain accommodation on campus only on sufferance from the Arts colleges. Why not establish a multi-faculty principle for the new colleges? This could apply both to their residences and to their academic undertakings. Indeed, it might be advantageous to have one college with a professional bias. I discussed these matters with colleagues in the professional faculties and got a favourable (if unenthusiastic) response.

A confirmation and detailed exposition of these policies came in a report that I asked T.H.B. Symons to make. (At that time, Tom Symons was dean of Devonshire House; he was shortly to become president of the new Trent University.) Symons had been unusually successful in creating an *esprit* at

Devonshire, despite a long record of neglect by the university of that residence, and despite also the tradition of hearty, boisterous living thought to be appropriate for young apprentices in Medicine and Engineering. In his report he emphasized the need to bring together the professional faculties and the Faculty of Arts and Science, to make each aware of, and sympathetic to, what the other was doing; and he envisaged a university in which all students had a college connection. This was far too delicate and expensive fare for the Board of Governors, but the recommendations were helpful in formulating my own ideas and in determining what was possible.

At this time, there appeared a champion of the college idea who was ready and able to give it a specific expression. That was Vincent Massey. The idea of a small residential college for graduate students had been forming in his mind for some time. When I was at Carleton, and he was governor-general, he had summoned me to Rideau Hall to introduce and discuss the idea; he had subsequently had a number of talks with Eric Phillips, whose acumen he admired and whose power he respected. I was enthusiastic about his proposal. I thought that his concept embodied ideas that had largely vanished from the university scene in Canada and that needed to be kept alive, if only as a reminder, a warning, and a counterforce. In Mr Massey's concept, the college would be small – far smaller than even the smallest residential unit contemplated in the university plan; it would be exclusively for graduate students, and this at a time when almost no attention was being given to graduate students; and it would be selective, just when the educational world was confounding and confusing the ideas of democracy and equality.

As the concept moved toward its final form, and as Mr Massey prepared to make a definite offer of the building to the university on behalf of the Massey Foundation, I could see emerging a central administrative problem. In his fear of government interference, particularly from a parochial provincial government, and in his reservations about the collective wisdom of the Board of Governors (of which he was a member), Mr Massey was insisting that the college have a high degree of autonomy. Yet it could not have complete autonomy, since the university would have to have the ultimate responsibility, and responsibility inevitably carries with it some degree of control. Mr. Massey was understandably unhappy that the university emphasized these practical, administrative problems. But a compromise was reached: the university was to have a strong voice in the administration of the college by reason of the *ex officio* presence of the president and the dean of graduate studies on the governing body of the college, and the appointment of the chief officer of the college, to be called the Master, was to be subject to approval by the Board of Governors. In addition, a determined effort was to be made to make the building pay for itself by reducing the number and the size of the rooms allotted to Senior Fellows (who would be the members of the Massey Foundation and some senior professors in the university) and by opening the college during the summer to students who were not members of the college.

Even this careful compromise did not altogether satisfy the board. At its meeting on December 17, 1959, it accepted the gift, but only after sharp, critical voices had been raised at the prospect of having a part of the university beyond the absolute control of the central governing body. Vincent Massey was not at the meeting, nor was the chairman; the vice-chairman, Henry Borden, who was fully sympathetic with the proposal, had to exercise careful diplomacy to gain its acceptance. I recall three strong voices raised in support of Mr Massey's idea: the chancellor, Dr Jeanneret, who rarely spoke at the Board of Governors, but when he did, spoke to good effect; Neil McKinnon, who thought that the college reinforced the very idea of the university; and Robert Bryce, an engineering graduate and mining executive, usually, in the board, the plain-spoken 'Schoolman', impatient of liberal frills, who spoke with sincerity and warmth of this latest example of the great generosity of the Massey family to the university.

At the time, the attitude of the board struck me as strange, but it was not untypical of the reluctance of an institution to accept a gift, no matter how generous, that demanded a departure from the accepted pattern. The board was not condemning a popular idea; on the contrary, it was expressing a common concern. Many looked upon the gift as a retrogressive step; a retreat into the colonial past. The college, it was said, was an English transplant, Vincent Massey's anglophile sentiments given a local habitation and a name; and the popular quip was that Massey was 'instant Balliol' or 'half Souls.' The appointment as master of the college of Robertson Davies – an appointment that I warmly approved – was thought to reinforce the popular view. Davies was a Canadian who had gone to Queen's University, but had taken his first degree at Oxford; and he wrote and spoke with an elegance and wit that struck many as distinctly unCanadian. An additional sense of irritation was the exclusively male character of the college, which drew sharp comments from women students and staff.

But the Massey idea persevered and prospered. The college had the asset of a good building, shrewdly designed by Ronald Thom, to express a sense of scholarly withdrawal within a direct, contemporary facade; students were carefully selected to represent both the sciences and the arts; it attracted good people to its senior fellowships, and it became the centre of vigorous scholarly life. When Vincent Massey died in 1968, he arranged for a substantial subvention to go to the college from the Massey Foundation, and this should, in time, provide the resources without which autonomy is a fiction.

The acceptance of the Massey Foundation's gift, and the swift steps taken by Mr Massey to launch the college, helped greatly in my propagation of the wider college idea. At the beginning of my third year as president, in the fall of 1961, I concluded that the climate was right to propose the idea of new colleges as a general principle. The necessity of limiting the growth of University College had been asserted; the professional faculties were not opposed to the extension of the college principle and, indeed, were, up to a point, in favour; and in Massey College, the Board of Governors had accepted the college concept in its purest and most uncompromising form. In the brief that I prepared for the board, I pointed out that the idea could be implemented gradually. New colleges could await the growth and expression of needs. This might mean delay in residential accommodation, but better delay than the harsh arrest of university evolution. With Mr Massey's enthusiastic support, my brief was adopted as a general policy statement for the university.

The plan developed slowly. New College emerged following the board's resolution, and was given two handsome co-ordinated buildings; but Innis College, which followed in 1964, was not so fortunate. Originally the idea was to make each of the two sections of New College a separate college, thus providing a home for Innis; but this was abandoned in favour of a single, consolidated foundation. Another building for Innis College was projected; indeed the architectural design – the work of Hart Massey – was awarded an anticipatory medal by a national body. But with increasing difficulty in financing undergraduate residences, the plans had to be abandoned and Innis, with a stoicism touched with relief, decided to content itself for the time being with temporary facilities and a controlled enrolment.

The two colleges developed in quite different ways. Academically, New College followed the pattern that I had envisaged: it appointed teaching staff in the two most heavily populated college subjects, English and French, and arranged for tutorial instruction in university subjects, particularly in mathematics and science. But Innis had no base for such formal arrangements, and had to devise its own academic pattern – at first, a laboratory to help students with their writing of essays, and later, when the Faculty of Arts and Science moved into a free, experimental phase, special courses given by staff members with an interest in unorthodox approaches. New maintained the traditional administrative structure, but Innis eagerly embraced radical concepts of student and staff involvement. Innis seemed to derive an ethos from its very name: Harold Innis had been a formidable scholar, but he had also been an individualist and a prickly nationalist.

For a while, public opinion added a third new college – the most controversial of all – Rochdale, a massive high-rise on the fringe of the campus that seemed, in design and ambience, to be a harsh parody of the college concept.

But there was no basis for the relationship, except a persistence on the part of the press. Actually, the university had resolutely opposed the attempt of the long-established co-operative residence movement, the responsible parent of Rochdale, to gain college status, since it was apparent that such status was desired only as a means of securing exemption from local taxes. The university was complicit to the extent that it informed the Central Mortgage and Housing Corporation that additional student residential accommodation was needed, since this no doubt eased the way for CHMC financial support. Rochdale did have a brief college existence. A group of academics, many of them from the University of Toronto, were involved in its planning and tried to develop within it, in company with a group of students, also largely from Toronto, a free university, where instruction, both abstruse and practical, was offered on a voluntary basis. But Rochdale was not hospitable to any structure, no matter how tenuous. It became an ugly, concrete wasteland, an urban campsite for the rootless and alienated, from which, nonetheless, genuine creative movements, particularly in the dramatic arts, emerged. It was occasionally said that the university administration had cynically contrived Rochdale in order to hive off the left-wing students. I would reflect on this during confrontations when, at a crucial stage, Rochdale reinforcements would arrive to swell the clamour.

New and Innis Colleges improved the quality of the education offered at the University of Toronto, but they made no contribution to the quantitative problem, which was uppermost in the minds of provincial officials. This problem had not, however, been ignored in the early work of the Toronto planners. In addition to smaller internal units, the Robinson committee of 1956 had recommended that 'one or more colleges should be established on the outskirts of the metropolitan area, which would be initially integral parts of the University of Toronto, but could in time become independent institutions.' Here the Board of Governors needed no persuasion; after the spring of 1962, when the province became aware of the need for concerted action and indicated its full support of the expansion proposed in a report of a provincial academic committee, Eric Phillips addressed himself with entrepreneurial zeal to the founding of these new institutions. At a luncheon meeting in the head office of the Canadian Bank of Commerce, Phillips, Neil McKinnon, at that time chairman of the finance committee, Frank Stone, the vice-president (administration), and I developed the general plan. We agreed to proceed with as much despatch as possible. Carl Williams, then director of extension, was asked to take general responsibility for making the plan a reality, at first as chairman of a planning committee and subsequently as a vice-president of the university.

The first college would go to the east of Toronto, where the main concentration of population lay, and where we could serve the city of Oshawa, which was insisting with some reason that it be considered as a site for a new institution for higher education. By Christmas of the year, two sites – one to the east in Scarborough, and one to the west near Erindale – had been selected, each symmetrically twenty miles from the main campus, each close to the likely concentration of population and main highways in its district, each affording a site that was varied in contour and not too grandiose in extent.

Like New and Innis, Scarborough and Erindale developed in different ways. Both were designed to provide all the facilities in staff and accommodation for a complete course in general arts. The staff of the colleges were to be full members of the university, with membership in the academic departments on the St George Campus, and the right (when appropriate) to teach and supervise graduate work. Scarborough bore some of the burdens of the first-born in a new endeavour. It had a buoyant faith in the power of closed circuit television as a medium of instruction, a faith not long sustained. Erindale grew more slowly, at first in simple utilitarian quarters – a far cry from the international grandeur of Scarborough. But, partly because of its cautious beginnings, it never experienced, as Scarborough did, a sense of separation from the main campus.

By 1967, the expanded college system had reached the fullest development that the times permitted. It was, viewed administratively, a complex and irrational system, a product of historical drive and accident, a series of answers to a variety of problems raised at various times through the 140 years of university history. At the centre was the main constituent college, University College, a state-inspired institution theoretically responsible for instruction in all subjects not taught in university departments, but without its own governing board or its own sources of income; three federated colleges – Victoria, Trinity, St Michael's – that were parts of autonomous universities that had surrendered their degree-granting powers in all areas except theology in order to draw upon the resources of the University of Toronto; two constituent colleges, New and Innis, with no officially separate staff, working informally with students through residences, special courses, laboratories, and tutorials; two constituent colleges, Erindale and Scarborough, that had many of the characteristics of separate universities, and that were indeed each larger than several of the autonomous universities in the province; and one college, Massey, that worked informally through residence and special academic arrangements, exclusively in the graduate school, and that enjoyed, through its financial resources, a considerable degree of autonomy.

Throughout the period, there were endless, inconclusive discussions about the responsibilities of the colleges and their relationships – academic and financial – to the university. I suspect that this will go on interminably, but that the colleges will remain distinctive societies. The college system is open; as the need and resources become apparent, new colleges can be founded. During this period, I had talks about two other colleges that did not come into existence. One was a college with an engineering bias that would have perpetuated in its name the brief-lived post-war engineering campus at Ajax. The second was a college with a bias towards Jewish studies, perhaps, like Trinity, Victoria, and St Michael's, with a separate theological division. Both ideas foundered because of lack of support; in the latter case, there was concern among many members of the Jewish community that a college with this bias would accentuate existing divisions in the Jewish community.

The idea of one other new college I never actively propounded, but I thought about it a good deal – a little private Utopia remote from the rag-and-bone shop of reality, but not beyond our grasp. It would be founded entirely from private sources for both capital and operating purposes, and would thereby be free of governmental pressure; its capital needs would be kept to a minimum – a group of renovated houses rather than a special building, and for library and laboratory facilities it would depend on the university. Its membership would not exceed three or four hundred, and admission would be based entirely on intellectual achievement and promise (with emphasis on the latter). The college would seek out students, not simply process applications; and it would have ample scholarship money with which to support the gifted poor. The staff would have a nucleus of full-time appointments, chiefly scholars who had roamed successfully across departmental boundaries, and they would be supported by cross-appointments from the university. The budget would be heavily weighted towards salaries, scholarly publications, and special lectures. The work of the college would be directed towards interdisciplinary seminars, with a basis in the study of major classical texts in the humanities, social sciences, and sciences, and each student would be expected on graduation to be proficient in writing English, have a good knowledge of two other languages (one of which would be French), and be acquainted with methods of quantitative analysis. In short, an elitist college on strictly egalitarian principles; a modern college with a sense of the past; a scholarly college with one eye cocked to the marketplace.

The genius of the University of Toronto is diversity, reflective of genuine needs and convictions. When the university was secularized in 1849, it did not become a gray, unitary institution; the state proclaimed a central institution, and then invited other foundations to join. The expansion of the college system in the sixties of this century was the secular equivalent of the federation movement in the eighties and nineties of the last century.

II

Erindale and Scarborough were contributions to the quantitative problem;

but they were integral parts of a university that had set limits to expansion and they were not free to respond directly to demand. Fortunately, by the time they were fully established, they were not alone in the metropolitan area; for the now independent York University had acquired a large campus north of the city.

Between 1956 and 1965, York had moved rapidly through three stages. In a first tentative and exploratory period from 1956 to 1958, it had emerged as a vague idea, in part an offshoot of the St Andrews conference on science and technology. Its two leading protagonists at that time, Air Vice Marshal Wilfred Curtis and Stanley Deeks, had been associated with that conference, Curtis as a senior executive with A.V. Roe, and Deeks as the conference's chief research officer. The organizing committee talked vaguely about an institution that would give work in aeronautical engineering and education.

I had had talks with Air Vice Marshal Curtis about the founding of a new university in Toronto when I was still at Carleton. A casual glance at the most conservative enrolment prediction showed that the University of Toronto would, by the middle of the decade, be swamped by students unless a second university existed in the metropolitan area. After the announcement of my appointment at Toronto in December 1957, I began to press for such a second university. In a speech I gave at the Empire Club on April 24, 1958, I urged the idea and speculated about the possibility of municipal support.

During the next two years, 1958–60 – the second phase – the initial concept was reduced to rational and practical dimensions. In conversations with academics, the organizing committee realized that the new university must begin with general work in the arts and sciences, where the need lay and the students already existed. Then came a series of specific measures to lay the groundwork of an institution: in March 1959, an Act of the Ontario legislature incorporating York University; an agreement in May 1959 between the University of Toronto and the new institution whereby it became an affiliate for a minimum of four and a maximum of eight years; and the selection of a president. It seemed to me (and to many others) that Murray Ross, the vice-president of the University of Toronto, was a logical choice. From the end of the academic year in 1959, Murray Ross took over as organizer and animating force, and, with my blessing, devoted almost all his time, even while still technically vice-president of the University of Toronto, to the promotion of the new institution.

The first essential step was to form a strong base in the community. The initial organizing committee was not widely known; it had, for instance, no resonant names from the Toronto business world and it had as yet no strong political endorsement. My suggestion of municipal support had been thrown out simply to arouse discussion; it was the provincial government, and in particular the prime minister, Leslie Frost, whose government had emerged triumphantly from an election in June 1957, that must be the real patron. The new idea also needed the endorsement of Eric Phillips. He had been sceptical of the need for a new university; and after my Empire Club speech on the subject, he had assured the mayor, Nathan Phillips, who was nervous about the financial implications of a new university, that the University of Toronto had the capacity to handle all the students in the metropolitan area for some years to come.

But public opinion was massing behind the new university; the organizers were suggesting the need for a large initial sum of money; and the Board of Governors was concerned lest all this subtract from the financial campaign that Toronto had then just launched. Eric Phillips decided to throw his weight behind the project. He doubtless had a great deal to do with persuading Robert Winters to become chairman of York's board. Winters, like so many prominent Liberals, had been defeated in the federal election of 1957, and was now established as a senior business executive in Toronto. Before his appointment on November 26, 1959, there had been an amalgamation of the old board (drawn from the original organizing committee) and a new board, bristling with prominent Toronto businessmen. The structure of the new university was now complete – a chairman who was a national figure; a president who had been a key person in the expansion plans of Canada's largest university; an impressive board; and the blessings of the public, of Leslie Frost, and of Eric Phillips. There followed quickly a financial agreement between the University of Toronto and York University, whereby York took over Falconer Hall on the Toronto campus as a home for its initial year, 1960–1, with the understanding that in 1961 it would move to Glendon Hall, an attractive location with considerable grounds in north Toronto, owned by the University of Toronto, and used at the time for teaching in the Faculty of Law and for field research in forestry and botany.

The third period – from 1960 to 1965 – was when firm foundations were established, and the general lines of development enunciated. Early in 1961, the provincial and federal governments decided jointly to give York 465 acres in the northern outskirts of Toronto, at the corner of Keele Street and Steeles Avenue, as a site for the university of the future. Planning and development followed quickly and, by the fall of 1965, the new campus was officially opened. The emphasis rapidly shifted from Glendon. Glendon was, however, retained and developed as a residential college. At the end of the academic year 1964–5, the affiliation between York and Toronto was amicably ended.

During the years from 1959 to 1965, there were minor irritations between the young and the old universities, irritations that at the time assumed dark,

glowering proportions. York was impatient to get financial support, and believed that there was an inadequate appreciation of the urgency and centrality of its needs. A joint meeting in November 1961 between representatives
of the boards of York and Toronto broke up in vague unpleasantness. A besetting York irritation was the refusal of the Canada Council to distribute
part of the interest and profits (amounting to some $7 million) from its un-
used capital funds to any university founded subsequent to the setting up of
the council in 1957. I had become chairman of the Canada Council a year earlier, and my position during the evening's discussion became more and more
uncomfortable despite my knowledge, which had been communicated to the
York board, that the Canada Council in this matter was bound by an official,
legal opinion.

The new university was propelled by a vigorous and uncompromising
idealism. It was to be resolutely forward-looking, unapologetically utopian.
At the installation of Murray Ross in January 1961, a chorus sang a secular
hymn composed for the occasion by John Seeley, a sociologist who was
briefly active in the development of York; it was declared that

> New-found vision lights the eye
> New-lit goals we shall descry.

Inevitably, idealism breeds arrogance and self-satisfaction, and a tendency to
compare favourably the visionary splendours of the new with the actualities
of the old. Whenever York's spokesmen talked about their new ideas and
contrasted them with the dead past, the University of Toronto sensed a
covert attack and bristled. Although, in its initial stages, York drew heavily
on the University of Toronto faculty, it was determined not to be unduly
influenced by the old university. In the fall of 1962, we proposed a joint discussion on development of professional education, since such close neigh-
bours should clearly strive to avoid duplication in expensive specialized
fields. But at the end of an exploratory discussion, I recorded in my personal
notes that it was a 'useless session; the York representatives were like a
group of virgins, nervous about our advances.'

Still, irritation seldom developed into serious tension. York had compres-
sed into a few years an evolution that had taken decades at Ontario's older
universities. Under these circumstances, it was a matter of wonder that more
serious conflicts did not arise. Perhaps the good relations were the result of
the policy of both universities to follow their own ways, and to avoid elaborate agreements. In the initial stages there was no basic conflict of interest, for
York's responsibility was to share with Toronto and other provincial universities the education of students in the basic disciplines, an area where no

undue duplication at that time could possibly exist. Later on, when York ventured into professional fields, it developed its own emphases and directions. Already by 1965, differences of style were beginning to emerge – in the social sciences, for instance, where York placed emphasis on the experimental and empirical as contrasted to Toronto's emphasis on the historical and textual. York was far more receptive than the older university to the Canadian renaissance in painting and sculpture. The older campus tended to turn a cold philistine eye on new developments in art; but York welcomed them enthusiastically. The competition was good for the older university and often provided the necessary spur to action. And, as suspicion waned, the two universities turned toward co-operative schemes.

York, unlike Toronto, was a unitary university, but it was from the very beginning devoted to the idea of creating a number of college units. The two universities in Toronto, then, were both attached to the college principle, the one by history, and the other by choice. If the colleges, particularly those recently founded, seemed at times to flounder uncertainly in their search for an identity, they did, at a minimum, provide a check to the centralizing and quantitative forces of bigness and a symbol that human values were more important than administrative efficiency.

5 / The Higher Learning

The defence and development of the college system emerged as an important policy concern after I had returned to Toronto. Having grown up in the system, I took it for granted; and my concern was more a response to an unexpected attack than the working out of a carefully planned program. The second major concern of these years, the development of 'the higher learning,' had on the other hand been long nurtured and carefully planned. Under 'higher learning' I include the activities in a university that go beyond instruction, and lead to the discovery of new knowledge and insights. These activities are associated with the graduate school, since graduate students are partners in the process of discovering new knowledge; with research, whether carried on by individuals or by groups; with the library, which is the laboratory for the humanist and social scientist, and the essential support of the scientist; with the university press, through which discoveries and insights are made widely known.

I was convinced that the world of the higher learning was the real sustaining atmosphere of the university, and that without it the university tended to dwindle into a trade school or a finishing college. I had a good deal of sympathy with Helen Gardner's reflection that 'students have come to an institution that has other ends than their education, and the education that they receive from the university derives its value from this fact.' The antithesis between teaching and research had not yet become in the fifties a platitudinous fixation. There seemed, at any rate, little chance that Canadian academics would be consumed by a passion for publication. The Canadian academic tradition was amateur and genteel; if you did not expose yourself in print, you were in a strong position to comment freely and sharply on those who did.

I was also convinced that only through the development of the higher learning could a university make an impact beyond its own immediate area. The university of Toronto should be a spokesman for the country in the intellectual exchanges of the world, where there could be no spurious coinage. Canada had never had such a university. McGill was certainly its best known university, and it had a style, an easy self-confidence, and a coherence that sprawling, untidy Toronto did not possess. But it was a fair question as to whether McGill's visibility came from its devotion to the higher learning or was the result of adventitious circumstances – the brief sojourn of a Rutherford, the receptiveness of its medical school to foreign students, the presence of the university in a cosmopolitan city beside which Toronto, until after the second world war, was a loose assembly of towns and villages, living on memories of Belfast, Edinburgh, and the frontier. But in the late fifties, McGill was no longer so favoured; it was beginning to be hemmed in by a resurgent French-Canadian nationalism, and could no longer rely on private benefactions to give it a special position. The city of Toronto and the province of Ontario were, on the other hand, becoming more responsive to the life of the mind and the spirit, if only as a reaction against the vulgar bulk of prosperity and rapid development. And the University of Toronto, having discharged its debt to the veterans through quick, efficient, economical programs in undergraduate training, was addressing itself, once again, to the continuing needs of scholarship.

Certainly the atmosphere for the higher learning was vital compared to what I had known as an MA student at Toronto in 1936–7. That was a bad time to enter the graduate school with the idea of preparing for a university teaching career. There were few fellowships and no system of financial aid. (I was fortunate to get a fellowship valued at $500, from which I was expected to pay fees, and for which I was also expected to teach a first-year pass section, three hours a week.) The prospects of employment were faint. Beyond all this, one had the sense of leading an unreal life. The graduate student felt like an unwanted relative, confined to the attic of the family mansion. The English department, under the stimulus of Woodhouse's energy and scholarly drive, believed in its graduate work and gave it proper emphasis. But in the university generally, and particularly in the humanities and social sciences, there was lethargy and a good deal of scepticism. The tone at Toronto was formed by teachers who had graduated from English universities, and England had always been sceptical of any attempt to pursue scholarship in an institutional system. There the important point was to give a good first degree, and then leave scholarship to follow its own natural evolution. With English dominance went the typically colonial attitude: if one really wanted to pursue formal graduate studies, one went to a leading American or European university; the resources in Canada for advanced work were slim and not likely to improve; Canadian universities should maintain a steady but modest flow of graduate students to Harvard, Oxford, and the Sorbonne, and concentrate on establishing a reputation as sound preparatory institutions.

During the fifties, the atmosphere changed greatly. In 1947, a committee on the reorganization of graduate studies prepared the way. The report was clearly forged by Harold Innis and Arthur Woodhouse, two members of the committee; it was nationalistic, sure of Toronto's pre-eminence in Canada, but aware of the need for fundamental change. It had immediate results. The library was strengthened by the addition of a wing to house expanded stacks and reading rooms and offices. Special research funds for the staff were increased, and money was made available for visiting lecturers. There was a feeling in the fifties that Toronto had emerged from a comfortable, self-satisfied cocoon, that the university had firmly established itself on the main trade routes of the mind. It was a more bracing climate, but it made tough demands. William Devane, chairman of the English department at Cornell, and later dean of Yale College, once remarked to me, 'You have a lot of good people hidden away up there, and you will now have to fight to keep them.'

The most conspicuous advance in the area of higher learning took place in the University of Toronto Press. Although the beginnings of the press went back to 1901, it was not really until 1945 that it emerged as an organization primarily concerned with the publication of scholarly books; that is, books not likely to be taken up commercially. But the dividing point in its history came in 1953, when Marsh Jeanneret became director. Jeanneret was a man committed to success on a grand scale and, in this respect, body and spirit were exact images of each other. In his regime, works of scholarship came first, but he also insisted upon going into a more general field of serious books, not technical or professional, but of sufficient interest to attract a wide reading public. I took it as a happy omen that my return to Toronto coincided with the opening of a new building for the editorial offices and the bookstore, and the launching of the press's most ambitious project: the publication in many volumes over a long span of years of the Dictionary of Canadian Biography. The University of Toronto Press had by that time become the means by which scholars, both at Toronto and elsewhere in Canada, could reach their fellow workers throughout the world, and no less important, it had become a creative agent helping to shape the cultural life of Canada. Jeanneret had a talent for attracting good assistants and colleagues and for making them as enthusiastic about the press as he was. He was an administrator of great practical skill and sagacity. In meetings of committees, whether with tough tycoons or impassive scholars, I would watch with delight as he nudged the members in the direction that he had already determined upon.

In 1958, then, there was a good basis for the development at Toronto of the higher learning. The most conspicuous inadequacy was the library. The new wing was a welcome addition that had eased the pressure; but it was not even an attempt to deal with graduate requirements, and I was fearful that it might be thought to represent the entire library expansion program for our time. It was too early to press for immediate action: there were other, more obvious priorities for which no case had been made. The concept of a research library, with collections built not upon daily use by a great number of readers, but on the potential use at some time in the distant future by an occasional scholar, was not part of the accepted academic gospel at Toronto or, indeed, anywhere in Canada. It was clear that I would have to depend upon reiteration, persuasion, and the growth of graduate work to make the need clear and compulsive. From the day I arrived at Toronto, I did not neglect any opportunity to emphasize the concept of the research library. Indeed, if I had a single, precise goal that I was anxious to achieve during my tenure of office, it was the planning and building of a library that could join the company of the great university libraries of the world.

In the meantime, the principal concern was the School of Graduate Studies. At the end of 1963, Andrew Gordon would complete his term as dean. The problems of the great expansion, which was already manifest, belonged to Gordon's successor. The dean of the graduate school had to have unusual qualifications. He was, in some ways, the least powerful member of the decanal group: he had no academic appointments to make since these were made in the undergraduate divisions, and, not being responsible for salaries, he had no large budget under his control. On the other hand, he was responsible for the most advanced work in the university, and he had himself to be a scholar of unquestionable achievement and authority. In addition, the job demanded strong personal qualities. For the big battalions of the budget, he had to be able to substitute weapons of persuasion and authority.

Andrew Gordon would not be an easy man to succeed. He had come to the deanship in 1953, following the death of Harold Innis. He was a short, slight man, whose rapid walk and energetic gestures seemed to be an overflow of intense intellectual energy. I am told by a favourite graduate student of Gordon's that his best ideas would emerge as he paced up and down interminably in his office. He was, one might say, an explosive Tory in his attitude; respectful of top authority and intensely loyal to the person who embodied it; contemptuous of the encroaching liberal gospel with its emphasis on egalitarianism and democratic procedures; in essence, an elitist who valued intellectual distinction above all else. In defence of his ideas he was often, by academic measurement, violent and abusive; and his quick, intense, concentrated outbursts in the Senate were one of the more attractive features of that solemn body. He was nonetheless a genial man who loved good food and drink and the companionship of his peers. In a community that winced at rotarian breeziness, he was never known by any other name than 'Andy.' When he retired in 1964, he refused to have anything to do with the ritual farewell dinner his office demanded. He finally settled, however, for a small affair at the York Club whose superb food he relished. The printed program was devised to fit the man – no arty embellishments: plain, modest paper, with a list of friends who had come to honour him, the menu translated into chemical formulae in which C_2H_5OH figured prominently, and a concluding tribute in verse which began

> A man explosive, volatile
> A tiger with a playful smile.

There was no heir-apparent to Gordon on the staff. Vincent Bladen, who had the qualities that were needed, had accepted the deanship of the Faculty of Arts and Sciences in the spring of 1959. Perhaps, I thought, it would be wise to go outside the university; Toronto was always in danger of becoming a cosy, self-contained, and self-satisfied world. I began to think about my friend Ernest Sirluck, who had left the English department as a junior lecturer and was now a professor in the graduate division at Chicago. We had talked informally about his returning to Toronto to succeed his mentor and fellow Miltonist, Arthur Woodhouse, and he was receptive to the idea.

I had known Ernest Sirluck since he came to the graduate school at Toronto in 1941, a tall, dark, commanding young man, immensely self-confident 'with,' as I noted at the time, 'an argument on every subject and a theory on most.' I had a city background, and had spent the last four years as a student and teacher at Cornell University, which had the reputation of being a cosmopolitan centre; Sirluck came from a southern Manitoba farm, and he had gone to the University of Manitoba, at that time the liveliest of the western Canadian universities, but not, in world terms, a notable centre. Yet this young man seemed to me to be immensely sophisticated, with an easy power of expression that I had not met before among graduate students. We became friends and members of a little, unofficial literary coterie. In it also were Earle Birney, who had finally found a firm academic post at University College after a difficult depression pilgrimage, had just finished a stint as editor of *The Canadian Forum*, and was preparing for publication his first volume of poetry, *David and Other Poems*; A.J.M. Smith, already an established poet, who was working on the anthology that was to become the starting point of any discussion of the Canadian poetic tradition; E.J. Pratt, at the full height of his career, probing in 'The Truant' the meaning of power in a war-torn world; on occasion, Pelham Edgar, now retired from his post as professor of English at Victoria College, relaxed and anecdotal, suddenly discovering in his pocket a letter he had written back at the turn of the century after a visit to some literary giant of the time; and Northrop Frye, whose scholarly reputation while a student at Victoria had burst through all college boundaries, now returned from Oxford and working on his first major book, *Fearful Symmetry*, a study of William Blake. This was exhilarating company for two young men with nothing to boast about except their future plans.

We both knew that the semi-bohemian life of the graduate student could not last long. In the summer of 1942, Sirluck and I addressed ourselves to getting commissions in the services. We had spent a year in the Canadian Officers Training Corps, but there was no assurance of a quick transition to the regular forces. We offered our services to the Navy, but were turned down. A trip to Ottawa to explore the chances of getting into Intelligence yielded nothing except a glimpse into a closed region of confusion. We resigned ourselves to a call to an infantry officers' training unit. That summer, Ernest got married – his wife was Lesley McNaught, a talented and beautiful young artist – and I stood nervously beside him in the little Hart House chapel. And finally in December, the call came. We tried to bolster each other's morale as we rode on a train to Trois Rivières, the most recently opened of the officers' training camps, where, during the next three months, grim expectations were grimly fulfilled.

Overseas, we met only a few times. Sirluck finally joined Intelligence, and became Intelligence Officer at 4th Division Headquarters. I remained with my battalion, the Argyll and Sutherland Highlanders, in the same division. A few days after the end of hostilities in Europe, we met in a little German town that breathed contentment and prosperity, seemingly untouched by the war; we strolled along the quiet streets, saying little, wondering at this sudden end to the movement and violence.

Now seventeen years later, as I thought about persuading Sirluck to return to Toronto, it seemed to me that he would be an ideal successor to Gordon. He knew Toronto and admired it, but had grown up academically in a major academic graduate school. He had established himself as a senior scholar in a field that was fiercely competitive. Moreover, he had the wide interests, and the curiosity about other disciplines, that a dean of graduate studies must possess. The graduate dean cannot afford to take a cursory interest in fields outside his own; he must have an informed layman's interest and knowledge, sufficient to spot strength and weaknesses and to ask questions, at times of an embarrassing nature. It seemed certain that enrolment in the graduate school would triple over the next ten years and that new and bold measures must be found to deal with such numbers. The dean would need administrative talents of unusual variety and toughness. I had no doubt about Sirluck's qualifications on that score. I remembered the SITREPS that he would turn out for the 4th Division – lucid and compelling analyses of resources, possibilities, and plans. At Toronto, during the next ten years, there would be plenty of opportunity in the graduate field for generalship on a high plane.

In these final years of the hierarchical, monarchical form of university government, one didn't worry too much about getting community involvement. Administration relied more on a flash of insight than on the deliberation of a committee. I wrote to Sirluck in June 1961, proposing that he should come in as associate dean of the graduate school with the right of succession to Gordon. I wrote that, 'The School of Graduate Studies is the fighting edge of the university upon which its scholarly reputation largely depends.' Sirluck accepted the proposal; he was appointed associate dean in December 1961, and finally joined the university in the fall of 1962. The apprenticeship as associate dean lasted two years, since Gordon was persuaded to stay on for an additional year beyond his term.

Despite the complaisant temper of the times, the appointment was an adventurous one. Sirluck had to work closely with Gordon, and Gordon was not given to soft compromise or charitable concessions. And he had to gain the acceptance of the academic community if he was to be an effective dean. In the first relationship there was no problem; Gordon recognized and valued intellectual excellence, and Sirluck qualified easily. On the wider front, there appeared the inevitable problems that arise when a vigorous, assertive, self-confident person takes over leadership. Sirluck was always in command; the arguments were there in serried rows and could be summoned in an instant. Less confident and less carefully organized men resented this display of strength. But these were early and, on the whole, minor problems; the important matter was that the graduate school now had a spokesman and leader of undisputed ability.

In my talks with Sirluck about the graduate school, I was able to assure him that all the omens were good; that the problems would not be, as in the past, problems of decent survival but rather of orderly expansion. The general enthusiasm for higher education was now beginning to find definite channels for action; and one of these channels was certainly graduate studies. Up until now, the conventional pose had been to assign the responsibility for graduate studies to the federal government, on the grounds that such studies attracted a national and international student body and were, consequently, a national responsibility. The federal government, whatever its political complexion, moved, however, warily and, except for specific research projects, threw the responsibility for graduate work to semi-autonomous bodies, particularly to the National Research Council and the Canada Council, and made no attempt to direct specific grants towards graduate work. The provincial government had never been thought of as an alternative source of support. The Province of Ontario sponsored a research body that had a minimal impact on the universities. Otherwise, it gave its emphasis to undergraduate studies. Its responsibilities, irrespective of political colouring, were to the ordinary citizen, who was conceived of as self-centered, mildly aggressive, and placidly parochial; his educational interests were believed to be concentrated in the schools, with some interest in the universities as handy conduits to prosperity.

But now the logic of a large-scale expansion in education was driving the province to a new attitude toward graduate studies. The chief problem in enlarging the system of post-secondary undergraduate education was to find the teachers. In Ontario, the total number of university teachers had to increase from a little over 2,000 in 1962–3, to about 8,300 in 1975–6, if the expansion was to mean anything more than an accumulation of buildings. We argued that most of the new teachers must come from our own graduate schools: traditional sources in the United States and Europe would be faced with similar needs and would not be able to supply the numbers we would need; besides it was about time we stopped being a colonial beneficiary and developed our own intellectual resources. In Ontario, we had at the established universities a foundation in graduate studies that could easily be built upon.

This was the central recommendation of a report entitled *Post Secondary Education in Ontario, 1962–1970*, prepared in the spring of 1962 for the Committee of Presidents of the Ontario Universities by a special research committee, under the chairmanship of John Deutsch of Queen's University. The committee's first and strongest recommendation was that immediate help, on a generous scale, should be given 'to provide for more generous fellowships and to help cover the heavy additional investments in staff, books, and equipment that the intensified graduate program would entail.' The committee recommended a 'crash program in graduate studies, a virtual doubling of the graduate school enrolment in Ontario universities during the next few years.'

The Deutsch Committee, although made up exclusively of university staff, was, to all intents and purposes, a government committee. At that time, the province had no bureaucratic machinery in the area of higher education. Traditionally, the universities had been a loose appendage of the premier's office, and this tradition had been carried on by Leslie Frost who, although retired as premier since 1960, was still influential in higher education through his membership on the government's Advisory Committee on University Affairs. It was Frost who had asked the presidents to produce a blueprint for the future, and the Deutsch report, succinct and persuasive, was the reply. But Frost did not stand alone in his interest in higher education. John Robarts, the new premier, had come from the portfolio of education. He had already talked informally with the university presidents. His successor as minister of education, to whom the university problem would go, was William G. Davis, obviously rising rapidly in the party, aware that for a good many years his department would be brilliantly spotlighted. Bill Davis had been a student at University College after the war. He had been a member of one of my English classes, and I recalled him as an attractive, able undergraduate, with a vigorous interest in campus politics and sport. Like Robarts, he was a conservative ready to take a chance on the future, prepared on occasion not to wait for the public wisdom to validate action. Within a few months of the Deutsch report, he initiated the most important part of its recommendations, a graduate fellowship program. It was to begin in 1963–4, and it was liberally conceived: the province would be able to pay 'all the awards recommended' in the humanities and social sciences; 20 per cent of the awards would go to non-residents; and the amount would be $1,500 for the normal September-to-May academic year, and $500 for the summer months. The ragged proletariat of academia had suddenly achieved security.

The authoritative documents of the sixties continued to emphasize the need for enhanced graduate support. In June 1965 appeared *Financing Higher Education in Canada*, a report commissioned by the Association of Universities and Colleges of Canada. The chairman of the four-man commission was Vincent Bladen, a person not likely to turn a deaf ear to the pleas of the university world. One of his chief associates was Wallace McCutcheon, now a senator, who had served briefly in the last Diefenbaker cabinet; although he was sympathetic to the needs of higher education, McCutcheon was not to be taken in by bland arguments. The report was concerned with the general picture, but gave a good deal of emphasis to research and stressed the expensive nature of doctoral work. This last point was driven home in setting out a suggested formula for allocating government operating grants to universities: if undergraduate students in their first and second year were to be given a weight of one, then doctoral candidates in their second or subsequent years should be given a weight of five. When the Ontario government finally moved from a special supplementary annual grant for graduate work to an overall formula, it adopted the heavy weighting for graduate students recommended by the Bladen report.

A few months after that report came the *Second Annual Review* of the Economic Council of Canada, in which education was ecstatically embraced as the chief source of economic growth. The report singled out five areas in which 'attention currently needs to be focused.' One of these was 'the more rapid development of facilities for a sharply accelerating flow of professional and other highly skilled manpower at the postgraduate university level – the level at which we have made least progress to date in the Canadian educational system.'

External support and encouragement were no substitute, however, for internal clarification and statement of intentions. The university's report on graduate studies in 1947 had concentrated on structure and had been almost laconically brief in its preparatory statement. We needed a report that would be thorough and reflective, that would see graduate education in a world context, and that would provide both a proposed program and a philosophical statement. In the latter part of 1963, at the end of Sirluck's first year at Toronto and in anticipation of his becoming dean in 1964, I appointed a committee to examine the graduate school and gave it wide general terms of reference: 'In the light of the new responsibilities of the School of Graduate Studies, and of development in graduate work elsewhere, particularly in the United States and the United Kingdom, to examine the academic, administrative and financial structure of the School of Graduate Studies and to make recommendations for change that may be necessary.'

The committee, which had eleven members, selected by a process of consultation with senior colleagues, was, I should think, the strongest internal committee in the history of the University of Toronto. Its chairman, Bora Laskin, professor in the Faculty of Law, was to become a member of the Supreme Court and then Chief Justice of Canada; two members, Ernest Sirluck and William Winegard, were to become university presidents; one, A.C.H. Hallett, was to become a college principal; and the whole group brilliantly represented the scholarly scope of the university. Charles Hanes, Northrop Frye, and Kenneth Fisher were senior scholars with international reputations; John Cairns, Harry Eastman, Robert McRae, and John Polanyi were younger men, each widely known in his field. The committee began its deliberations early in 1964, held some forty meetings, sent special delegations to look at graduate schools in the United States, the United Kingdom, and Europe, and submitted its report late in 1965. Then followed several months of open discussion, the eventual appointment of a special committee to bring in recommendations about specific proposals, and in May 1966 the final endorsement of the revised report. This was the procedure that was to be followed for all the major reports of the sixties: the full exposition in the report of a general philosophical position with a proposed program of action; widespread discussion extending over several months and involving as many interested groups as possible; and, finally, the appointment of a committee to formulate specific proposals, which were then either formally endorsed, amended, or set aside.

The Laskin Committee had no uncertainties about the value of graduate studies. Like the committee of 1947, it took a strong nationalistic stand: graduate studies were a 'national imperative' because 'such studies must be relied upon to establish the country's intellectual horizon.' The implication, although not coarsely spelled out, was that the imperative was strongest at Toronto. From this point on, the committee was concerned with methods of improving graduate studies and integrating them more firmly with the university, with eliminating, once and for all, the atmosphere of remote prestige in which such studies had hitherto existed. The initial decision was whether graduate studies should be carried on vertically through departments or division, abandoning the central structure that already existed; or whether the central structure should be strengthened, while recognizing that the basic work must be done on a departmental basis. The committee came down on the latter side, on the grounds of preserving standards, and, more pragmatically, on the grounds that this would give the university a stronger basis for dialogue with the government. To a special plea of some of the professional schools to be looked upon as different and, therefore, unassimilable in a single graduate school, the committee replied: 'A university setting acquires meaning for a professional school by enabling it to transcend its practical function; it is not required to abandon that function.' A strong central graduate school should not, however, create sharp divisions between graduate and undergraduate staff; and the committee reaffirmed the traditional Toronto pattern by which appointments were made to a department, with responsibility presumed to exist both for undergraduate and graduate work.

In its specific structural proposals, the committee tried to preserve a balance between a tidy centralism and widely distributed responsibility, between efficiency and involvement. An initial reaction among many academics was that centralism and efficiency had triumphed: that the replacement of the old all-inclusive council by a smaller representative one was a regrettable departure from academic democracy; that the proposed involvement of the dean in academic appointments gave him powers at the expense of the departmental chairman that would be reinforced by the extension of his central bureaucracy; and that the establishment of a Research Council closely linked with the graduate school would formalize procedures and stultify creative work. I thought that most of the criticism was unjustified and that it reflected an emotional response to change, rather than a close reading of the report. The university, as a whole, thought so too, for the main recommendations were finally accepted; and the structure has, I think, brought coherence, sense of purpose, and widespread involvement.

A major theme in the report was the need to recognize interdisciplinary developments and to be willing to break through departmental structures for the sake of creative work in graduate studies. The university was already moving in this direction through the setting up of small units of an interdisciplinary nature. This process was to continue throughout the sixties. Sometimes the units, known either as centres or institutes, were directed towards a set of specific problems, as in the cases of Criminology, Urban and Community Studies, Applied Statistics, Bio-medical Electronics, Immunology, Quantitative Analysis of Social and Economic Policy, and Industrial Relations; sometimes they were a method of introducing a new discipline, initially better adjusted to graduate than to undergraduate studies, as in the Philosophy of Science and Technology, and Linguistics; sometimes they represented a fusion of various departmental resources in one area, as in the Study of the Drama, Medieval Studies, Medical Sciences, and Environmental Studies and Engineering.

Normally, the recommendation for the setting up of a centre or institute came from a committee, and the president got involved at the later stage of financing. But I had a more direct role in two of the centres – Culture and Technology, and Study of the Drama. The Centre of Culture and Technology, as Emerson said of institutions, was the lengthened shadow of one man – Marshall McLuhan – and was a means of keeping him at Toronto and enabling him to pursue his own peculiar constellation of interests. I had known Marshall McLuhan since he came to the English department at St Michael's College just after the second world war. I was then teaching full-time in the same department at UC, and we were both resident on the campus; the Bissells in the dean's house at University College, and the McLuhans in a house on the St Michael's College campus. Corinne and Marshall McLuhan were a warm and hospitable couple and liked to have informal evenings of talk over drink and food. Marshall was an enthusiastic and provocative talker, ranging through English literature with an easy authority, full of information and insights about the great moderns – Pound, Joyce, and Eliot. His first book, *The Mechanical Bride*, which appeared in 1951, puzzled his colleagues in the English department, and was widely dismissed as just another squib about advertising (a grossly astigmatic view: the book is scathing and serious). In 1953, McLuhan launched an interdisciplinary seminar with the help of a grant given by the Ford Foundation in the perfunctory discharge of its Canadian obligations. At the same time, McLuhan and Edmund Carpenter, an anthropologist, published a magazine called *Explorations*, in which the interests of the seminar were reflected brilliantly by writers from all over the world, many of them famous names in their fields – David Riesman, Northrop Frye, Siegfried Giedion, Kenneth Boulding, and many others. The magazine declared its point of view in a simple foreword: '*Explorations* is designed, not as a permanent reference journal that embalms truth for posterity, but as a publication that explores and searches and questions. We envisage a series that will cut across the humanities and social sciences by treating them as a continuum. We believe anthropology and communications are approaches, not bodies of data, and that within each the four winds of the humanities, the physical, the biological and the social sciences intermingle to form a science of man.' Every issue contained an article by McLuhan, and the last two issues, numbers seven and eight, were presumably written in large part by Carpenter and McLuhan themselves. McLuhan was gathering a large international audience of which, characteristically, Toronto was unaware – the city and, at times, the university, having a remarkable ability to seal themselves off from the rest of the world. I became aware of McLuhan's reputation when I visited Wayne State University in Detroit in the spring of 1959 to speak at its graduation exercises. The president arranged an informal lunch with a representative group of the faculty. At the end of the meal, he made some unexceptionable remarks about the good relationships between Canada and the United States, and then invited the audience to ask me questions about Canada. There was a prolonged silence; clearly no one knew enough to shape a respectable question. Then someone asked; 'Could you give a brief summary of the ideas of Marshall McLuhan?'

In the early sixties, McLuhan published his two major books, in 1962, *The Gutenberg Galaxy*, (astutely taken up by the University of Toronto Press) and in 1964, *Understanding Media*; and finally Toronto grasped that McLuhan was a writer of extraordinary world influence. I thought that it was important to keep him in Toronto and to work out financial and administrative arrangements with St Michael's whereby he would have a special university status. John Kelly, the president of St Michael's, shared my point of view and we came to an agreement quickly. The university would establish a Centre of Culture and Technology, of which McLuhan would be the director. He would retain his professorship in the English department in the college, with reduced teaching responsibilities. But by this point the graduate school had become alarmed by the plethora of research centres, and Andrew Gordon was the last person in the world to have any sympathy with McLuhan's unorthodox probes. Sirluck, beginning his second year as associate dean, acted as intermediary. 'The Dean suggests,' wrote Sirluck, 'that if the President would like to establish such a centre in the University at large, the School would have no objection.' This was academese for saying that the graduate school would not give academic credit for work offered in such a centre. Sirluck added, conscious that he would be succeeding Gordon: 'Next year we can try to thread him through the portals guarded by the Executive Committee of the School.'

The centre was so threaded, and has had a tranquil and productive existence. It is now housed in a little coach-house behind some surviving mansions on Queen's Park and is reached by a circuitous route through backyards and parking lots. McLuhan is happy in his obscure retreat. He would explain that in these days of instant electric circuitry, nineteenth-century hardware is a dead loss. A phone call from London, New York, Los Angeles, or Athens turns his academic village into a global headquarters.

The Graduate Centre for the Study of Drama had diverse origins. The language and literature departments at Toronto – both modern and ancient – had always offered good work in dramatic literature. Yet since the days before the second world war when Wilson Knight, in his own Shakespearian productions, tried to demonstrate on the stage what he expounded in the classroom, there had been a cold area of indifference between the academics and the small but pleasant theatre that had been built as part of Hart House. In the forties and fifties, Robert Gill had brought that theatre to brilliant life. He had come to Toronto from Carnegie Tech to fill a post described as director of drama, but he had not been given academic status; his job was to produce and direct four plays a year, drawing upon whatever undergraduate actors were available and, in the process, presiding over what amounted to a one-man school of theatre. I was a member of the Hart House Board of Syndics, a mixed lay and academic body that answered for the theatre, but in practice confined itself to drawing up a budget. The theatre was allowed a modest deficit, beyond which it was not permitted to go. In short, it had to depend largely on box office revenue. It was, therefore, a commercial venture with a small public subsidy. Under these restrictions, Gill produced miracles, maintaining high standards in his choice of plays, and in his productions stooping only occasionally to box office demands. But with the development in Toronto of other little theatres, ticket sales to the general public declined; on the campus the sixties was a philistine era, with students preferring rock concerts and political rallies to the theatre. I thought the solution was to relate Hart House Theatre more closely to academic life and to banish forever the bogey of commercialism. We had no ambition to found a professional theatre school in competition with those already in existence; but, at the same time, we were sceptical of undergraduate courses in the theatre that vanished into aimless amateurism. In our plan, Hart House Theatre would be linked to graduate studies in the drama, and would be used to reinforce and illustrate the study of the literature.

There was a good deal of confusion and misunderstanding about this centre, prolonged and intensified by garbled press reports. It was thought of as a denial of the past and a callous abandonment of student participation. Actually it was a logical outgrowth from the past, and, far from abandoning the students, it gave them, both in Hart House and in a new experimental theatre that was provided, opportunities and scope never known before.

II

All the major documents of the sixties emphasized the centrality of the university library and drew attention to Canadian inadequacies. The most forceful statement came in the report of a commission appointed to study the development of graduate programs in Ontario universities, all the more telling because two of the three commissioners, John Spinks, the chairman, president of the University of Saskatchewan, and Kenneth Hare, at that time master of Birkbeck College, University of London, were scientists, and scientists did not usually take the lead in pressing library needs. Here is the key passage written with an unqualified intensity rare in commission prose:

The library is the heart of the University. From it, the lifeblood of scholarship flows to all parts of the University; to it the resources of scholarship flow to enrich the academic body. With a mediocre library, even a distinguished faculty cannot attain its highest potential; with a distinguished library, even a less than brilliant faculty may fulfill its mission. For the scientist, the library provides an indispensable backstop to his laboratory and field work. For the humanist, the library is not only his reference centre; it is indeed his laboratory and the field of his explorations. What he studies, researches and writes is the product of his reading in the library. For these reasons, the University library must be one of the primary concerns for those responsible for the development and welfare of the institution. At the same time, the enormous cost of acquisitions, the growing scarcity of older books, the problems of storage and cataloguing make the library one of the most painful headaches of the University administrator.

By June 1966, when the commission discussed with the Ontario presidents a preliminary version of its report, the University of Toronto had finally reached a point where it was prepared to launch the Research Library for the Humanities and Social Sciences. The plans were a culmination of ten years, beginning formally with a committee on library facilities for the entire campus under the chairmanship of R.R. McLaughlin, dean of the Faculty of Applied Science and Engineering, which had made its report shortly after I returned as president. This report had envisaged library expansion in the humanities and social sciences on the existing site, with the erection eventually of a separate science library on the site then occupied by the main building of Applied Science and Engineering. But events had rapidly outstripped this concept. After 1962, with the establishment of a new priority for graduate school development, the theoretical basis for library expansion changed; and after 1964, with the launching of the graduate fellowship program, the theoretical basis and reality approached each other much more rapidly than we had ever anticipated.

Although the need for library expansion had always been acknowledged, it was not easy to establish an acceptable scale. A large proportion of my correspondence from 1958 to 1960 was devoted to trying to put library needs into perspective, and I wrote lengthy memoranda on the subject to all those who, I thought, might influence the final decision. My principal allies were Carl Williams, who became the chairman of the users' committee for the library; Ernest Sirluck, fresh from work on the planning of the new library at Chicago, a storehouse of information on all technical and bibliographical matters; and, of course, the chief librarian, Robert Blackburn, meticulous and unswerving in advancing the cause.

One of the persistent objections to any large-scale library expansion was the idea that electronic technology would shortly make all conventional libraries obsolete. The sixties were a great era of faith in technology; magazines like *Time* and *Fortune*, beloved of the business community, printed articles about how all the books in the world could be reproduced on an infinitesimally small surface and then made available instantaneously to readers anywhere on the globe within reach of the necessary hardware. (There was no estimate ever given of the cost involved; it could be assumed, however, that it would exceed astronomically the cost of the most elaborate book-oriented library.) But even the most sophisticated technology (which is always just around the corner) will never eliminate the human being. It is he who receives and interprets the messages, whether encoded in statistics or in the metaphors of Plato. The library is essentially a place where human beings work in close proximity to the material that they need; it is not a storehouse of books, but a place where people work with ideas and information. In all of our plans, therefore, we gave emphasis to study space for the individual, which we compared to laboratory space for the scientist. Where the new technology had proved valuable, for instance, in the application of computer techniques to the card catalogues, in bibliography, and the rapid retrieval of factual information, we could in fact say that we had taken the initiative, and were far advanced in the field.

Other inhibiting factors were simply part of the inheritance of a complex and established university. There was, for instance, the question of a site. Unlike the new campuses, we could not plan in an untrammeled fashion. We had to fit our buildings in to existing conditions, and we had to recall that we were still very much a part of the city, and subject to its rules and regulations. We looked briefly at some of the large open spaces on the existing campus but turned down the idea quickly; these spaces were sacred and could not be violated. We then shifted to the new campus west of St George Street. This was not initially hopeful. The area bounded by Harbord, Spadina, College, and St George had been set aside for instructional and residential buildings, and we had always indicated that we did not envisage a move north of Harbord Avenue. But the planning division was convinced that the site at the northwest corner of Harbord and St George was the best for our purposes. It provided ample space, and eventually would be at the centre of the campus. The site, however, was not cleared, and before us lay complex negotiations with the current occupants – government bodies, fraternities, an optical college, and private homeowners.

The selection of the architects gave some problems as well. The firm of Mathers & Haldenby had done the extension of the main library in 1951 and the recently completed University College library; and in doing the National Library in Ottawa, the firm had acquired an official imprimatur. But the senior partner and principal designer, A.S. Mathers, died suddenly and the Board of Governors thought that the firm should seek some assistance in the area of design from an allied architectural firm. I was of the opinion, as I said in a letter to the chairman of the property committee, O.D. Vaughan, 'that the library requires the insights and the flexible approach of a young architect adept in the use of contemporary idiom and prepared to try a variety of design concepts in the search for the best solution.' I thought that there were 'half a dozen architects in this city who could answer our needs.' But the board decided to look for the design ally in the United States; specifically to a New York firm, Warner, Burns, Toan and Lunde, that had recently built successful libraries at Cornell and Brown.

The extent of the financial aid we could receive from the province was, in those non-formula days, unknown. All we could be absolutely sure of was $1.5 million still in our Canada Council account. In the fall of 1963, the Board of Governors passed a resolution that any new library building should, for the time being, meet only immediate needs and should not exceed in cost $10 million. We had already projected a building estimated to cost twice that amount and designed to take care of the foreseeable future. Later in that year, the atmosphere changed, when Henry Borden became chairman of the board. Henry Borden liked to plan on a large scale and to move quickly and adventurously. His interest was medicine, but he respected the priority that I gave to the library. He had good relations with the provincial government, and in the new minister he had a man prepared to listen to bold designs. Everything now moved rapidly. The original plans were revived and amended in the light of fresh expansion factors – more rapid increase in graduate enrolment, and an increase in the projected number of students to be admitted to the School of Library Science from 100 to 400. Discussions were begun with the New York architects and their relationships with the Toronto firm were clarified. The total complex would be approximately 800,000 square feet gross, 650,000 for the main library, 100,000 for Library Science, and 50,000 for a rare book library. The rare book library could, we conceded regretfully, be omitted if further reductions had to be made.

As I read the preliminary report of the Spinks commission, everything seemed to confirm and support our library plans. Then I noticed, with chilling apprehension, the phrase, 'provincial library.' My presidential colleagues noticed the phrase too, but without apprehension. This could be interpreted as meaning a separate library under provincial jurisdiction. It would presumably be located in a neutral area. In the final report of November 1966, the commissioners recorded some of the geographical fantasies entertained by my colleagues at other universities: 'Near the geographical centre of the province, perhaps somewhere between Sudbury and Port Arthur; a service area on Highway 401 west of Toronto.' If this idea were to be taken seriously, it would mean the end of the Toronto plans. The government would have to concentrate its financial support on the provincial library, and, what was worse from our point of view, would have to draw heavily upon Toronto's research collection to give the provincial library any scholarly authority. On all counts, it would mean the disappearance of Toronto as a major centre. I was enraged at the concept, which seemed to be a cynical, conspiratorial design to cut down Toronto to the provincial average.

I said all this, privately and passionately, to the commissioners, particularly to Gustave Arlt, the eminent American humanist who was the third member with Spinks and Hare. He denied that the commission had any desire to stand in the way of Toronto plans, but he saw the possibilities of misinterpretation. In the final published version of the report, this crucial sentence emerged: 'We had learned of the advanced state of planning of the new Humanities and Social Sciences Research Library at the University of Toronto, and it occurred to us that a great economy could be effected if the plans for this building, while still in their present flexible state, could be expanded to allow this library to serve as the Headquarters Provincial Research Library rather than to locate it, at great new cost, in some remote hinterland or other region.' In the meantime, I had discussed the nature of the 'provincial expansion' with Robert Blackburn. He had done an analysis of what it would mean in additional space to provide service to privileged users from other universities, centralized bibliographical services, and acceleration of the acquisition and processing of new material. Thesee changes would mean, in rough terms, an extra three floors, and an estimated additional expenditure of $6–8 million.

The new concept would bring problems in jurisdiction, and I made it clear to the minister that we were happy with the original proposal, and had no desire to assume provincial responsibilities. In a letter of October 19, 1966, I wrote to him as follows, 'If the government is fearful of the tremendous expense involved in the expanded provincial concept, and is doubtful about the efficacy of the concept, either as a working arrangement or as a means of controlling expenditure elsewhere, and if, above all, these doubts give rise to delay, then I can assure you that the University of Toronto would be quite happy with the limited proposal.' But Davis was attracted to the provincial idea: it would give Ontario international leadership; it would justify the expenditure on the Toronto building, even on this expanded scale; and it would discourage dreams of grandeur elsewhere in the province. In the late fall of 1966, the full provincial concept at an estimated cost (including related buildings for Library Science and the rare book library) of $41 million was accepted, subject to confirmation by the provincial government's Advisory Committee on University Affairs. The advisory committee, which had never had a full-time chairman, and was not yet involved in the determination of capital expenditure, was not looked upon as a formidable barrier. In the fall of 1967 I left for Harvard on a year's leave of absence, convinced that my major goal had been achieved, and that I could, on my return, face the swelling political problems with a jocund heart.

On my return in June 1968, I found that the final decision had not yet been made. In March 1967, the advisory committee had acquired a full-time chairman, Douglas Wright, former dean of engineering at Waterloo; and, in the provincial system, he had found a heady scope for his quantitative skills. Before the committee was the Toronto scheme, and new library proposals from five other universities. Among them, the Toronto proposals seemed to be significantly more expensive. We countered effectively by demonstrating that the provincial estimates were based upon inaccurate figures, and that the remaining differential, between our library and the other libraries, now quite small, could be accounted for by the size and complexity of the building, which was the result of explicit provincial directions. Final approval came through for the library on November 21, 1968.

Work began on the building in what was almost a conspiracy of silence. Then, as its size and extent became apparent, there were sullen murmurs of criticism. The planners (both professional and unprofessional) said it was grossly out of scale with the rest of the campus. (This was palpably true; the building had been designed to fit specific needs and not to satisfy theoretical concepts of symmetry and proportion. Besides, the long-term plan called for high-rise instructional buildings – for Innis College and graduate studies – to the north and west of the library that would help to restore the balance between the old and the new campuses.) Midway through construction, it became apparent that, for some time to come, there would be little money from the government for new university buildings; and those not naturally enthusiastic about a research library resented such conspicuous expenditure in a period of growing scarcity.

The *Globe and Mail* editorialized indignantly about the extravagance of the library. (The paper always left the impression that the research library alone cost approximately $42 million. Actually over $5 million of this was for the School of Library Science, which, as a matter of convenience, was built next to the library and joined to it; and a very large sum – certainly no lower than $5 million – went into the provision of special provincial facilities. The Robarts Library, conceived of as a University of Toronto library, omitting the Thomas Fisher Rare Book Library, thus cost about $28 million.) In protesting against the use of taxpayers' money to support the mysterious and remote activities of the mind, the paper moved with the popular wave of anti-university feeling in the early seventies.

In my report for the year 1959–60, referring to the inadequacy of the library, and the excellence of other facilities, I had quoted Prince Hal's comment about Falstaff's diet: 'But one half pennyworth of bread to this intolerable deal of sack.' Now this state had been greatly remedied. Concentration of large library resources had always been the single, clearest mark of a great university. The library was both indispensable resource and declaration of intent. It enshrined the very idea of the university.

The principal section of the library complex – the research library – was named after the retiring premier of Ontario, John Robarts. Early in the sixties, when Ontario was searching for a centennial project, he had discussed with me his own favourite idea – a central provincial library in Toronto that would provide a headquarters for all libraries, both institutional and public. I pointed out to the premier that given the expansion of the University of Toronto, particularly in graduate studies, we must, under any conditions, greatly develop our library resources, and I feared his proposal would simply lead to costly duplication. If the province persevered with its project, then, of course, finances for any large scale expansion at the University of Toronto would disappear. He quickly saw my point and did not develop his idea. The University of Toronto project went ahead with his support and could not have been built without it.

I was greatly pleased as well that we were able to go ahead with the building of the rare book library. Although our book holdings had long been nourished by private collections, many of great value, it was only in recent years that we had set aside a special rare book area, at first a cramped and obscure room in the old library building, then, during the days of rapid expansion, rented quarters some distance from the campus. Now we had a room of renaissance splendour wedded to modern technology. The rare book library immediately attracted gifts – most important, a Shakespeare collection assembled by the Montreal financier, Sidney Fisher, regal in variety and scope but carefully shaped by Fisher's scholarly interests, and a collection of modern British writers assembled by his brother, Charles. The library was named, at the request of the brothers, after their great-grandfather who had come from England to Ontario in the early nineteenth century to establish a family tradition devoted to the trinity of business, music, and literature.

The building of the library was the final, climactic stage in the development of the higher learning at the University of Toronto. The library was our major commitment to the future, and there was no way now by which that commitment could be altered. It would grow steadily in importance; it would be absorbed and proudly taken for granted, like the Widener and the Bodleian, and the protests it had aroused would fade away like the headlines of yesterday's newspapers.

6 / The Professional Schools

Within the university, the colleges were the dominating influence. Their students generally ran the undergraduate paper, provided most of the participants for dramatic and debating events, and had a firm hold on the Rhodes scholarships. But to the general public, largely unaware of this special society that surrounded the formal program of instruction, the university was, first of all, an institution that trained professionals, particularly engineers and doctors.

Within the faculties of Engineering and Medicine, the tradition was strongly practical – brisk, no nonsense, efficient. The Faculty of Applied Science and Engineering had developed from the School of Practical Science, which had existed outside the university during its early phase in the late nineteenth century. The emphasis asserted in the original name was carefully nurtured. The engineers always proudly declared themselves to be members of a 'school', in the post-war years affectionately spelt 'skule.' 'Skule' denoted a place of lively basic activity, not given, as most faculties were, to woolly and theoretical speculation. Medicine was less assertive about its superior practicality. But that faculty too was strongly oriented towards practice, and might well have expressed surprise if it had been suggested that this was not its whole duty. The medical buildings on the campus, austere and institutional, were overwhelmed by the network of hospitals beyond the campus in which practical work was carried on.

The discovery of insulin had brought great fame to the university, but the discovery seemed to be an event not closely associated with the Faculty of Medicine. Charles Best, the co-discoverer, subsequently had developed his own institute where he pursued his researches in an intimate atmosphere, apart from the rest of Medicine: he was wary of the faculty and fearful of bureaucratic interference. He had a feeling that his faculty was not really concerned with fundamental research, and that it gave little heed to the recognition that came in regular waves to him from universities and learned societies all over the world.

The Board of Governors always took a special interest in Engineering and Medicine. When I rejoined the university as president, both the chairman and the vice-chairman were graduates of Engineering and naturally had a special feeling of affection towards that faculty. When Eric Phillips described the board's task as that of containing 'areas of chaos,' he undoubtedly had in mind primarily the activities of the Faculty of Arts and Science. Engineering and Medicine could be chaotic in their own way, but unlike Arts and Science, there was never any doubt about their having a clear and important goal. Medicine aroused the board's interest most easily. In part, it was social – a doctor with a university appointment and a large practice was likely to be one of the few academics that a governor would know; he might be a member of the same club in the city or a fishing partner in the wilderness. In part, it was the fascination of medical politics: governors always served on the boards of various hospitals and saw the constant pull between patient care and instruction and research; in hospitals, too, they were no doubt fascinated by the complexities of medical finance, which had its own dense jargon. Behind all this was the realization that whatever doubts one might have about the value of a university education, there could be no doubt about the value of a medical education. It provided the leadership and the intelligence in the fight against disease.

As a result of my years with Sidney Smith, I knew more about the professional faculties and was on easier terms with the deans and staffs of these divisions that I was with those of the Faculty of Arts and Science, of which I had been a member. I had never enjoyed the meetings of the Faculty of Arts and Science when I was a member, and I never learned to enjoy them when as president I became their chairman. Intricate questions about the academic status of students (the bedrock of these discussions) bored me, and the debates struck me as usually undisciplined and opaque. The dominating figures were the college registrars, long-suffering, patient men, learned in the academic law and its numerous exceptions, usually sympathetic to students; the other participants tended to be uninformed, emotional, or coldly technical. I found the atmosphere of the professional faculties more relaxed, the procedures more orderly, and the discussions less windy.

It did not seem to me in 1958 that the major professional faculties required special attention. Engineering was confident and buoyant. It had benefited greatly from the popular educational reawakening and its plans for expansion and development had been clearly determined. It had strong leadership in its dean, Roly McLaughlin, a man of wide cultivation and interests, who was quietly determined to shift Engineering from its tradition of rough practicality to an emphasis on research and the role of technology in society. He was largely responsible for the faculty getting a special grant from the Ford Foundation which gave impetus and direction to a swelling research program.

Medicine was far less assured and self-confident. The dean, J.A. MacFarlane, sensed the changes in the offing – the break-up of the old standard mechanized curriculum, the emphasis on medicine as part of a united social effort, the need to shatter the encrusted economics of the profession. MacFarlane welcomed change. He had great human warmth, was impatient with procedures when they stood in the way of whatever was fair and sensible, and could advance his ideas with a celtic dash and incisiveness. But he was nearing the end of his tenure as dean and he knew that he could only initiate, certainly not complete, the changes. Dentistry, another large and related faculty, was just about to enter its new building, and Roy G. Ellis, the dean, towered patiently and surely over its affairs.

Among the small professional divisions of the university – and Toronto had acquired over the years a great number – there were, however, persistent problems. In general, these concerned the firm establishment of academic credentials and standards, and the articulation of the division with the university as a whole. A professional faculty should not act like a special guest in the university; it must make the university, and not the profession, its first loyalty. In 1958, the most immediate and compelling problems among the small divisions were those of Music; and I made the resolution of those problems a first call on my time and attention.

In 1958, the Faculty of Music was a small, rather indistinct enclave in a large whole known as the Conservatory, royally anointed recently by act of the governor-general. To most people, including the university staff, the conservatory was not really a part of the university, and, in an important sense, they were right. The Royal Conservatory of Music of Toronto had developed from an independent musical school that made ends meet by conducting an elaborate examination system, accepted as authoritative throughout the whole country. When in 1919 the conservatory, nervous about its financial position, had joined the university, it had brought with it the examination system and a concern for music as a general cultural force. It had brought little concern with, or comprehension of, music as a university discipline. Within such an atmosphere, a university faculty was slow to emerge. It existed in effect as a small alien group within the conservatory, dependent upon the conservatory for its precarious financial existence.

This situation created tensions and aroused jealousies, and in the early fifties the newspapers had realized, in an obscure sort of way, that music in the university was a source of news – of bad news, of course. At the meetings of the Faculty of Music that I had attended as Sidney Smith's assistant, the atmosphere was outwardly benign. Ernest MacMillan, the dean, presided with a relaxed dignity, like a conductor conscious that he was in charge of an orchestra made up exclusively of virtuosi. The two senior professors were Leo Smith and Healey Willan. Both had had their training and experience in England, but had become devoted to the new land. Smith was a little man, sweet and gentle in manner; Willan was more robust and had a constant twinkle in his eye and in his speech. (I knew that both men held strong views about issues and men and could find abrasive words when aroused, but this I never saw.) The third senior figure was Arnold Walter, as assertively teutonic as Smith and Willan were unassertively English; and this cultural opposition was no doubt the source of some of the tensions that surfaced outside the quiet waters of the faculty meetings.

My general goal when I became president was to bring Music more firmly and obviously into the university and this could best be done by enlarging and emphasizing the faculty, which was concerned with university instruction and research, as distinct from the old conservatory, which was concerned with part-time non-university work. The problem of Music was part of a larger problem of clarifying and empasizing the function of the University of Toronto in the area of the fine arts. I thought that the university had three general responsibilities here: first, the study of the history and theory of the arts; second, formal training in the techniques of composition; and third, the setting of high standards in the choice and production of works of art. The first was wholly, and the second partially, a responsibility of the classroom and seminar; otherwise the responsibility was of a general nature, in which the central administration had a major share.

The university had traditionally taken little initiative in these matters. Most of the activity in the arts was of a voluntary and amateur nature, and took place most conspicuously in Hart House, which had, over the years, developed a fine collection of Canadian paintings, brought music of a kind and quality not available elsewhere in the city to the student body, and stimulated a good deal of creative work. The Hart House approach, unpretentious, almost casual, a sort of democratic elitism, was valuable, and had a profound effect, but it needed to be supplemented in other divisions by a university approach formalized through academic policy and strengthened by financial support. In Music, we should be making a major contribution to the professional world and we should be a centre for experimentation. In opera, for instance, which brings together so many of the arts – music, writing, acting, design, and the dance – the university could play an innovative role.

The initial problem was reorganization of the structure. I began with a series of interviews in the old ramshackle conservatory building on College Street, with its long, narrow corridors, its little concert hall like a renovated gymnasium in a rural school, its general atmosphere of continuous, self-absorbed bustle. I soon found that the faculty and the conservatory stood for two strongly different points of view. The conservatory carried on its old tradition of genteel, amateur instruction combined with a program of technical training and performance for the specially talented. We were repeatedly told that the pattern that had emerged was unique and invaluable and that great care should be taken not to disturb it. This was, of course, the inevitable stance of those who have grown up with a certain way of things and have a feeling for its intricacies and an understanding of its ambiguities. It was clear to me that, whatever we did, we should not lose the existing relationship between the full-time academic and the part-time amateur and professional. Many of the great names in Canadian music had come out of the conservatory. Musical genius, especially in performance, had little to do with academic ability; and it would be stupid to sacrifice all this on the altar of academic respectability. But, nevertheless, the university's responsibility was to create a faculty that could stand along with other faculties: full-time students meeting prescribed university qualifications, a staff sufficiently large and diverse in abilities to meet the needs of both undergraduates and graduates, a building appropriate to the special needs of the discipline, and a budget based on demonstrated need, not put together hastily from private revenue and arbitrary university grants.

The solution of the administrative problem (as a special consultant agreed) was the separation of the faculty from the old conservatory. The administrative division furthermore would be spelled out for all to see and understand in the physical arrangements: a proposed new building would be primarily for the Faculty of Music, since it was a full member of the university, but special arrangements would be made for the School of Music, as the old conservatory was renamed. This decision was received with some bitterness. The new building would have to be constructed from the proceeds of the sale of the old conservatory property, which now had become of great commercial value. (We knew that we had a ready purchaser in the provincial government, since the site was a natural area for the expansion of the Ontario Hydro offices immediately to the south, and the proceeds of the sale – about $3 million as it turned out, at that time a sum that could command respect – belonged morally, one could argue, to the old conservatory, even though all its resources had been transferred legally to the university.) Certainly, any solution had to contemplate special quarters for the old conservatory, near enough to the new building to permit joint use.

In our complex, federated campus, in the centre of the city, the selection of a site could not be an exercise in abstract theoretical planning. We had to work out an equilibrium from a complex of pressures: proximity between the new building and quarters for the old conservatory; a site that would not obstruct the growth of other active divisions, or eliminate essential breathing space on the campus; ease of access by public transportation since the public, both as audience and as student body, would make heavy use of both buildings. Some people raised the question of parking: this seemed to me to thrust problems soluble ten or twenty years before on a future that could not even entertain them. The final selection of the site has proved to be a happy one. The two divisions are close together near a central intersection and two subway stations; the new building for the faculty is unobtrusive but not crowded, with the prospect, given planned demolition in the future, of an open prospect on Queen's Park; the school is housed in a large and commanding Victorian edifice, newly renovated to its needs, that had once housed McMaster University and opens directly on to Bloor Street.

The money used for the new building was 'free' money. That is, there was no need to draw upon the campaign resources or to ask the government for special grants: the money from the old conservatory property was automatically doubled by the Canada Council under its capital grant program. In such a case, the possibility of opposition to the move from the Board of Governors was remote. But the board (not noticeably tender to the arts) could at least theoretically have held back a portion of the money from the sale, which had been absorbed in the university's general funds and was not tied to a specific building. Fortunately, one of the governors, James Duncan, who was also chairman of the board's conservatory committee, was a strong protagonist of the use of these resources for a new building for Music; and there was an unwritten law of the board that each member, especially a powerful one like Duncan, had veto or initiating power. At the time, I was unaware of another circumstance that may well have strengthened Duncan's hand. He had recently resigned as president of Massey-Harris under pressure from the holding company, Argus, of which Eric Phillips was senior executive. Under these conditions, Phillips may have been prepared to make concessions in an area of no business importance; and Duncan pressed the case of Music with unusual vigour. (In his memoirs, Duncan is concerned only with his business activities and makes no mention of the incident or indeed of the university at all.)

James Duncan and I had a strong ally in the dean, Boyd Neel, who had come from England in 1953 to succeed Sir Ernest. Like another recent cultural import from the United Kingdom, Tyrone Guthrie, he took a more shining view of Canadian accomplishments and possibilities in the arts than

Canadians did themselves; and he insisted on a building of major proportions with full facilities. He was particularly emphatic in his insistence on an opera theatre. Even I became hesitant here, for the stage he envisaged had to be capable of taking large productions, and this meant a structure on the scale of a major opera house. But Boyd Neel had his way, to the great advantage of Canadian musical life.

The general agreement has worked well, although the old conservatory was unhappy about losing its place of eminence; and the ancient tensions and jealousies lingered on without, however, precipitating a crisis. Even a series of sullenly critical articles in an evening paper in the spring of 1963, written by a former student of the conservatory, could not get any response. The articles had the usual characteristics of hurried journalistic exposés: a hodge-podge of editorial quotations, an air of omniscience, and a vague suggestion of horrors yet to come. There was much insistence that I must answer the charges, and the paper printed a picture of me in full academic regalia, taken some time before at a convocation; the implication was that I was pondering the paper's dark accusations. But I made no statement, and the attack collapsed under the weight of its own pretentious inanity.

The new building was opened officially in March 1964 with a special week of music. The idea was to emphasize the faculty as a creative force. An opera was chosen not likely to appear on any popular repertoire – Benjamin Britten's *Peter Herring*. The main compositions were Godfrey Ridout's dramatic symphony *Esther*, and Ernest MacMillan's *Chorale Ode*, a setting for choir and orchestra of Swinburne's *England* that he had composed in 1918 when he was interned in a German prison camp and had later submitted for a doctor's degree at Oxford. The performance was a tribute to Sir Ernest, after whom the main theatre had been named. By then he had retired from his musical activities. When he arose at the end of the performance, a rather slight figure with a neat white beard, many of the audience cast their minds back over the last thirty or forty years during which he had presided, with easy and unquestioned authority, over the musical world of the city and, to a large degree, of the nation. We listened to the music with a sense of pride and gratitude: it was the work of a young man, self-confident and assertive, expressing his deep sense of patriotism while held captive in the enemy's land. But it belonged, we thought sadly, to an age that would never come again, and Swinburne's poem, written during his last faded years, when emotions no longer welded the tumbling words, floated vaguely on the waves of the music.

In Toronto, music had always been the first of the arts, nourished and treasured when the other arts languished. The movement of the Faculty of Music from the periphery to the centre, and the provision of facilities that were among the best in the university world, had an ever-widening effect. The MacMillan Theatre became as much a city as a university facility, a constant reminder that the university had a responsibility to go beyond standard repertoires.

My second commanding concern among the professional faculties was Law. Its emergence as a full faculty had been the dramatic event of the fifties, a story that can be summed up briefly. The study of law had long been established at the University of Toronto, but it had been pursued independently of the profession, as a liberal discipline in the Faculty of Arts. Graduates of Toronto's law course were given no special concession at Osgoode Hall, the law school run by the Law Society of Upper Canada, which was solely responsible for the full formal teaching of law, both theoretical groundings and professional preparation. This was not, however, a cause for grievance. The university's honours course was taken voluntarily by students who willingly spent an extra year to get what they believed to be better preparation for practice. By the beginning of the fifties, however, cracks had begun to appear in the smooth Osgoode wall of containment. The dean of Osgoode Hall, Cecil Wright, and a senior colleague, Bora Laskin, were unhappy about the heavy domination of practical education. They had both taken advanced Harvard degrees and were wedded to the idea of law as a philosophical and logical discipline as well as a system of codified regulations and restraints. They thought that in Ontario, as elsewhere in the world, the study of law should be the responsibility of universities, with only the technical articling left to the profession.

In this issue, Wright and Laskin found a strong, eager ally in Sidney Smith, himself a Harvard graduate and a former Osgoode Hall lecturer. Together they worked out a coup whereby Wright and Laskin left Osgoode for the university and, simultaneously, the university established a separate law school to receive them. Although I was Smith's assistant at the time and had been progressively drawn into the main decisions, I knew little about the plot. It was conceived and implemented by Smith and Wright, who were close friends.

Cecil Augustus Wright was always known as 'Caesar.' Although the nickname partially defined the man, the man enhanced the nickname. He was imperial in his mastery of his subject and in his exposition of it, and he cast a cold eye on those who disagreed with him. Still, one was conscious that behind any ringing declaration lay a grinning reply or a reasoned objection; and his conviction and shrewdness were tempered by the irony and humour that were always on the verge of taking over. He needed these qualities to deal with his colleagues. Council meetings of the faculty, which I attended occasionally, resolved themselves into interminable arguments, and I only gradually realized that these were not violent brawls but boisterous pillow fights. But on the question of law education and the place of the Faculty of Law in the University of Toronto, Caesar was uncompromising; and no sooner had I arrived on the scene as president than he informed me that Law was unhappy. The faculty then was housed in Glendon Hall, a pleasant home but cramped, and distant from the campus. The eager revolutionaries, it seemed to them, had been received and sent off into an obscure retreat.

I soon discovered that there was no burning enthusiasm for Law in the Board of Governors; the Smith-Wright coup had been tolerated, not supported. There was, on the other hand, a good deal of pro-Osgoode sentiment: Law was a craft to be learned as quickly and efficiently as possible, not a proper university discipline; the prospective lawyer should study mathematics or classics or political science at the university and then address himself briskly to the learning of a tough trade. This was not a benighted point of view; indeed it was close to the familiar Oxbridge notion that the best preparation for a life of affairs was an immersion in a theoretical and unrelated subject. This did, of course, ignore the very point that Caesar was trying to make: that Law was an essentially liberal study, and if it was abstracted from its philosophical and political context, it would become a mechanism for money-making and for settling minor disputes. The board's doubts about Caesar's point of view were reinforced by personal irritation. Members of the board did not like Caesar's ridicule of respected members of the law profession, and his persistent reminder that the current location in Glendon Hall was demeaning, irritated members of the property committee.

I knew it was unprofitable to use theoretical arguments with the board, and I fell back on practical pressure. York had established itself on the campus but must quickly find a more ample home, and the site of Law was ideal for its needs. If York moved to Glendon Hall, we had then to find an appropriate site and buildings for Law on the main campus. This program was accepted. Flavelle Hall, once a large private home but for some time now a part of the university, was renovated, and a new wing was started to house a law library and classrooms, with a separate moot court building nearby. I thought that the whole abrasive issue had been laid to rest. But there were protracted and niggardly arguments about the cost, especially for construction of the moot court, which was thought to be ostentatious and expensive. Law thus moved back to the main campus in the fall of 1962 with no great sense of triumph. There was a feeling among its members that they had clawed their way back, that the university would continue to regard them as tolerated intruders.

Although the new faculty rapidly developed strength – it had a small and carefully selected body of students, and a vigorous staff, widely known in their various fields – it never did come to feel completely at ease on the campus. The staff, with their predominantly Harvard training, thought of their faculty in Harvard terms, and that meant holding a separate and powerful position in the university. When the new law library was set up, there was bickering about what constituted a law book: it seemed as if Law embraced all the social sciences, and if one accepted Law's criteria, the main library would have been savagely denuded. Law also was constantly finding anomalies and injustices in the university's policies: why should graduate work be so strongly supported and, when formula financing was introduced, be given such a heavy weighting? was not Law a proper graduate activity since almost all the students had good honours degrees? why did Canada Council policy, determined by academics, rule out research in the law as eligible for grants? But the main grief as the years went by was that new law faculties of splendid amplitude were springing up on other campuses – their very existence made possible by the Toronto coup which broke the Osgoode Hall monopoly – while Toronto's faculty was confined to quarters that now seemed in contrast to be inadequate, and to an annual budget squeezed and pummelled in the yearly financial battle of a large, diverse university. An opportunity for big-ness on a grand scale might have opened up briefly when the Law Society de-cided to give up its academic undertaking and concentrate on professional preparation. I heard of discussions between Caesar and the Osgoode Hall au-thorities, but they were abandoned at an early stage and never came officially to the attention of the university. This outcome was on the whole fortunate: Toronto had no need of another large faculty. York University was a natural heir to Osgoode; but the many-chambered building for law that rose rapidly on the York campus naturally intensified the Toronto sense of neglect.

If the staff of Law saw themselves as inadequately recognized, they did not respond with sulky self-absorption. They were active in university affairs, often giving leadership and providing skilled direction. Caesar Wright was chairman of the committee that worked out the relationship of Toronto with York; Bora Laskin took on the demanding job of chairman of the committee on graduate studies and insisted on writing most of the final report; Martin Friedland was a patient, skilful, determined, yet conciliatory chairman of the committee that prepared the way for a university-wide discussion of a new university constitution; and Albert Abel gave careful and wise advice on uni-versity problems that had legal implications.

I discovered quickly how many questions in the university did demand a nice legal approach. We were moving, without being entirely aware of it, from a society of status and rigid hierarchy to one in which we had to seek for balance between various elements, whose rights and traditions could not summarily be denied. One incident early in 1960, initially of minor significance, illustrated this. A young girl was turned down for membership in a fraternity. She was black, and she believed that her rejection was an act of racial prejudice. The papers picked up the story, and one played up the incident as an example of the widespread racial prejudice that it said existed in the provincial university. Our initial disposition was to say, with technical correctness, that this was not our business, since fraternities were not officially recognized at Toronto as academic ancilliaries of the university. (Each year I would explain to incredulous travelling American secretaries that we didn't concern ourselves with the moral or academic state of their fraternities.) To the public, however, fraternities were part of the university scene no matter how immaculate our denial; we had, as a matter of fact, denied our theoretical assumptions by seeming in some of our activities (for example, in the annual student yearbook) to accept fraternities as part of the community; and we saw that we had to make a far more positive statement.

I had never been a member of a fraternity, and looked upon them as divisive units that made little contribution to the university; in this crisis, I saw a chance not only to reassert the university's position of neutrality, but to point out that we could, if we chose, refuse a student permission to join a fraternity (as indeed one college already did.) This attitude, which I explained in a press interview, aroused as much of a storm as the incident of alleged discrimination. I was visited in my home by a graduate of the university, a prominent fraternity man and a minor pillar of the law profession, and lectured at with heavy unction. Did I not realize that fraternity members controlled the centres of power in this country, and that the opposition to them was politically motivated and came from communist-dominated agencies for the improvement of the lot of the blacks? I was angered and more determined than ever to take a strong moral stand on the fraternity question. But in the subsequent discussion in the Caput, the disciplinary body of the university, Caesar Wright cut through the mental fuzziness of both defenders and attackers. We should reiterate our legal position, he argued, and then give body to our theory by denying fraternities the few privileges they enjoyed or appropriated, such as inclusion in semi-official publications or use of the university's name. A statement was made; the uproar died down; and the rush of events – the appropriation of fraternity buildings for expansion, the widening social basis of the university – pushed the fraternities more and more into the background.

With the growth of the student power movement in the late sixties, the disciplinary problems became more tangled. For clear criminal offences, some of us thought that we could simply call in the civil courts and leave it to them to examine and assess judgment. This, after all, would be in accord with the current student battlecry against the old theory of *in loco parentis*, by which the university acted not only as fatherly disciplinarian but as fatherly protector. A brutally clear example of an offence that could be treated in this way was the stealing of books from the University Bookstore, of which there had been a number of incidents. In several especially flagrant cases, charges were laid against students by university officials and the cases referred to the courts. To my surprise, Caesar Wright objected strenuously to the procedure. A charge, he said, was not an automatic response to a criminal act: one considered the circumstances, the person involved, and the probable penalty. (In this instance, if the charge was upheld and a penalty assessed, the criminal record thus sustained would prevent the student from entering the United States, which, for a graduate student looking for a position or for further study, could be very serious.) To me, all this discussion was a demonstration that the law was not an *a priori* fixed response to the event but a flexible pragmatic assessment of the human situation. It was a valuable lesson at a time when the whirl of events seemed to call for reassertion of fixed principles.

II

It is a universal maxim among academic administrators that Medicine is the most difficult of all the faculties. In discussions of the nature of the complex university, someone will eventually say 'that's the university with a medical faculty'; and the result is good-natured laughter, such as follows a joke about mothers-in-law. The difficulty arises, first, from the fact that much of any medical faculty structure lies outside the university, entangled in hospitals and government agencies, and, second, from a tendency that had become a way of life at Toronto, to rely upon part-time teachers whose loyalties and incomes lie elsewhere than in the university. I decided not to get deeply involved in the internal politics of Medicine. That would mean a drain of time and energy at the expense of neglecting basic university programs. But I was concerned, as I was in the cases of Music and Law, with bringing Medicine more firmly and centrally into the university. Medicine should be a unifying discipline, part science, part human calculus, part mystery; and the great doctors that I knew at the university – Joe MacFarlane, who retired as dean in 1961, Duncan Graham, the retired Sir John and Lady Eaton Professor of Medicine, and his successor, Ray Farquharson – possessed in common a wise and ample charity that came in part from the teaching and practice of their profession.

Radical change in the university, as elsewhere, comes from the realization that the policy one has been faithfully following, hitherto unchallenged, is leading to disaster. In the spring of 1963, John Hamilton, who had succeeded MacFarlane as dean of medicine, wrote a letter in which he pointed out that the faculty, generally believed to share, with McGill, primacy in the country, was actually slipping badly into a secondary position. It was a story familiar in academic life; our memories of the past are durable and often brush aside the realities of the present. The main cause of decline was the continuing reliance on part-time teachers, the split between the clinical and the basic sciences, and the lack of facilities for research. The faculty was an agent for the profession and not an integral part of the university – in a way not unlike Law before the acceptance of the university involvement.

I was generally aware of these developments, not through a close study of the local scene, but from discussions I had listened to far from the university campus. On several occasions, I had been asked to be a member of a panel selecting young medical scholars for a career in academic medicine. This was the exclusive project of a small American foundation. The invitation to join the panel was attractive because it included wives, who were expected to take an active part in the selection process, and involved a three- or four-day stay in a hotel carefully selected for the elegance of its service and the charm of its situation. Canadian students were eligible in one region of this competition, and a Canadian representative was always invited to sit on the panel. (Almost all my releases from the treadmill of administration came as a result of American initiative and generosity. A fellow university president, a Canadian who had worked for many years in the United States, remarked to me, as we journeyed together to one international conference sponsored by an American foundation, 'Canada's a good country to have come from.') The culmination of the selective process, which consisted of interviews, conversations over meals and drinks, and a party that could grow naturally or collapse in grim self-consciousness, was a seminar in which aspects of the relationship between medicine and the academic life were discussed. In these exchanges, the panel was to be on the lookout for those who would go into academic medicine – teaching and research; the type to be avoided above all was a young doctor who would quickly give up the austere academic life for a lucrative private practice. Although Toronto had often been successful in the competition (my successor as president, John Evans, was a Markle Scholar), I got the impression that we were not looked upon as a university that nurtured academic medicine. We were known rather as the home of the high-powered specialist and the skilled practitioner. This was not to be taken as an indictment, since specialists and practitioners carried the burden in the hospitals, and the ultimate end of medicine was surely to alleviate human suffering. But the Markle Foundation believed that unless the university devoted itself intensively to teaching and research and produced graduates who would continue the process, medicine would become a repetition of procedures or an exercise in human politics, and the faculty would lose its power of renewal.

The realization of the failing academic strength of Medicine coincided with mounting pressure to expand. Expansion was certainly the price of any potential increase in aid from the provincial government, committed whether it liked it or not to some form of health insurance that depended upon the provision of far more doctors than the existing Ontario medical schools could produce. But there was strong resistance to expansion within the medical faculty – part inertia, part a real fear of slipping standards. The decision to move to a first clinical year of 250 (from the previous 175) was taken not by the faculty, but by the Board of Governors.

Although I had not taken the initiative in urging the expansion, I was in agreement with the board's decision. The problem was similar to what we had faced elsewhere – making sure that the inevitable increase in numbers was accompanied by measures to assure quality. But the metod of taking the decision exposed the danger of the current system. The medical faculty finally gave its approval, although in a resigned mood of *fait accompli*. The Senate had not debated the question, and, according to the simple, arbitrary constitutional theory of the university, this was not a matter for its concern; it was a quantitative and financial problem, so long as academic policies and standards were assumed to be unchanged. This was an illustration of the dangerous bifurcation in policy that ran through the whole university, and that could easily have led to a bitter confrontation if we had had a more battleworthy Senate. But although protest still simmered away in the Faculty of Medicine, the rest of the university was undisturbed, even though a decision had been made that would fundamentally alter the campus-wide balance of resources.

Henry Borden, firmly established as chairman of the board, addressed himself to the problem of medical expansion. He was at home in the Faculty of Medicine and relished its problems which, in their extent and political involvement, were closer to the world of business than the problems in other faculties. He saw the problem of expansion as falling into two areas: the provision of space on the campus for the basic sciences and for the research activities of the clinical sciences; and the expansion of the hospital empire in order to provide more 'teaching material' for an enlarged student body. Of the first there could be no doubt; a new building of a size never contemplated before was conceived, planned, and built in two years – a record of speed for the university – and the result both in efficiency and appearance was a satisfactory one (at least when it opened in 1970 there was no chorus of faculty disapproval, the usual first stage in the accommodation to a new building).

About the hospital expansion, there was not the same unanimity. The scheme involved taking over from the federal government in 1966 a huge complex known as Sunnybrook Hospital, north of the city, and then converting it into a university hospital, in the sense that the university would be entirely responsible for its administration, and the teaching staff attached to it would be full-time members of the university. This venture was peculiarly Mr Borden's; he carried out the negotiations with the federal government, and with the members of the family who had originally owned the Sunnybrook ground. He set up the Sunnybrook board and stiffened it with members of the university's board specially appointed for this purpose; and above all, he persuaded the provincial government to accept this scheme and support it in a generous fashion. It was a scheme that called upon all of Henry Borden's formidable entrepreneurial skills. However, it aroused concern and sharpened doubts in the medical fraternity. We didn't need, they argued, to add another hospital to our bulging network; and the special status of Sunnybrook was bound to create jealousies among the other teaching hospitals, which had looser but historically longer ties with the university, and financial distortions within the university itself. I was concerned that the sudden protrusive priority given to Medicine would upset the balance of expansion and would set back my special project, the research library. But Henry Borden recognized the library needs and at the crucial moments of decision when his opposition or his indifference would have killed the proposal, he came to my support.

On the whole, the changes brought the medical faculty more firmly within the university. If Sunnybrook created a distant outpost of which much of the university was only vaguely aware, the Medical Science Building, which took over the dominating position on the campus occupied formerly by the old Engineering Building, became, through its facilities for meetings, a university centre. A strengthening of academic ties, Sirluck and I thought, might well come through the development of graduate studies in the clinical sciences, an area that heretofore had tended to live to itself. The idea here was to unite clinical experience and knowledge with the pure sciences, to provide an alternative route for the medical graduate to general practice and specialization. The Centre for Medical Sciences was established as a structure for this purpose. The medical faculty was now not just a distinguished (but aloof) guest who found the university a convenient host; it was a member of the family much taken up with outside interests, but still joining in common enterprises.

The bringing of the professional faculties closer to the university was the positive side of the policy. But I came to believe strongly that the university must also accept a negative side. We should look at our professional faculties and determine if there were any that should not continue to exist. There might well be duplication of work that was already being done in established departments of other faculties; work that was being carried on more successfully in neighbouring universities; or work that no longer clearly belonged in a university. It is always easy to work out schemes for strengthening a particular academic activity, no matter how dubious; but it is painfully difficult to work out schemes for its elimination or translation. Once established in a university, an activity rapidly develops a sense of identity, and after graduating a few generations of students, it acquires protectors and apologists.

At various times we looked critically at a number of the small faculties: at Forestry and Physical and Health Education, because we thought they might flourish better at Erindale or Scarborough; at Business, because York had made Business an overriding priority, and we wondered whether there was a place in the same city for a comparatively small enterprise; at Child Study because we could find no successor for its charismatic founder, William E. Blatz; at Food Chemistry, really 'Household Science,' renamed by a committee anxious to banish the Victorian blandness of the old name.

We made no change in Forestry and Physical and Health Education. In Child Study we worked out an arrangement whereby it would have a closer relationship with the College of Education. A look at Business ended with a decision to strengthen it, not to reach for bigness and comprehensiveness, as York was doing, but to build an effective postgraduate research centre. It often puzzled me why the Board of Governors, with such a strong business bias, should not have pressed for a heavier commitment in business education. It may have been the resistance of our social sciences to what they looked upon as academic bowdlerization; or it may have been the indifference of businessmen who had grown up in a tough competitive atmosphere and were suspicious of academic intrusion. York's board was also strongly business in composition, but the businessmen were younger than ours and more at home with the new, easy relationship between the business and academic worlds. York had elected to be a university with a brisk, business profile, and we had no desire to challenge it.

This left Food Sciences for consideration. We concluded that here we should take strong action – absorb the pure scientific part into the relevant departments of the university, and abandon the other part, what might be described as the union of general education and the domestic arts. For students who wanted to follow the latter course, the University of Guelph offered a milieu and facilities that we could not provide. The proposals precipitated a series of protests in which students, staff, and, above all, the fiercely devoted alumni, joined. In the spring of 1971 we arranged for an open hearing in the Senate chamber over which I presided with a dismal sense of duty.

Under difficult conditions, the meeting was restrained and friendly; at least no one accused my advisers or me of male chauvinism. The hearing revealed sharp disagreement about the role of the faculty, but made it clear that action could not yet be taken.

Thus, the negative policy could report defeat or, at least, a stalemate on all fronts. I began to wonder whether, under the traditional governing structure, the university could radically change itself. There seemed always to be the possibility of an endless series of appeals. Somewhere this process must end, and, increasingly, during my final years of office, I placed my hope in the single, representative body that was clearly emerging as the goal of structural reform.

7 / The Winds of Change

The years from 1958 to 1967 were the final period of the old feudalistic university that was based upon certain rigid assumptions that went unquestioned. The first of these assumptions was that the universities were separate, self-contained entities that existed outside of the political process. They were wards of the prime minister's office, and not subject to any direct interference by government. The second assumption was that the university existed as both financial corporation and academic process, and that the two must be kept rigidly separate. The former was the responsibility of laymen who knew at first hand about the mysteries of finance, and the latter was the responsibility of the teaching staff; but ultimate power on any question must lie with the lay board. The third assumption was that students were not active participants in the running of the university; it was their happy lot to receive and to enjoy what had been decided for their benefit.

The system was authoritarian, but benign, and under it Toronto prospered. On the provincial level, Toronto was the prime minister's favourite ward, quixotically dealt with from time to time, but never scorned or neglected. Internally, conflicts between lay and academic, between board and staff, were rare; staff accepted the doctrine that their freedoms – to make appointments, to determine curricula, to criticize the university and the world about them (in a gentlemanly manner) – were dependent upon not meddling in financial affairs. Students embraced the doctrine of *in loco parentis*; they resented not paternalism, but a mean and distant paternalism.

In this system the president, living in a fixed and unchanging world, could work with confidence and despatch. If he won the confidence of both Board of Governors and Senate, he was granted large areas where he could exercise his own initiative. On the whole, he was happy to leave negotiations with the province to the chairman of the board; he thereby remained an academic to whom political intrigue was thought to be foreign and distasteful.

But this system could not survive if the assumptions were challenged. And all of them, in varying degrees of urgency, were now being challenged.

The first to be challenged was the laissez-faire institutional individualism. The university had been to this point like a proud old four-master making its way by its own skill and energy, only vaguely aware of the distant authorities who had despatched it on its voyage. But navigational methods had long since become more sophisticated and new perils demanded more central control, possibly even movement in convoys.

The provincial government was initially reluctant to abandon the old ways. Carleton, the only new institution since the war, had been permitted to struggle along without significant help or encouragement; it was ten years in existence before, in 1952, it was given official provincial status as an institution of higher learning. During that period, there was lively movement in a number of areas; the establishment of a new college or university (the distinction was not clear to the eager founders) became a community obsession. In January 1956, the minister of education, W.J. Dunlop, called a meeting of the province's university presidents to pronounce his official disapproval of the rush to found new colleges. Bill Dunlop had grown up in the University of Toronto and before entering the government had presided for decades with paternalism over the university's expanding world of extension studies – instruction given outside of formal classes, either for a degree or for disinterested self-improvement. Possibly he felt that this process could continue, and absorb the need. A proper university was the culmination of long years of growth, and the minister thought it was absurd to think of establishing one by fiat.

During my two years at Carleton, I took little interest in the wider picture, concentrating all my efforts in bringing Carleton fully into the family circle of universities. But at Toronto one had to think constantly of the provincial scene, if only for the sake of survival: the university was hovering between two courses, each a rapid descent to disaster – bloated expansion, or the draining off of resources into a multitude of new foundations. The government showed no interest, as yet, in developing a provincial scheme. Under these conditions, it seemed best to take some immediate local action to shore up the institution against ruin. That action was the establishment of York, which was a combination of community aspiration and University of Toronto effort. Evolutionary developments among the existing universities also relieved the pressure. The Ontario Agricultural College at Guelph – still attached at that time to the University of Toronto by tenuous threads of sentiment and legality – began to formulate plans for a separate institution; and at Waterloo, a process of separating the existing college from the University of Western Ontario and creating a complex federation of colleges was under way, energetically led by the man who became the first president of the new university, J.G. Hagey. More difficult to assess were the regional pressures for new institutions. In southern Ontario, the demographic map pointed to two regions where new institutions were clearly needed: the Niagara Peninsula, centred in St Catharines, and the area east of Toronto, centred in Oshawa. The former provided the basis for Brock University; but the latter encountered a rival in Peterborough, which made up in spirit and drive what it lacked in population. A number of university presidents thought that, in the light of the population distribution, Peterborough's claims should be looked at coolly and critically, and as the president of the largest university in the province, and the one believed to be closest to the government, I inspired some snarling outbursts in the Peterborough press. An editorial declared that Toronto was besotted with the idea of bigness, that we cheerfully contemplated a city university of 40,000 or 50,000, and to accomplish our purpose would oppose the foundation of any new institution. Robertson Davies, then the editor of the *Peterborough Examiner*, wrote to me in a tone of mild but firm expostulation.

But the Peterborough affair had a fortunate outcome. Tom Symons went from Toronto to be the first president of Trent, the institution that finally emerged; and two of our senior administrators, Joe MacFarlane and Moffat Woodside, were active in the early stages of its planning. Strong population pressure is not always the best parent of a new university; indeed, the very absence of such pressure enabled Trent to achieve an early and lively individual identity.

With the growing number of new institutions, and the pressure for more still mounting, it became clear the province should prepare a comprehensive plan. But the province had no resources for collecting information, analysing the data, and determining policy. The Department of Education was exclusively concerned with secondary school education. For the universities, there was the beginnings of a grants committee, made up of a few civil servants and government appointees, but it was casual, tentative, and fumbling in its approach. The animating force of the committee was Leslie Frost, who had stepped down as premier in November 1961 and had been succeeded by John Robarts.

Retired from active politics, Frost made the universities his main interest. His own university career had been interrupted by the first world war and he had never graduated. During the long years of his premiership, he had rarely if ever dealt directly with academics; his commerce had been with the chairmen of boards of governors, who tended to be businessmen, well disposed towards his party. For the university presidents that he now saw frequently, he had formal respect, part benign, part amused tolerance. They were to him senior schoolmasters venturing uncertainly into the world of affairs; and he would address them, in a friendly, patronizing way, as 'Doctor,' the word drawn out and emphasized with a relaxed rural Ontario drawl.

No doubt part of his interest in the universities arose from his awareness that higher education was a rapidly expanding area over which the government had as yet no machinery for control. At first he spoke to us more in his capacity as the ex-provincial treasurer, for whom a balanced budget was the noblest work of the politician, than as a leader of higher education. On the financial front, he was tough and unswerving. I remember a fierce tongue-lashing when he was incensed by the release of figures the university presidents had prepared on the future cost of higher education, with the final cut that, 'This will do you no good.' The next time I saw him at a social gathering, he made a point of coming over to shake my hand, smiling warmly and saying in tones that could be heard throughout the room, 'I wonder if this fellow is still mad at me!' This was an example of the Frost charm and inborn small-town friendliness that made it difficult for any opposition party to turn him into an authoritarian symbol.

It was Leslie Frost who, realizing that the government had no plan for expansion or means of devising one, summoned the presidents and asked them to say what should be done. The request came late in March 1962, at a time when my institutional budget was being worked out in detail, and I could at the same time look forward to some administrative diminuendo before the convocation exercises swallowed up everything in a world of speeches and dinners. As chairman of the committee of presidents, I had major responsibilities in implementing the governmental request. I did not view this responsibility cheerfully. The presidents then had little experience in working together. They concentrated on getting along with their own deans and governors; and association with their fellow presidents was confined to annual meetings of the national body, the National Conference of Canadian Universities and Colleges – mainly an academic conference with strong talk during the day and strong drink in the evening. In Ontario, the presidents of the old established universities with clear government affiliations, Toronto, Queen's, McMaster, and Western, had met on a few occasions – a sort of self-constituted security council. But when we met, we tended to commiserate with each other and to reinforce our fears for the future. Now there had been added a fresh group – heads of recently established institutions, men who were suspicious of the old guard, convinced that the hope of the future lay with their institutions.

I did not see how a group of presidents, each a fierce defender of his institution, could work out a plan that reflected accurately a system of provincial priorities. What we must do, I thought, was to turn the problem over to a representative academic group. Such a group would not be burdened to the same degree with institutional aspirations and prejudices, and was likely to command a greater variety of professional talents than the presidents could. The selection of the chairman for the research committee, as it was called, was important. He should come from one of the older universities, preferably not from Toronto; he should be acceptable to government; and he should have a talent for resolving discord. Given this formula, John Deutsch, the vice-principal of Queen's, was an inevitable choice. He had previously been a respected senior civil servant on whom authority sat easily; and his manner, undemonstrative, self-assured without being prickly and contentious, seemed to proclaim that there was no problem that could not yield to reason and good will. Almost as important was the selection of a good secretary. Here again, the choice was inevitable. Frances Ireland had worked for Sidney Smith; she could turn raw words into a finished statement, and she had become increasingly familiar with both the politics and metaphysics of higher education. I had given her a special independent status in my office so that she could work on the major issues. She had been secretary of a policy and planning committee at Toronto that I had set up, in effect a senior seminar on problems in higher education, to which I would take ideas and from which I could derive them. More and more we had turned to provincial problems; and Frances Ireland had reduced our discussions to order and dignified them with supporting evidence.

We were requested to prepare a report, and less than two months later, on May 16, we presented the completed document, brief, succinct, and specific. Behind it lay years of careful preparation in groups and committees within universities and in national bodies. Its brevity and clarity were based on ideas long meditated and on statistics thoroughly checked and analysed. No doubt we needed government initiative to launch the study; the universities still had no formal provincial structure and, even if they had, they would not have tried, on their own, to formulate provincial policy. This was the first – and the most significant – example of government and university co-operation; and from this point on the problem was to devise some structure whereby that co-operation could be assured and strengthened.

The presidents asked the research committee to examine the problem of additional institutions of higher education. This they did in a special study called *The City College*, which was released in October 1964. The development of junior colleges in the American manner – the incorporation of the last year of secondary school and the first year of university in a middle institution – was attractive to those who wanted a controlled, interlocking system. There were other arguments as well, of a more reputable nature, for the concept. Junior colleges spread widely throughout the province would reduce the expense of higher education during a student's early years. They would provide a time for self-analysis before a student was forced to take a decision about his area of specialty, and they would be a cheap and effective way of meeting the great demands for general education without over-expanding the university. (Presumably many students would find the junior college years sufficient and would not go on to university; they would decide to pursue a vocational training or take a job directly.)

Nevertheless the presidents as a body came out strongly against the junior college idea. We were concerned that it would weaken both the secondary school and the university; and it would play down an area of education where the country was notoriously weak – vocational and technical education. Any new colleges should have their own justification. They should not be adjuncts of the university.

There was a good deal of journalistic opposition to the presidential recommendation, and some opposition from within, particularly from Murray Ross. The journalistic outcry was that universities were selfishly defending their own powers and arbitrarily denying to thousands of students the precious prize of the BA. We were, of course, concerned with defending the integrity of the university, and for this there was no need of apology. But in addition, we were saying, 'Rid your minds of the snobbery of the university degree; realize that there are other talents besides the verbal and the mathematical and that this country desperately needs people who are trained to do intricate practical tasks in industry and the arts.'

The position taken in 1964 was a crucial one; and events have justified it. The new colleges of applied arts and technology, with their strong vocational bias, are happy to go their own way and do not aspire to turn themselves into universities. The universities retain their strong unfragmented faculties of arts and science. Quebec, I think, supplies an object lesson of what happens when a new institution is thrust between the secondary school and university. Students from the collèges d'enseignement général et professionel – the equivalents of the proposed Ontario junior colleges – enter university at an advanced stage with vague credentials that the university must accept. In the United States, there are increasing difficulties arising from the differences in training and aptitude between those who enter university directly from secondary school, and those who transfer from junior colleges.

If the universities have a special and important task to perform for which they alone are responsible, then, it was felt, they should be the concern of a special arm of government. No such arm existed. The Advisory Committee on University Affairs was advisory only, and the Department of Education was constructed to supervise primary and secondary school education. We were distressed at the prospect of being absorbed in that empire with its central court and its obeisant ambassadors despatched to the provinces to carry out the imperial will. It was a fear of such absorption that had swollen our outcry against the system of junior colleges, for this would have meant an interlocking system, which involved bureaucratic control from the top. The theme of a separate minister and department became an insistent one in our deliberations and finally, after some reluctance, the government accepted the idea. At the time, Bill Davis merely assumed a second portfolio, that of university affairs, but the way was now clear for separate administrative machinery and, eventually, for a separate ministry.

The most delicate and crucial problem, however, was the nature and composition of the advisory committee. At that time, it was so small, unrepresentative, and isolated that it could be mischievous. The committee of presidents believed in the concept of a 'buffer' committee – an independent body between the university and the government – that made recommendations to government about the total amount of money that should be allocated to universities; but we wanted to learn from what we understood to be the United Kingdom experience of such a body. We wanted the committee to be defended against government interference by having its own staff; and, more important, we wanted the committee to work closely with the university in devising general policy. We realized that the latter goal could be achieved only if universities worked closely together and developed a strong unified voice. This had not happened, I gathered, in the United Kingdom, where the Grants Committee moved closer to Treasury than to universities. When Lord Robbins, who had been working on his report on the future of higher education in the UK, paid us a brief visit, he had some caustic things to say about the Committee of British Vice-Chancellors: 'They maintain a careful anonymity, a cultivated non-existence. Compared to them, the deer in Windsor Forest are positively ferocious.'

The strengthening of the advisory committee meant to us the addition of new members, with a strong academic representation, the development of a separate research resource, and the appointment of a full-time chairman. All of these objectives were amicably achieved. But the more complex and important task was to develop among the universities an effective central body that would carry weight both with the universities and the government. We aspired to the impossible – a body that had no legislative powers, that in the last resort admitted institutional freedom of action, and yet spoke collectively and strongly to the government. And we were still dogged by the dogma of the divine right of presidents: presidents alone could speak for their institutions; they could not suffer the intrusion of another voice since it might be a dissident one.

I was much concerned about the problem of finding a collective, authoritative voice that would give this central body the right to speak for the universities. The presidents argued that they alone could fuse the decisions of the two supreme bodies of their individual universities, the lay boards and the academic senates. But, on the provincial field, boards and senates were being by-passed by faculty associations, representative organizations of the teaching staffs, which were quick to realize that many of the most important decisions must now be made on a provincial basis. Some of my preisdential colleagues held out against any recognition of the faculty associations on the sound constitutional grounds that they were responsible alone to the legally established bodies in their institutions. But hard political facts could not be resisted; and in the selection of academic representation for the advisory committee and proposals for the full-time chairman, we conferred with the faculty associations amicably and with an agreeably close approach to unanimity.

In the spring of 1966 I was succeeded as chairman of the committee of presidents by J.A. Corry, principal of Queen's. It was a relief to lay down the additional burden, since the work was demanding and the means to do it inadequate. There was as yet no fixed constitutional structure to the committee and no clear basis for establishing one. There was no secretariat. It was a question of trying to perceive a consensus and hoping that action would be subsequently ratified. Under such bizarre circumstances, we accomplished a good deal. As so often in the history of higher education in Ontario, the Queen's point of view, idealistic but with a shrewd pragmatic hold on the actual, was influential, especially as it was expressed in Alex Corry, most humane of constitutional theorists.

All these developments on the provincial front had enormous implications for the system of Toronto's institutional government. All the old assumptions were being challenged. The university could no longer exist as a separate entity, and would have to work closely with fellow institutions and with government. Moreover, the ponderous internal system of separate powers and complex interlocking committees was not well adjusted to the tempo of change. The province could not wait until the academic snail completed its prescribed journey. And internal decisions about general financial policy could no longer exclude faculty, who had already seized some of the power on the provincial front. The Board of Governors and Senate seemed to me to be increasingly peripheral, solemnly going through formal drills in full-dress uniforms while the fighting troops were locked in bitter conflict a few miles ahead. The first internal priority was to bring the faculty into all phases of decision-making, and this meant, at a minimum, the addition of some faculty to the board.

The doctrine of faculty representation on the Board of Governors was not a comfortable one at the University of Toronto. Indeed, to most members of the board it was not even a question for negotiation. It struck at the very heart of sound university government, namely that the lay element should occupy a position of pure independence, godlike in its remoteness and omniscience. The board was conceived of as being similar to the board of a business corporation, but with a paternalistic zeal and a power of initiative never dreamt of by any business board. It was at Toronto a combination of cabinet, executive, and supreme court, and its authority was unquestioned and mysterious.

The principal argument against faculty participation was that faculty were bound to act out of self-interest. If they were admitted to the board, the board would become a battleground for warring factions, and cease to be a disinterested body serving the university and the country. In its devotion to this point of view, Toronto was squarely and uncompromisingly in the American tradition. When I met my American presidential colleagues, I would occasionally introduce the idea of faculty representation on the governing body. It would be greeted with scorn as if I were an excommunicated priest who had stumbled into a conclave of bishops. 'Would you,' replied the best known scholar-administrator in the United States, 'like to be operated upon by your brother-in-law?' He presumably thought that the question carried its own crashing negative. But I reflected that I wouldn't object in the least, provided that I was sure of my brother-in-law's professional credentials.

Eric Phillips believed devoutly in the separation of powers and the necessity of maintaining the purity of the lay body. The Act of 1906 establishing the modern structure of the University of Toronto was, for him, a magna carta, assuring efficiency by giving ultimate power to the lay board. I knew and understood the theory but I had increasing doubts about whether, in the new environment, it could survive. On the national front, faculty associations were urging the setting-up of a national commission to examine university government. During the year 1962–3, when I was president of the Association of Universities and Colleges of Canada, I urged that that association, largely controlled by presidents and senior administrators, should work with the faculty in establishing such a commission, and I then became the chairman of a joint steering committee created to implement the proposal. I kept Eric Phillips informed of these activities. He was usually relaxed and tolerant about my national activities in educational politics because they seemed to him harmless diversions. But the commission on university government was a different affair. It would presumably visit individual campuses and summon board members to appear before it. Eric had no intention whatsoever of appearing before an unofficial body of academics, and he was not going to permit any tampering with the Toronto constitution. I tried to allay his fears by explaining that university government was now the great topic for faculty discussion, and that it was better to have the questions pondered by a national commission rather than raised with partisan bitterness within the university. He was only partially placated, and it was fortunate for him and the university that his chairmanship came to an end before the commission began its active hearings.

The steering committee spent a good deal of time in looking for two commissioners. They thought, with typical bland Canadian self-deprecation, that the deliberations of the commission would command more attention if the commissioners came from outside Canada; and we concluded that one should be from the USA and one from the UK. In the event, we hit upon an effective team. The American was a young political scientist, Robert Berdahl, from San Francisco State College, and the representative from the UK was Sir James Duff, retired as vice-chancellor of the University of Durham, but still active on a number of educational fronts. On the surface, the choice of the two men seemed deliberately perverse. Berdahl was youthful, even more youthful in appearance than in fact, and he had an enthusiastic, eager, confident manner. Sir James was thirty years his senior; in appearance he looked like a stout, kindly English country squire (which indeed he was); he spoke slowly, with sparing precision and a strong suggestion that others should do likewise. But the two men worked together famously. Berdahl had written a book about the British universities and their relationship to government, and spoke and understood the language of British academic life. Sir James had wit and understanding, as well as deep knowledge, and he valued the younger man's energy and resourcefulness.

The report was released in March 1966, a little anticlimactically since the *Globe and Mail* had already secured the main outline and had published its conclusions. The crucial passages were clear recommendations for faculty membership on boards, and for the creation of strengthened senates that would be firmly in control of academic policy. Given the prior newspaper publicity, there was little interest shown during the official press conference in Ottawa. The only persistent questioner was a young woman who came from the Canadian Union of Students. She was fluent in the language with which I was to become familiar during the coming years – the report, she said, was authoritarian and 'an Uncle Tom document,' but she was cheerful and unaggressive, had no supporters or claque, and we were disposed to listen to her with unvexed tolerance.

The report was a British document, an urging upon Canadian universities of British practice. We must get rid of the separation of lay and academic and establish strong ties between them, without undermining the final authority of the lay body. These are typical British constitutional ideas adapted to universities: power carefully controlled by the nature of representation and by a complicated process of discussion and review before a final action is taken. Certainly the ideas were more liberal than those embodied in the structure at Toronto.

As chairman of the steering committee, I had been familiar with the work of the Duff-Berdahl commission, and knew the main recommendations long in advance of the release of the report. Toronto was obviously the classical example of the old-fashioned, discredited ways that were described in the report, and the publication of the report would strengthen the internal movement for reform. My main concern was to avoid a clash between board and faculty. In the spring of 1965 I proposed the setting up of a middle body between the Board of Governors and the Senate, consisting of representatives from the board, the faculty, and the administration. It would be free to discuss any matter, but would concentrate on general policy, particularly on such complex problems as academic priorities, government relationships, and faculty appointments, where finance and educational policy coalesced. It would be advisory to the president and would have no legal status or powers; but it would inevitably carry great weight. The body, known as the President's Council, was established, and for the next five years enabled the university to deal in an intelligent and coherent way with its main problems.

But the council was a temporary device. In September 1965 I suggested in a memorandum to the chairman that we 'give some thought' to the possibility of asking the government for a special commission to look at the University of Toronto Act of 1906. I gave three 'good reasons' for the proposal. First, 'It would anticipate a campaign that might well be launched to investigate the university.' Second, 'It would place any examination on a sound procedural basis. The 1906 Act must obviously be amended in hundreds of places so that the specific problems of the Board and the Senate would be seen as part of a wider context.' And, third, 'If the university proposes such a commission, and provides proper facilities first, we would stand to benefit. I am convinced that the university is going to be more and more in the public domain. Instead of fighting this movement, we should do our best to go along with it and thereby influence it.' But the proposal drew no response. The prospect of faculty membership on the board, acceptable to some of the governors, was repugnant to most; and there was no doubt now that any commission even distantly conscious of the mood of the academic community would recommend faculty membership on the senior body of the university.

Since the board was reluctant to launch a full-scale investigation of university government, the initiative had to come from elsewhere. I could use the President's Council to start a few controversial hares. The Duff-Berdahl recommendations were radical in a Toronto context, but they were largely a codification of British practice, and surely we could generate something from our own experience.

During the previous few years, I had been moving towards a theory of university government that was different from the Duff-Berdahl theory. I finally set down my ideas in a paper that I gave to the President's Council in December 1966 and elaborated a month later in a formal paper at a meeting of the Association of Universities and Colleges of Canada. In brief, I argued that there was not now (if indeed there had ever been) two worlds in university affairs; that there was only one academic world, of which financial affairs were an indissoluble part; and that the university should have one representative, authoritative body to deal with all matters. I talked about the 'double innocence,' a phrase that gained considerable currency at Toronto during the next few years – innocence among the academics of financial matters, and innocence among lay people of academic matters.

The idea, as I discovered later on, was closer to the French than to the British mode. But its real significance was that it was based on my own experience, and was not a theoretical elaboration. I was unhappy about the role of the president as pacifier and reconciler in a world that was increasingly fragmented. His traditional responsibility of keeping the peace between Board of Governors and Senate had not been difficult, especially since each was ignorant of the other. But now he was faced with unofficial bodies of great potential strength that he could not ignore – a faculty association, already exerting strong influence on the crucial provincial plans, and a student organization now sullenly withdrawing from its old subsidiary role and establishing itself as an independent body. Given so many separate and distinct bodies, was it not likely that the presidential authority would be hopelessly shredded and the university reduced to a perpetual state of conflict?

The proposals that I made were usually described as the unicameral system. That was unfortunate, since the emphasis was not on the creation of a single body, but on a representative body of final, indisputable authority. Whatever subsidiary bodies came into being afterwards would feed into the main body.

An underlying thought in the working out of my position was reluctance to have the provincial English university used as a Canadian model. Shortly after I became Sidney Smith's assistant, I had been granted a travel fellowship by the Carnegie Corporation, designed to broaden the knowledge of young administrators who might some day take on senior executive responsibilities. I spent the early part of the summer of 1951 touring the English provincial universities. It was, on the whole, a dispiriting experience. The universities were unapologetically assertive about their seniority in the Commonwealth (with, of course, proper deference to the special positions of Oxford, Cambridge, and London) without having, as far as I could see, a strong basis for their self-esteem. Their spokesmen were convinced that Canadian universities were American offshoots, degree factories presided over by academic tycoons. They thought of themselves, on the other hand, as models of constitutional government where everything proceeded by order and precedent, with wisdom and restraint the final issue. I returned with the feeling that the Canadian system of pragmatic and tempered absolutism had many virtues, among them speed and despatch; and the new concept I emerged with almost twenty years later was a development of the Canadian and not an adaptation of British experience. It was a continuation of the Canadian emphasis on directness and decisiveness, expressed now in a communitarian context.

In my working out of the new proposals, I had not given serious thought to the inclusion of students – and the Duff-Berdahl commission had taken the orthodox paternalistic attitude. Students were not mature enough to help in the formulation of university policy; besides, their role of learning was all-demanding and left no room for the perplexities of running a university. (But the report did take note of student discontent, and ruminated that 'some variation of the Berkeley disturbances might occur in Canada during the coming years.') To the student radicals, the report was an apology for the old regime. Sir James Duff wrote to me sadly: 'I feel sometimes that Duff-Berdahl was out of date almost before it appeared. Faculty alienation was never, it seems to me, as formidable a problem as student alienation is becoming.' Sir James's words were to be an epigraph for the next five years.

8 / Student Power

Although the student question was, from about 1967 on, to take a sudden sharp twist and present the university with a whole new set of problems, the years immediately before had not been uninstructive blanks. In 1963 and 1964 we had been very much concerned about the degree of autonomy given to the official student organization, the Students' Administrative Council. With the rapid growth in student numbers, it had attained a great financial power, since each student paid a compulsory fee. Under the rules and procedures of the Board of Governors, the SAC was a financial subsidiary, a non-academic unit responsible to the board. In point of fact, there was little financial control, but the theoretical power was there and the SAC now began to assert its independence.

I was sympathetic with the students' demands for financial autonomy. The students had their own special interests and they should be free to develop them in whatever way they saw fit. The insistence on financial control (combined with a policy of benevolent non-concern in what the SAC did) repeated the fundamental flaw in the university structure – the separation of financial responsibility from an administrative and moral responsibility, with a constant threat of interference from above and waywardness from below. There had in practice been no conspicuous examples of either. The real irritation was that the students were forced to deal with financial officers immediately responsible to the board; and they resented this as demeaning (especially when financial officers read them moral lessons on the necessity of economy and the danger of spending hard money on soft causes). Besides, the students pointed out, after reading the University Act with great care, they were enjoined by the Act to make representations solely to the president, not to his delegates.

The controversy was, by comparison with the quiet years before, lively and intense, with an occasional foretaste of what lay ahead. In the fall of 1964, with the main issues still unresolved, the SAC produced a handbook for incoming freshmen that went far beyond the usual innocuous indiscretions. In a meeting with the student executives, I railed against it as 'a sick piece of buffoonery.' Some members of the board resisted any loosening of the financial ties with the SAC, and they had law and moral conviction on their side. But the board (as it was to do frequently in the years ahead), finally succumbed to the urgency of the times. By the end of 1964, the SAC had become a financially independent body, with lines of communication directly to the president. From now on, I would have the ultimate responsibility for the development of student power within the university; and I welcomed this, because I believed I knew students and could work easily with them.

My confidence went back to the ten years I had spent as dean in residence at University College. During those years, the number of students I had worked with was at first very small, only about forty or fifty, but that number grew gradually into two hundred or so. I had been in daily touch with a representative group of students whom I knew far better than those I met in the classroom. In class, the traditional discipline was strong. Students simply took it for granted, and even the most casual student felt its power. But outside the classroom, these passive and undemonstrative young men and women erupted into normal human beings. They were, in the fifties, a non-political group, not greatly concerned about collective rights, and shrinking from responsibilities. I tried to avoid paternalism, but, at times, it seemed to be not only required but desired, if the residences were not to become a boisterous clubhouse. In the event of any disturbance, I tried to take action coolly and swiftly, emphasizing the residences as an academic arm of the university that could not tolerate disruptive members. The students I considered as fully responsible adults and, in my dealings with them, there was to be no camouflaging or superior moralizing.

From my residence experience, I had derived the idea of students as anxious to live their own lives, with no great concern for the institution of which they were briefly members and no desire to shape the nature of the academic community. They could from time to time develop a collective urge to break out of the community: usually this resulted in a 'high jinks' episode, a sudden descent on the outside community, noisy and largely innocuous, with newspaper reporters sweating out lurid stories with headlines that collapsed overnight. But by the middle of the sixties, the collective concern seemed to broaden and became more serious.

In my address to the students at the opening of term in 1958, I had commented on the apathy of the preceding years, ridiculing the concept of the all-round student, urging a more critical, socially involved attitude, what I described as 'angularity.' (The speech was favourably received; speeches in favour of non-conformity are always well received since everybody sees himself as a doughty non-conformist.) The kind of involvement I had in mind was slow in coming. By 1965, with the Berkeley disruptions vaguely in the background, some events took place that pointed to a changing attitude – the arrival of my 'age of angularity.' On May 28 of that year Adlai Stevenson came to the campus to receive an honorary degree. A year or so before he would have been universally welcomed as the clear spokesman of American idealism; but now the shadow of Vietnam had fallen, and Adlai Stevenson, as United States representative to the United Nations, was engaged in defence of American intervention. A small faculty group drew up a protest against the award of a degree to a defender of American imperialism. On the night of convocation we prepared for violent confrontation, but the protest consisted only of a 'silent vigil' with a handful of protestors, in academic dress, ringing the approach to the hall. Stevenson seemed a little nervous and troubled. When we had met him at the airport, almost his first words had been, 'Here am I travelling around the country out-Goldwatering Goldwater.' As we passed the solemn protestors, he suggested – not too seriously – that he should get out and invite the dissidents into the hall to hear his speech. The protestors quietly dispersed, and inside the crowded hall, the audience listened intently to a skilful defence of American foreign policy. Stevenson protested that this was not his aim. 'I did not come here,' he said, 'to defend the effort of the United States to help Vietnam defend itself, or to save lives and hold the situation in the Dominican Republic.'

Another indication of a shifting mood was the introduction of the mass meeting – the 'teach in' – which in the United States had developed as a technique of political immersion. The Toronto version, launched in the fall of 1965, was in the tradition of the 'silent vigil' – correct, ordered, and academic. A committee of staff and students organized an 'International Teach-In' on the topic of 'Revolution and Response.' It was designed to look at the areas of revolutionary ferment – Russia, Latin America, Vietnam. In the choice of speakers the committee sought scrupulously to obtain a balanced point of view between revolutionary ardour and judicious conservatism, although inevitably eloquence, dedication, and idealism were on the revolutionary side. The program began with small seminars and sessions; but the final, climactic form was a series of mass meetings in Varsity Arena, each with a capacity audience of some 6,000 and extensive media coverage, beginning on Friday evening and ending on Sunday afternoon. The formal speeches were followed by a question-and-answer period carefully controlled and directed. At one point there was talk of disruption by a group of left-wing students, disgruntled by the committee's decision to deny the platform to a non-official American spokesman on Vietnam, but the controversial speaker was given a forum elsewhere and the crisis passed off. Those of us who worked on the Teach-In had a sense of buoyant satisfaction. We had, so we believed, harnessed the energies of the university in the cause of general enlightenment. It was also a source of satisfaction that we had given a potentially disruptive technique a serious academic setting. The first Teach-In was followed the next year by one on China and, in the fall of 1967, by one on 'Religion and Morality.' On all of these staff and students shared the initiative and the work. Although the idea was preserved on a smaller scale in the fall of 1968, it had by then clearly lost its momentum, and disappeared from the academic scene.

The student leaders were beginning to look inward, to locate the establishment not in some distant and comfortably unassailable foreign country but at home, specifically in the university, which had now, in numbers and complexity, become a little state. From 1965 to 1967, the symptoms – sporadic, irritating, even distressing at the time – were appearing, even though they added up to no major movement. In the spring of 1965, I was asked to talk to the newly elected Students' Council about university affairs. I was aware that the old, relaxed atmosphere had changed. When I entered the room at Hart House where the meeting was to take place, a student officer was angrily protesting against the positioning of my chair at the head of the table (not by my direction). 'What does he think he is,' he was saying, 'a school teacher lecturing kids?' I sensed, as I spoke, an undercurrent of resentment. Shortly after, the president's representatives on the SAC, traditionally two younger members of the staff with a sensitivity to student problems, warned me of the growing militancy of students. I responded by recommending to the President's Council that it invite student representation. This the council agreed to do, and the students responded positively but with a surly wariness. At their instigation, we agreed that we would publish minutes of the President's Council meetings, but that the minutes would be confined to an account of proposals and decisions and would not give personal ascriptions. Nevertheless a version of the meeting appeared in the columns of The Varsity with names of speakers prominently displayed, and villains (i.e., those critical of students) and heroes (i.e., those laudatory of students) neatly typed. The President's Council exploded in hurt indignation, and the experiment in student representation came to a halt.

I tried unsuccessfully to explain our position to the students. Their obsession at this time was the iniquity of secrecy in high places, and they could not associate themselves with any group that tried, in any way, to restrict information. They were basically right. It is difficult to occupy a half-way house between secrecy and full disclosure. But at the time they seemed to us to be indifferent to agreements and to assert themselves with a maddening self-righteousness and arrogance.

This discussion took place in the fall of 1966, and until the close of the academic year in 1967 the student position was cloudy and vaguely menacing. At one point a small group, with support from the SAC, presented a petition signed by a thousand or so students, calling for subsidized ˙textbooks. After a number of discussions, I finally told the group that the university did not accept student petitions as mandates for action; that the university was, whether they liked it or not, closer to a corporation than to a political democracy because it was governed by an appointed body; and that further discussions were useless. The students then sent a letter to me full of savage vituperation, with a copy to the press, which declined to publish it.

The final incident of the year was a masque of misunderstanding between youth and middle age. It grew out of a 'Psychedelic Festival,' organized by the students of University College, and ostensibly designed to show the impact on art of the new electronic and mind-expanding environment. There had been a carefully worked-out agreement between the principal of the college, Douglas LePan, who was concerned about any encouragement of the use of drugs, and the student sponsors of the festival. Yet the restrictive boundaries were soon crossed and the festival plans moved into full discussion of drug culture. There was an inevitable logic in this. Nevertheless I refused to petition the federal government on behalf of Timothy Leary, the high priest of the drug culture, who was then under indictment in the United States and therefore not able legally to cross the border. To the president of the Students' Council, Tom Faulkner, a high-minded young man planning a career in the church, the principle of freedom of speech took precedence over every other principle. My opposition was clearly based on dusty legalism.

None of these incidents, although disturbing and even painful at the time, had any wide reverberation. At the end of the academic year of 1967, as I prepared to take a year's leave from the presidency as Harvard's first Mackenzie King Professor of Canadian Studies, I was concerned, but generally optimistic, about working out arrangements with the students. I had reached two firm conclusions: that student government should be given complete autonomy; and that the president of the university should always talk frankly and seriously to students on any university issue. All this was based on the existence of the traditional *entente cordiale* between administration and students, and the continuation, in a modified form, of the current form of government. I did not think that students really wanted to be part of the governing structure, or that if they became part they would be comfortable and able to play an effective role.

One of the reasons for accepting the Harvard offer was a wish to get back to the old easy relationship with students. There was no way back at Toronto since there I was a political and administrative figure and would always remain such to each new generation of students. I could not, of course, transfer any Harvard experience intact to Toronto, but I believed that I could retain enough of it to give me a renewed sense of confidence in dealing with students; and on the assumption that students were basically the same anywhere, I could learn a good deal about them.

Harvard gave me a good vantage point. I was initiating a new course that attracted publicity in the press and at Harvard itself, and the enrolment of around seventy gave me a representative cross-section of students, the more so since the course was thought of as general education open to all undergraduates irrespective of specialization. We lived, moreover, in close association with students in the guest professor's suite in Quincy House, and were surrounded daily by undergraduates. I had informal talks with students in our own house's dining room and junior common room and at other Harvard houses. Most of the students were indifferent to, if not contemptuous of, student government. In comparison, Toronto was a tough and demanding school for young politicians. Harvard had a hard core of activists, but it was difficult to reach them since they were not organized and were not visible. I managed an informal session with the editors of the undergraduate newspaper, The Crimson, which seemed to me to be vastly superior to the Toronto equivalent, The Varsity. At that time, the editors were much incensed by President Nathan Pusey's reference to the activists as 'Walter Mittys of the Left' and were anxious to find out my attitude towards student dissent.

Harvard, during the year 1967–8, seemed a less volatile, explosive academic society than the one I had just left. It was true that the year had begun with the Dow 'lock-in' – a recruiting officer for Dow Chemicals, makers of napalm, much used in Vietnam, had been detained for several hours in his office by protesting students. But the punishment was mild: 'admonishment' for most of the participating students and 'probation' (slightly more severe, but carrying no real penalty) for those who had actually obstructed. What interested me about the event, besides the rarefied distinction between participation and obstruction, was student acquiescence in a decree made by a disciplinary board on which they had no representation. At Toronto, I reflected with a touch of superior pride, students had passed beyond this; they would not be a party to a disciplinary regulation affecting them directly unless they had helped to formulate it.

The major student disturbance in the United States during that academic year came at Columbia in late April. In severity and intensity, it expressed the growing repugnance to the Vietnamese war, now swollen into a major conflict. Although there was a general condemnation of the student violence, few found virtue in Columbia's administration. It had seemed to inherit the incubus of guilt that had fallen on all official acts. The Columbia disturbances had deep reverberations in Harvard. Archibald Cox, of the Law School (five years later summoned to examine a social cataclysm of even more shattering dimensions), was appointed to write a report. He emphasized (as did most Harvard teachers and administrators) the impersonality of Columbia, especially by contrast with Harvard. Harvard had its 'house' system, which assured continuous association between students and staff, and the inference (sadly shattered next year) was that this couldn't happen here. Whether or not it was truly convinced of its immunity, the Harvard community was fascinated by the Columbia affair, and for several weeks little else was discussed in common rooms.

I shared fully in the concern. Indeed, I felt even more deeply involved since, unlike my Harvard friends, I saw the events not as safely distant but as a direct, menacing commentary on my own university. Columbia and Toronto had some similarities that the present crisis illuminated. Both were big, complex universities in an urban setting; both had devoted more of their energies to strictly professional goals than to the development of a humane community; both had boards of trustees with final powers, made up largely of senior business executives in the urban area. As the Columbia disturbance moved to a climax, the analogies with Toronto became sharper. It was clear that once the university community burst through the customary restraints the president and the board lost their authority. At Columbia the board had declared that the president had ultimate disciplinary power, but this was a little like maintaining, in the midst of a successful revolution, that the old regime still prevailed. The board itself was powerless to act; it rapidly withdrew from the scene, and ceased issuing ultimata; the president, thought of as a creature of the board, lost his powers; and the resolution of the conflict was left to the faculty.

This was a scenario that could repeat itself in Toronto and, therefore, another compelling reason for establishing a single representative body as the final authority. In the event of a deep disturbance like that of Columbia (no university was exempt and at this time the possibility filled the foreground), what one needed was a mediating power that could command respect and wield authority. Deep movements of opinion, even when they took the form of illegal action, could not be dealt with adequately by disciplinary bodies composed of administrators and academics, operating in a void.

The Columbia disturbances were also a terrifying lesson in the ways of student power; of how a little trickle of dissent could swell into a raging torrent. The Columbia issues – the proposed erection of a gymnasium on land that adjoined the black community, and Columbia's participation in projects related to the war effort – did not of themselves arouse widespread indignation and sympathy. But an uncertain or peremptory response from the administration could (and in this instance did) create a sudden alliance between the systematic agitator and a substantial proportion of the student body, all of whom, it could be assumed in a large university, had suffered at some time from an arbitrary or inept bureaucracy. And such a large body, swept along by a gathering sense of indignation and self-righteousness, would attract staff in increasing numbers. The result would be a community divided within itself, leaderless and drifting.

I had already been thinking about these problems in abstract when I was writing my report for the 1966–7 academic year. The report appeared just before the Columbia disturbances, and acquired a brisk topicality from the events. In one passage in it, I distinguished between radicals and revolutionary saboteurs: I argued that the former were a healthy force, and the latter an alien intrusion of diseased romanticism. Popular comment emphasized the negative rather than the positive side of the observations; and I found myself cast in the role of the self-exiled general meditating measures to crush the revolutionaries on my return.

Actually the analysis was reasonably accurate. The student radicals were in the main academic tradition of protest and dissent, now organized more carefully, far less respectful than their predecessors had been of authority; the revolutionaries saw themselves as part of a worldwide ferment, and 'Columbia today, Toronto tomorrow,' was a battlecry in a campaign to overthrow the world establishment. The task, I thought, was to avoid an issue that would unite radicals and revolutionaries and could then gain support from the non-political majority. But a defensive posture was not enough. The radicals resented my analysis; they didn't like the traditional, non-revolutionary role assigned to them and were eager to demonstrate their sympathy with those who proclaimed a bolder faith. What I must do was to enlist the radicals in the process of reform, to make them a part of the self-renewal of the university, to give them an active role in the new government that was bound to emerge. When I had left Toronto for Harvard, I believed students should be looked upon as a separate group to be dealt with seriously but not to be thought of as part of the official machinery of government. By the time of my return I was convinced that in the interest of the university they should be brought into the central councils. The problem was that the students might decline to play such a role. Would they not prefer the excitement of irresponsibility to the boredom of responsibility? Would they not always be suspicious of administrators even when – perhaps especially when – they came bearing generous proposals?

On my return, my first priority was to establish a firm association with the new student leaders and to win their co-operation in the revision of the university structure. To do this, I needed a great deal of time and I needed it at once. Reluctantly I decided that it would be impossible to attend meetings of the Association of the Universities of the Commonwealth, which were being held later in the summer in Australia. Christine agreed. Both of us had looked forward to the trip and to the meetings, but by the time we would have returned in September, the students would have formulated their strategy and I would know very little about them or their leaders. The new student leaders were a different breed from those I had known only a year before; it was as if a great dividing line separated them from their predecessors.

II

The chief difference was that the old *entente cordiale* had disappeared. The students had decided to play a tough adversary role and to organize themselves for political warfare against an enemy that was generally associated with the administration. To my amazement they read and took seriously an American document called *The Student as Nigger*, in which the lot of the student was, with solemn venom, equated with the lot of the negro in American society. I thought it was monstrous that these affluent young Canadians should see themselves as suffering the privations of the blacks. But they did not understand my disgusted amazement. When I gave my annual speech to the freshmen in the late September of 1968, a big banner faced me, strung across the balcony in Convocation Hall, with the words 'Welcome Home, Charlie' – a reference to the sanctimonious paternalism of the old slave owners.

Still, beneath an initial common front, there was apparent from the very beginning the division that I had noted in my report between the radicals and the revolutionaries. The student leaders had noted the distinction I had made and protested their solidarity. But it was a tenuous and nervous solidarity and I had to see that it did not harden into something durable.

The president of the Students' Council and the leader of the radicals was Steven Langdon. After my first meeting with him in July, I described him as 'a tall, delicate, blond, good-looking lad, slow spoken, fiercely idealistic.' His closest associate was Robert Rae, the son of one of my classmates, Saul Rae, who at that time was Canadian ambassador to Mexico. My first impression of

Bobby Rae was of 'a rather diffident, mild youth who makes extreme statements to keep up his courage.' Like most young people at the time, Langdon had little historical sense or awareness of the evolution of the reform movement in the universities. He thought of me as an old-fashioned Tory, redeemed in part by a Methodist conscience, an analysis that would have amused my academic colleagues and puzzled my associates on the Board of Governors. Langdon quickly acquired a messianic complex, fed by the enthusiasm of his followers and sustained by his considerable intellectual power, his impressive appearance, and his slow, incantatory style of public speaking. A pinkish Rupert Brooke turned into a gray John Knox in shirtsleeves. Rae I came to know much better, since later we sat together on the Commission on University Government. He had a quick mind, a talent for easy public discourse, and, unlike almost all his contemporary radicals, a lively sense of humour.

On the whole, I had good cause to be grateful for the leadership of the student radicals. They were a far cry from Mario Savio and Mark Rudd, the Berkeley and Columbia torch-bearers. I never lost touch with them, and, in the final analysis, they preferred discussion and compromise to violence and intractability.

The leader of the revolutionaries, if they could be said to have one, was Andy Wernick, a graduate student in sociology from Cambridge, England, whom I described after our first meeting as 'a Marxist with a cheerful, appealing dogmatism.' But Wernick, who thought of himself in apocalyptic terms, moved rapidly away from the centre. He believed that in dealing with members of the administration civility was servility, and he became for me a voice behind every raucous clamour and an energy behind every impossible demand. Perhaps today in the pleasant places of Trent where he teaches sociology, he may reflect, from time to time, about the days when he strove to destroy the establishment by which he is now nourished.

The years 1968 to 1971 were drenched with the jargon of the far left. *The Varsity* was continuously under the editorship of sympathizers with the extremists, and the editors enjoyed an intoxicating freedom. The paper, comfortably subsidized by student fees, was responsible neither to the student organization nor to the university government. Its columns were splattered with the cant of the new dispensation. I once amused myself by stringing together a number of these phrases into a sentence and managed to pass it off as sound currency even among some of the traditional radicals: 'Hopefully students can secure a meaningful, relevant, and viable role in participatory decision-making; thereby they can prevent alienation and the repressive tolerance of bourgeois liberal society; and create an educational experience that gives an alternative to the assembly-line, value-free rigidity of impersonal industrialism and the soft liberalism spawned by American imperialistic colonialism.'

In the meantime, I was pushing ahead with the establishment of a body to look at university government. That seemed a simple enough matter. The President's Council had already gone on record during my absence in Harvard as strongly in favour of such a commission; the students' position was that they could not really participate in university affairs until the system had been throughly examined by such a body and revised; and at the first meeting of the board that I attended after my return, on June 27, a general resolution approving a commission had been passed. Nevertheless, five months of negotiations and discussions were to elapse before the commission actually emerged. During this period, it seemed at times that we would have to relinquish forward movement and hope that the *status quo* could be preserved and suitably garnished for general acceptance.

The first obstacle to the establishment of the commission was the opinion, strongly held by a number of board members, that any body set up to look at university government should be solely a creature of the board. It should, in its wise condescension, consult students and staff, but should formulate its own conclusions. This impossible point of view died quickly when two of the strongest members of the board, Wallace McCutcheon and Vacy Ash, insisted that there must be representation of students, staff, and governors, and supported a formula of representation agreed upon at the President's Council.

At this time, a new obstacle to board approval and participation appeared. The establishment of a commission on university government had been reported in the newspapers; there were enthusiastic editorials approving the step and giving their blessing to the solution that I had frequently advocated – a representative unitary body. In my own comments to the press, unduly expansive in a sense of relief at the setting up of the commission, I had made it clear that I anticipated some version of my proposals as the probable outcome of the deliberations. The board was irritated. I was to be a member of the commission, and before discussions began I had already declared myself on the major issue. Although my own opinions were well known and had been expressed inside and outside the university, I realized that I had acted indiscreetly and had raised an unnecessary barrier to the success of the commission. The board's sensitivities were further bruised by the natural tendency of the newspapers to emphasize the revolutionary nature of my proposals; they talked not about the establishment of a new body but about the abolition of the old one. The Board of Governors had never had a popular following, and the press now contemplated its immediate demise with undisguised satisfaction.

The board meeting on September 26 was ominously well attended. (Attendance was normally erratic and some members rarely appeared.) I sensed a coming storm when Beverley Matthews, always my sympathetic supporter, said he thought that in these days of stress, the board should express its confidence in the president. He was obviously trying to head off an attack. There was some desultory comment and then George Drew, who had been grimly turning over notes and clippings, began to speak. Behind his words was the authority of a former premier of Ontario who had appointed several members of the present board, a former federal leader of the Conservative party, and a recently retired Canadian High Commissioner in the United Kingdom. He spoke as if he could see across from him the combined shades of Mackenzie King and Tim Buck. There was, in his opinion, a threat against sound and thrifty government of the university which he, when premier of Ontario, had, with the assistance of Eric Phillips, firmly established. I was a party to this subversion; and I was doing so in an arrogant manner. He quoted:

> Upon what meat does this our Caesar feed,
> That he is grown so great?

I reflected that this was probably the first time that Shakespeare had been quoted in the Board room (which spoke well for Drew, although he did not seem to be aware that often Shakespeare puts his most ringing rhetoric in the mouth of his least forthright character).

It was not easy to reply. George Drew was a voice from another age and he had no knowledge of the discussions that had been going on for years about the changes in university government. Besides, I had a guilty conscience about the newspaper reports. I had let down my guard carelessly and had unnecessarily complicated the process of setting up the commission. The storm swept on. The acting chairman, O.D. Vaughan, greatly distressed, tried to arrest it. But Drew persisted, moving stolidly through his notes and clippings. No one joined him in his attack, and no one came to my defence. At the time I viewed the attack with a fascinated objectivity – it seemed like a crudely written and awkwardly staged melodrama – but later in my office, with my two closest associates, Jack Sword and Don Forster, both of whom had been present at the meeting, I exploded in anger. I thought, and probably said: 'If the board wants to hand me an issue that will unite the whole university against it, I shall accept the offer.' When I met Christine afterwards to go to a dinner I was still in this mood; and aroused by my account of the humiliating two hours I had just spent, she welcomed the fray.

George Drew continued, so I learned, his campaign against me with dogged virulence but could enlist no supporters within the board; and his representations to the government were politely ignored. My own wrath rapidly cooled. I had found him a shy, friendly man, who reserved his explosions for public occasions. When I retired three years later, he came to the board's farewell dinner. He was one of four Ontario Conservative premiers, all of whom were present, who had presided over the government of the province since 1943. I said to him at the end of the pleasant evening: 'It was good of you to come, George; I know you don't value my work as president highly.' He demurred politely and we parted on friendly terms.

In the meantime, a more general problem had arisen. The Students' Administrative Council now proposed that both student and staff representation on the commission be increased from two to four; that board representation be maintained at two; that the board representatives and the president have no voting rights; and that alumni and administrative representation be abandoned. The registrar, Robin Ross, and I met to expostulate with the students. Had they not argued that no examination of the university structure could carry any weight unless it involved the highest legal body, the Board of Governors? 'That was so,' replied Rae, 'but with the rapid evolution of events, the board has been made irrelevant.' I didn't think the students were serious. They were simply pushing matters as far as they would go in a burst of youthful iconoclasm. Besides, I thought, the staff would never go along with them. I was reassured by a decision reached at the President's Council and agreed to by the executive of the Association of the Teaching Staff: that the number of staff and students should indeed be increased, but that the president and the board members should have full voting rights. This was a compromise that I believed I could sell to the board.

The compromise resolution was to be put to an open meeting of the Association of the Teaching Staff on the evening of October 3. In the past, I had not attended meetings of the association except towards the end of the academic year, when I would give a general review and try to anticipate the course of the immediate future. I did not propose to change this practice, but some vague forebodings made me change my mind and I decided to go to the meeting. There were about 150 faculty members present in Cody Hall, the auditorium of the School of Nursing Building, not a commandingly representative group in a full-time faculty that numbered about 1,500, but nonetheless the official voice of the staff and empowered to make decisions for the whole. When the compromise motion was put, I was asked to speak in its support; and believing there was no need for a strong appeal, I underplayed my arguments and may have given the impression that I was not committed to the proposal. Langdon and Rae spoke against the motion; their main point was that the students and staff made up the university and should, therefore, have the power to shape and control it. I was still not worried about the result. The questions put to me were hostile. ('Will the president please explain in what sense the board represents the public?') Still I was confident of the outcome. But when an amendment was moved and seconded, disfranchising the board on the grounds that it was the only section of the university that would not be affected by the changes (presumably because it would no longer exist), I suddenly became aware of a great faculty hostility towards the board and saw that the students could draw upon strong emotional support. The amendment was approved by a vote of approximately 90 to 50. I immediately left the meeting, shaken and distressed; it seemed impossible now to bring together the various parts of the university.

From this unhappy meeting stemmed many of the problems of the future: a coolness in the board to any co-operative approach to the examination of university government; a student belief that staff had accepted a simple concept of student-staff parity in the running of the university. I was appalled by staff naïvety. The commission was about the distribution of power in the university; yet at the very outset, the staff was prepared to set aside the principal power in the university as established by a democratic legislature. Here surely was a triumph of emotional pique over considered judgment. How could those who were cool and objective in appraising the past be so undisciplined and crudely emotional in judging the present? The answer – it was to become a litany of the times – was that this was the voice of the minority.

During the next few days, staff groups met to see what could be saved from the wreckage. I thought that the staff vote was a clear declaration of loss of confidence in me. I was told that this was not so; but I could not see how protestations of support could make up for a sharp repudiation of a policy to which I was committed.

In a few days, I recovered my confidence and believed that time and persuasion would get us back on the main road. Besides, the rush of events left no time for introspection. The library problem was still unsettled: we had to revise the estimates sharply before we could expect government approval. The council of the Faculty of Arts and Science had become the locus of student protest, and itself was bitterly divided over the recommendations of the Macpherson report on changes in the curriculum; I was *ex officio* chairman of the council, but I had lost touch with the current issues, and the council, once a relaxed and friendly body, easily dominated by old associates, had become a huge, unhappy concourse pushed into extreme positions by young turks or recalcitrant traditionalists. The public debate with the student activists went on continuously, in an open-air discussion with Langdon on the function of the university; in a formal debate in Hart House – 'Resolved that student power works against the best interests of the university' – in which I sincerely supported the winning negative; in more jocular fashion in the student float parade, which had as its theme, 'How I learned to stop worrying and love Claude.' Other distractions were of a happier nature. Bob Blackburn, the chief librarian, had suggested that Sidney Fisher was looking for a permanent place for his great Shakespeare collection; I spent a day with Fisher in Montreal, got an agreement that most of the books would go to the new library, along with substantial financial support, and returned jubilantly prepared to face any number of crises.

But the major problem remained: how to persuade the Board of Governors to go along with a commission that relegated the board to an inferior status. The President's Council had agreed to accept the proposals and the alumni (like the board, deprived of a vote) had said they were willing to nominate representatives. The final decision to co-operate did not come until the board meeting of November 7; and it owed much to the reconciling offices of Beverley Matthews and Arthur Kelly. But it was a cautious agreement. The board would send 'observers,' not delegates, and it reserved its right to act independently. In the board generally, there was distaste for the use of the word, 'commission,' that had already been appropriated by the students; the correct designation, the board pointed out, was a student-staff committee. To the university community, such a distinction and reservation meant little. This was the body that would make recommendations about the structure of university government, and it now moved to the forefront of concern.

One final crisis remained before elections could be held and the commission begin its work. Initially it had nothing to do with the commission, but it quickly became entangled with it.

Ever since the setting up of a formal mediating body for the province, the Committee on University Affairs, each university had made a presentation of its case. As the provincial body became more firmly established, the presentations became more formal; by this time they took the shape of written briefs. These presentations had always been made in closed session, since much of their substance was an estimate of future building requirements, and this involved speculative sums that, if known, could become firm commitments in the public mind. Toronto's brief for this year had been prepared hurriedly and a little casually; there were many other demanding problems and I was not yet convinced that the appearance before the provincial body was anything more than a mandatory ritual. The provincial committee was chiefly concerned with establishing the level of the operating grant for the next year; and that depended on a political decision that, in all likelihood, had already been taken.

At a meeting with Steven Langdon late in November, I told him about the provincial brief and suggested that he might like to come along as one of our delegates. He declined on the grounds that the Students' Administrative Council was absolutely opposed to secrecy in the conduct of university affairs. I respected the position to which he was bound and thought nothing more of the matter. A week later I read in the morning paper (now better informed about student politics than I was) that the SAC was incensed by administrative secrecy and that unless the brief were made public, there would be a sit-in. 'Secrecy' is a dark and ominous word, and I realized that the students had, by its use, acquired an immense moral headstart. I was determined not to hand them an issue and told them that I was quite prepared to release the brief. But to do this I needed the postponement of our meeting with the provincial committee, and the consent of that body, and the consent of the Board of Governors, to the release of the brief. The first two were easily secured but the third posed problems. The Board of Governors was in no mood for further concessions to students. Besides, the brief contained some general statements about our proposals for reform and the probability that they would result in the establishment of a new governing body. George Drew quickly fastened upon this phrase and now returned to the attack. At this point Wallace McCutcheon assumed the role of arbitrator: skilfully he piloted a crucially amended version of the brief through the board, with the understanding that it could now be made public. The threatened sit-in collapsed.

In accordance with a pledge, I invited the SAC to an open session on the brief. This developed into a series of meetings, but led to no major revisions in the main thrust. In so far as we had planned to discuss changes in particular areas, however, we were compelled to return to the status quo. The students accomplished this by the simple, effective device of rallying the vested interests in those areas. It was a nice illustration of how movements of protest are often indistinguishable from alliances against change. There was a piquant epilogue to the incident. Having fully participated in the discussions and become a party to the recommendations, Langdon at first refused to become a member of our official delegation, despite what I took to be a clear agreement; but he finally relented, came to the presentation, and spoke of student needs with characteristic effectiveness.

In retrospect, I speculated about why this incident should have taken place at all. The most charitable explanation was that the students were genuinely apprehensive about the secret brief. They had an elaborate mythology about the administration, a principal article of which was that we planned to turn the university into a graduate school and slowly eliminate undergraduate work; and possibly they feared that the brief contained a dark program for carrying out this design. But the real explanation, I suspect, is that this was simply a game whose goal was to demonstrate the ineptness of the administration. One needed a simple emotional issue, and an opponent paralyzed by an initial error. It was a dangerous game that could confuse, arouse bitter emotion, and hopelessly obscure a rational program of reform. With that crisis behind us, I was determined to avoid a repetition. The Commission on University Government had now been firmly established; the faculty and student elections for representatives had been held; and the board and the alumni had nominated their observers. Throughout the campus there was a feeling that an important hurdle had been surmounted and the way was clear for reform. But I knew that the university could be easily drawn away from the main path in pursuit of an elusive or imaginary quarry.

The key was, as I had argued earlier, to keep the traditional radicals from coalescing with the revolutionaries. The commission was the main guarantee against this because the traditional radicals were now committed to it, whereas the revolutionaries looked on it as a sell-out to the establishment. Yet to understand a danger is not to avoid it, and, on a number of occasions, I was unable to prevent radicals and revolutionaries from making a common front against the administration. On those occasions orderly reform would recede, and reaction or anarchy would threaten to dominate the scene.

III

The first of these occasions came early in February 1969 and, at the time, puzzled me by its sudden savagery. Looking back now, I can see that it had a rationale in terms of the ebb and flow of student politics. The commission had held about half a dozen meetings. The meetings had been theoretical and philosophical, about the nature and goal of the university, the structure of the academic community, and the role of the president. The expected division of opinion had appeared – between the university as committed participator and the university as objective critic – but I thought all was going well. Then, in a meeting on February 4, we heard our first witnesses, a group of students known to have strong political convictions. Andy Wernick was the climactic voice. He was grim and intense: he sketched a swift Marxian cartoon of Ontario society and ended up by declaring undying war on the commission and all it stood for. He was clearly urging the student members to return to the true faith and to resist the blandishments of the administration. Bobby Rae abandoned his usual jaunty self-assurance and observed grimly that Wernick was right. The prophet had spoken and the erring disciples had heard and were ready to return to the sanctuary.

It was against this background that Clark Kerr, who had been president at Berkeley at the time of the 1965 disturbances, arrived on the campus. He had come, at the invitation of a group devoted to American studies on an interdisciplinary basis, with my warm concurrence. I knew and admired Kerr. I thought that his book, *The Uses of the University*, was one of the best on higher education in recent years – a lucid account of the developments of the complex university. It was not, as the student critics declared, a paean to bigness and complexity, but a clear account of what had actually happened. Among American university presidents, Kerr was, I knew, an advanced liberal. Shortly after the disturbances at Berkeley, I had heard him talk to a small group of fellow presidents about the events that at the time had seized and held the newspaper headlines of the world. In his calm, Quaker way, he was patient and unvindictive, skilfully unwinding the various strands in the skein of student protest. Someone had asked him what the whole affair meant, and he had replied, 'I think the university must become much more sharply aware of moral issues and goals.'

At the time Kerr came to Toronto, his liberal credentials were, I thought, apparent to all. He had fought Ronald Reagan, the Republican governor of California, over his punishing policies towards the universities, and had, as a result, been removed from office. In the Democratic party, his strong anti-Vietnam views were well known. Besides, the Berkeley disturbances were by this point three years old and seemed to belong to a mythical past. Surely there could be no controversy over his appearing on the campus. But I had forgotten about the Canadian time lag; I had forgotten too, as the Stevenson incident should have reminded me, that heroes of American liberalism can expect a mixed reaction in Canadian universities; and I did not appreciate the confused and worried state of student politics despite the warnings implicit in the last CUG meeting.

Kerr was to give the first of two lectures on the night of Wednesday, February 5, in the theatre in the Royal Ontario Museum. Before the lecture, Christine and I had a dinner party for him at our home to which we invited ex-Berkeley staff members and their wives. One of our guests, Lewis Feuer, had come to Toronto because he was gloomy about Berkeley; he had just concluded a major study of student protest movements in which he had seen them as part of the eternal clash between generations. I had some vague apprehensions about the evening, but I had put them aside. That afternoon, I had seen a poster prepared by Wernick's group (a tangle of revolutionaries embraced under the flat designation of the Toronto Student Movement) announcing a debate between Clark Kerr and Mario Savio, the student leader during the Berkeley disruption. It seemed only a faint possibility that the group could have resurrected Savio, now fallen into obscurity, and brought him to Toronto to confront his old antagonist.

Our little party arrived at the back of the theatre just before the lecture was to begin. N.S.C. Dickinson, my assistant, reported a full house, and then added that there were some 'queer characters' in the first few rows. As soon as I began my introduction, I realized that the queer characters were not concentrated in one group. They were widely scattered and had come prepared for reckless hostility. The action began in the manner of guerilla theatre (satiric miming of the ways of the establishment), appropriate enough in view of the surroundings. Two students rushed up on the stage, one presenting Kerr with a bouquet of artificial roses, the other hanging around my head a chain of marshmallows – the marshmallows symbolizing, so I had learned, the soft saccharine approach of Canadian liberalism. Rather relieved by the tone of the gesture, I tossed the marshmallows to Christine, who was sitting in the front row with our dinner guests. She ate one and passed the rest along the row in a spontaneous gesture that aroused much delighted comment. (Just as she finished eating her marshmallow, she recalled with a shiver of apprehension that LSD was often camouflaged in sweets.)

For the first twenty minutes of his speech, Kerr encountered a thin orchestration of jeers, shouts, and bursts of cynical laughter. Then, at a signal from the conductor, the sound swelled into a crescendo. A man in the middle of the audience rose and launched into a harangue to an imaginary audience; towards the rear somebody turned on a tape recorder at its highest pitch (it was, I learned later, a record of some of the Berkeley confrontations); people rose everywhere shouting, protesting. Even under normal circumstances, the museum theatre has a claustrophobic atmosphere; it is a windowless, sub-level, narrow space, and shouts and sudden violent movements are accentuated within it. How to restore order and peace? I knew the police could be summoned in a minute; but since the museum was officially outside university jurisdiction, I would have to call the city police, and I drew back at the thought of what might happen in this confined space.

Then quiet suddenly returned. The protestors abandoned pantomime for reality. Wernick walked up on the platform and moved towards the microphone before which Clark Kerr was standing. I held out my hand to him, hoping that I could persuade him to leave, but he spurned it and continued toward the microphone. I stood in his way and pushed him gently back. Immediately half a dozen supporters were on the stage. I took the mike and shouted, 'It's ironical that the first people to demand free speech are the first people to deny it to others'; then, anger getting the better of discretion, 'We have had enough fascism this evening.' This aroused the audience to a frenzy and the group on the stage writhed and shouted in an ugly ballet. I concluded that I had forfeited the chance for peace and, as the hubbub continued, suggested to Clark Kerr, who was patiently leaning on his lectern, that we leave.

He firmly and quietly said that he was prepared to wait it out. Then I saw Rae and a fellow student member of the Commission on University Government, D'Arcy Martin, walking down the aisle. They came on to the stage and Rae whispered, 'Suggest to the audience that you give Kerr fifteen minutes and Wernick fifteen minutes.' He spoke with confidence. I followed his advice, and peace descended as suddenly as it had been broken.

Clark Kerr turned to his manuscript – 'As I was saying,' he began, and there was a relaxing wave of laughter. He then brought his speech to a speedy conclusion. The rebuttal was, unfortunately, not confined to Wernick, who spoke with nervous ineffectiveness. He was followed by an American girl who had come from the United States as a sour Marxian missionary to the unconverted, and then by Philip Resnick, the official student theoretician of the far left. Other voices and other views demanded to be heard and it was some time before I could bring the meeting to a conclusion.

The Clark Kerr incident was an important milestone. I thought at first it would split the radicals and the revolutionaries. Although the radicals were worried about what had happened ('It was bad tactics and it was counter-productive'), they tended nevertheless to find justifications and explanations ('It was no worse than many political meetings'). The incident left a deep impression on me, however. I knew something from my army days about the terror that arises when, under stress, normal human safeguards suddenly disappear. This was a different and more mysterious terror. Christine never forgot the experience – the feeling that an ugly genie of hate had suddenly enveloped the room.

The incident also greatly increased my concern about the possible use of force to gain student political goals. The sit-in – the physical occupation of an area central to the work of the oppressor – had been hallowed by its use during the civil rights struggle in the south; and it had now been transferred to the North American campus with its accompanying high moral tones. There were, however, certain basic distinctions between these two uses of the technique. The blacks had been denied basic rights as citizens – the right to mingle with other citizens on the basis of equality, the right to vote freely in elections; but students had not been denied any basic rights. Certainly they had, and always would have, grievances, but these were of a nature that could be settled over a period of time by discussion and negotiation. Then – and this was an even graver distinction – those who had participated in the civil rights sit-ins were willing to accept the consequence of their illegal acts; whereas the students declared that they were taking part in a legitimate action and should not be subject to any discipline or legal strictures. They distinguished between peaceful and non-peaceful sit-ins; their sit-ins were peaceful and non-violent since they avoided damage to property or injury to individuals. I found the distinction unreal. Physical occupation always involves, at the minimum, a deprivation of somebody's freedom of action.

Certainly the experiences of 1969 underlined the inevitable drift of academic sit-ins to violence. In February, there had been the sudden explosion at Sir George Williams. When police were called in to eject protestors during a sit-in, the retreating students savagely wrecked computer installations and destroyed records. In April occurred the Harvard 'bust.' The administration building was seized and the resident administrators forcibly ejected; the police raid that followed left in its wake some broken heads and, more grievously, a sense that holy ground had been desecrated. The disturbances at Cornell in April carried overtones of a latent destructive violence. A group of black students, enraged by a real or fancied injustice, had seized the students' union. When they finally emerged from the building, they were shown in newpaper pictures carrying rifles and improvised weapons. A chill of apprehension spread throughout the USA. An incident such as this might be the prologue to a bloody race war.

Throughout the spring of 1969 the unrest on American campuses continued. In May, the *New York Times* reported that the disturbances had reached a crescendo with a widened repertoire of issues – student-staff parity in governance, admission of minority groups to university, the so-called 'open' university. The student revolution had caught the attention of the world. At an international conference in Denmark that I attended in May (the Bildenberg Conference, normally devoted to economic and international affairs), the major topic was campus unrest.

In September 1969, as we began to prepare for the new year, the atmosphere was uncertain and obscurely menacing. The Commission on University Government had come through a number of crises and was working on its final report; a moderate student had been elected president of the Students' Administrative Council; but little groups on the left had coalesced and hardened and tended to take over the ideological debate. The university world (particularly the world of the University of Toronto) seemed more than ever to be a world of its own, isolated from the workaday conservatism of Canadian life – a little like an eastern European state where subversive ideas flourished and romantic revolutionaries found eager audiences. No doubt this view was part illusion, fed by rumour, gossip, and a natural relish for imaginary horrors. But illusions could turn into reality if enough people believed in them.

The clearest response to this atmosphere was a paper entitled 'Order on the Campus,' prepared by the Committee of Presidents of the Universities of Ontario and released to the press on September 18. The paper had been under consideration since the preceding March, when it had been thought of as 'a reflective essay with a bite.' It had finally emerged as a working paper for the development on each campus of an appropriate statement of policy regarding the handling of incidents of violence or the obstruction of the university's due processes. Once the document appeared in the press, however, it lost its provisional, tentative nature and immediately became, in the eyes of the public, a statement of a tough, new policy to deal with dissent. To all left-wing students (and many in the centre) it was a 'repressive' document that ran counter to the moderate, liberal ideas that had hitherto guided campus discussions.

The statement was, in a sense, an American document reflecting the shocked response to American campus violence, and proclaiming our intentions not to be caught up in a similar sequence of events. One statement in particular aroused shrill outcries: 'Violent action is unnatural to the university and yet the only response by which violence can be contained is the exercise of counter-violence.' To the student revolutionaries, violence (and there could be endless discussions about what constituted violence) directed against the establishment was legitimate (since many of its processes were 'dehumanizing' and 'alienating' and needed to be changed); whereas counter-violence was a blind response by insensitive power.

The document set out a precise procedure to be followed in the event of an obstructive or disruptive action. Although the procedure involved consultation by the president with 'a standing committee of faculty members and students,' it seemed, in its bare outline, rasping and bellicose.

The presidents' statement was a grand, overall approach; on the Toronto campus, I was attempting to formulate a more specific policy. I was convinced that the extreme left would shortly launch a series of disruptions, both at general university events and in the classroom, and I was determined that we should announce a clear policy of containment and counteraction. The problem once again was that we had no clear authoritative centre that could formulate a policy. The old disciplinary body, the Caput, had lost its effectiveness: it was composed exclusively of senior academic administrators and it existed in its own right with no clear relationship to any larger and more representative body; it still proclaimed its divine powers long after belief in the gods had vanished. Yet until a new disciplinary structure was devised, we had no alternative except to use what already existed.

We were not concerned about the handling of specific offences – the stealing of books, or cheating on examinations, for instance; these were clearly recognizable and could be dealt with by formal judicial procedures. The problem was the handling of 'disruption' that involved mass action for political purposes, did not overtly endorse violence although by its nature it invited violence, and was directed towards the obstruction of academic life. I believed that this problem would be capable of solution only when the government of the university had changed; when we had a supreme representative body that could be seen to reflect the university community. Such a change was at least a year away. In the meantime, we could hope for some help in the report of a special committee on disciplinary procedures which, under the chairmanship of Professor Ralph Campbell, had been deliberating on the problem for almost a year. While awaiting that report, I had some time before appointed a special committee to recommend an interim reconstruction of the Caput, but the committee had repeatedly foundered on the same question, the proper response to disruption.

I was determined not to let matters drift further, all the more so when at almost the first opportunity a disruption did occur. At a dinner for University College freshmen, the final event of a program designed to familiarize new students with the university, a group of zealots arrived suddenly, interrupted the proceedings with incoherent questions, and then nursed the swelling disturbance into pandemonium, finally bringing the event to a halt. This was the Clark Kerr incident over again, but much closer to the heart of the university. I summoned the Caput, still the only disciplinary body, and got approval of a statement providing for action by the Caput in the event of disruption, with suspension or expulsion as possible penalties. There was no opposition in the Caput to the proposals, but the atmosphere was less than enthusiastic; one college representative left the clear impression that what we were dealing with was a university plague that did not cross the borders of his college.

Just before the term opened formally, all these strands came together: the appearance of the presidents' statement, the University College disruption, and the Caput pronouncement. There was an initial silence and then the Students' Administrative Council issued a fiery denunciation. I must repudiate the two statements, it demanded; both were repressive and undercut the report of the Campbell committee that was shortly to appear and was to be the basis for future university policy.

There now followed ten days of continuous tension, fitfully illuminated to the public by newspaper stories. One could describe these days as a teach-in which was always on the verge of violent eruption. There were three main public events. The first was a meeting of the committee on the reconstruction of the Caput which took place on Tuesday, September 23, after the publication of the two official statements and the SAC response. I was not a member of the committee and was not under any obligation to attend the meeting; but under the unusual circumstances, I thought it best to do so. The committee meetings were open, but had hitherto attracted little interest. Now one could anticipate a burst of popularity, and the registrar, Robin Ross, had accordingly shifted the place of the meeting from the small committee room in Simcoe Hall to the larger debates room in Hart House, which had a capacity of three to four hundred. When I arrived, the room was filled with onlookers, most of them members of the New Left Caucus, the latest umbrella organization of the revolutionaries. The representatives from the SAC on the committee were members of the caucus and got their inspiration there, not from the SAC, which was divided in outlook. One of them was Bob Barkwell, a medical student, easy-going and friendly; he had picked up the leftist doctrines, as a generation or so earlier he would have picked up fundamentalist religion, and he spoke with the rapt intensity of the 'saved.' The other, Gregory Kealey, heavy-set and dour with a reddish, drooping moustache, was a student at St Michael's College in history with a high academic standing; he expounded the doctrines of Marx, Marcuse, and Fanon with heavy, untroubled seriousness. The committee had just begun its proceedings when Barkwell, on a point of personal privilege, read a statement declaring that the committee had already resolved not to extend the jurisdiction of any disciplinary body to political and social offences, and that I had therefore completely ignored the committee in issuing the Caput statement. In reply, I pointed out that the committee had in fact not reached any formal agreement and remained sharply divided on the issue, and that, in any event, the Caput's jurisdiction could not be contracted without formal legal action. Then followed some speeches from other representatives, largely supporting the Barkwell statement. Steven Langdon, now a graduate, just back from a trip to Africa, rose like a classical presence from the past, saying that the repressive atmosphere he had found on his return to Toronto reminded him of South Africa. The SAC representatives then solemnly withdrew. The crowd, exploding with malicious glee, shouted at the rest of us, 'Get out!' A shrill female voice urged that the meeting reconstruct itself and elect a new chairman. Wernick, hitherto silently watchful, moved up behind the table where the committee members sat, accompanied by members of his palace guard. Robin Ross, the chairman, calmly held his ground and his temper, maintained the committee in being for twenty minutes or so, then formally adjourned the meeting. I made a final speech, saying that the university would move forward by rational discussion and not by the deliberate chaos we had witnessed; and then, with the remaining committee members, departed amid a sullen silence.

The second session of the 'teach-in' took place the following afternoon at a mass meeting in Convocation Hall called by the New Left Caucus, with the support of the official students' organization, the SAC. I had been comforted by strong supporting editorial comment in the daily newspapers; and I had been briefed by Gary Webster, another of the student members of the Commission on University Government, who had clear left sympathies. He assured me that the New Left Caucus did not want a violent confrontation, but was convinced that I was intent on its elimination. He suggested that in any remarks I made I should urge continual discussion within the university of the nature of disruption. Thus sustained, I went to the meeting with a certain jaunty optimism. The hall was full and the crowd was not completely hostile. But the first vital hour, from 1 to 2 pm, when classes were not generally held, was consumed by the chairman, Steven Langdon, in the reading of long resolutions from a variety of campus organizations. By the time I spoke, most of the audience had left for classes, and there remained a hard core of leftists. The questions were hostile and aggressive. I became progressively less effective in reply and finally walked out in complete dejection.

The problem had now become a question of confidence in my leadership. This had been dramatized by the drawing up by the Students' Administrative Council of a series of demands (the important ones being the repudiation of the two disciplinary statements), which were to be satisfactorily answered by Wednesday, October 1. The penalty for an unsatisfactory response was presumably to be the occupation of Simcoe Hall. Given the difficult nature of the issues, and the apparent absence of any overwhelming internal support for my stand, I was not optimistic. In the meantime, we had secured the early publication of the Campbell report, which was thought of as the new magna carta of discipline. I could thus emphasize the fact that this report would henceforth determine the direction of policy, although on the subject of demonstrations and disruptions it was fuzzy and inconclusive. But I still needed a statement that would be clear and positive without denying the validity of the actions of the last few weeks.

Robin Ross had prepared a draft statement and he, Ernest Sirluck, and I reviewed it and agreed upon the final version. It was essentially a personal statement – in a sense a political plea for understanding and confidence, which emphasized my general commitment to greater student and staff participation in all aspects of the university, and my determination to invoke the same principle in working out any disciplinary procedure. There was no repudiation of recent documents and, in the case of the presidents' statement, only a recognition of 'the apprehension it has raised among some members of this university, particularly when we do not yet have a system of government that is adequately representative of the whole university community.' The statement did not meet the SAC demands. I had no idea as to how it would be generally received, but it represented my views simply and noncombatively and I was happy with it. When the final version was completed around midnight, before the student deadline, I had a feeling of confidence.

On the morning of the day of the mass meeting, Wednesday, October 1, that late-night optimism vanished. *The Varsity* appeared with black headlines, declaring that all attempts at compromise had failed; in an editorial it urged a sit-in to test whether the administration would then use counterforce. Don Forster, among my advisers the closest to the teaching staff, reported much ambivalence there. The gloom deepened during discussions in my office on security measures. When, at noon, I went over to Hart House to a luncheon held annually for the presidents of faculty and college student societies, I was convinced of disaster and reflected to the gathering with gloomy objectivity on the failure of the university to find any common front and, in particular, on the split between Arts and the professional faculties. The current discussions originated almost exclusively with Arts students and the professional faculties seemed to be remote and indifferent.

On returning to my office, I heard that Convocation Hall was packed and that a large contingent of engineers, both students and staff, had arrived early and had taken over the strategic front seats – at previous mass meetings the pre-empted territory of the New Left Caucus. (That was a cheerful sign; a reply, as it were, to my remarks at the student luncheon on the apathy of the professional faculties; although if the engineers had, in fact, taken over the meeting, the ultimate consequences might be bad, since the split in the university would thereby be emphasized.)

Robin Ross came to my office to escort me to the meeting like a kindly padre escorting the condemned man to the gallows. As we entered the hall, I was prepared for the boos and taunts that had echoed through the week. It was some time before I was conscious of the fact that the audience was cheering. The cheers rose in a great crescendo as I walked to the platform. Gus Abols, the SAC president, and personally a moderate, whispered, 'I don't think there is any doubt about where this audience stands.' The president of the Engineering Society, Art McIlwain, had been elected chairman of the meeting – another good sign since he had not been involved in the political manoeuvres of the previous few days and could be counted on to take a neutral point of view. He asked Abols to read out the SAC demands and then asked me to reply. Copies of my statement had been distributed to the audience and, as I read it, there was an intent turning of pages and, from time to time, loud cheers. A motion was made and seconded to accept the statement as an adequate response to the SAC demands. There followed a series of speeches, a few aggressive and to the point, most tediously anticlimactic. The audience listened for a while with good-humoured patience, then shifted to mockery and continually called for the question. The motion was put, and passed with a thunderous 'Yea.' The audience burst into 'For He's a Jolly Good Fellow' and surged out in great high spirits.

What had begun in such a melancholy fashion, thus ended on almost a convivial note. Everybody, except the hardest of hard-core leftist, was happy. If the SAC thought they had won approval of their tactics, I was not disposed to split even so large a hair or to look such an amiable gift horse in the mouth. The health of the university was more important than maintaining a public image of toughness. On the evening of the mass meeting, we held an impromptu celebration in my home in which many of the student activists joined. It followed a reception for Julius Nyerere who had arrived that afternoon to give a speech and receive an honorary degree; his flashing smile and friendly, easy ways seemed to pronounce a final benediction on the events of the week.

The law and order crisis solved no problems, either theoretically or administratively. We found it impossible to establish a democratic successor to the Caput, since the SAC insisted that student members on such a body be appointed by the Students' Council rather than elected by the students at large; and the staff believed (rightly, in my opinion) that this would mean, in practice, directed students who hewed to the party line. But, at least, all the energy and time had been directed to a central issue, and the university had debated the main propositions. Any final solution, I still believed, would follow the setting up of a single representative body which could then confer authority on proposals.

The discipline crisis had come, in large part, because of my actions and statements; I had been prepared to take full responsibility for them and to work out a resolution. But the next crisis, the day care centre episode, emerged like a small black cloud suddenly smudging a blue sky. Its origins seemed petty. Yet it came the closest of any of the incidents of those years to disrupting the university and to undermining the delicate negotiations that were going on at that time on the recommendations of the Commission on University Government.

The day care centre crisis was fueled in part by a number of small political groups who were far more militant than the New Left Caucus. They had associations with outside party organizations and two of these, the Maoist Canadian Party of Labour and the Trotskyist League for Social Action, had a small vociferous organization on the campus known as the Worker-Student Alliance. By themselves, these groups had little impact. A few months before, they had mounted a picket line in front of Simcoe Hall following some labour trouble in the operating of the kitchens at New College – not directly a university matter since the kitchens were run by a private catering firm under contract. A little gloomy group had circled in front of the main door, brandishing militant signs and raising from time to time a ragged cry, 'On

Strike, Shut It Down.' But they had been ignored by the rest of the university and beyond an occasional scuffle with the campus policemen, there had been no cause for alarm. A subsequent incident had looked more threatening. One morning as I walked down the hall to talk to a colleague, I had glimpsed a swirl of hair and jeans mounting the main staircase next to my office. A few minutes later, an excited secretary reported that the group had swept through the waiting room and had established themselves in my office. I debated as to whether I should summon the campus police to eject them or should return to face them. I decided on the latter. There were about a dozen students forming a half circle around my desk, but sitting quietly and, I concluded, unmenacingly. They had come to demand the re-hiring of four waiters who had, they declared, been singled out by the caterers for punitive action because of their strike activities. I repeated the official position, that this was a matter for labour arbitration and not for university coercion. They responded with a chorus of abuse. I decided to make no further reply and asked them to leave before my next interview, fifteen minutes away, contemplating with melancholy intentness the unpredictable course into which I had thrust myself. After a few minutes of nervous silence, and a promise from me that they would have a chance to talk to the university administrator concerned with labour problems, they got up and filed out.

The day care crisis was not essentially the work of this group – motherhood, it has been frequently observed, unites all parties – but at crucial moments, they nudged it into extremism.

It was late in March 1970, and I had some reason to feel relieved and modestly cheerful. Long-drawn-out and acrimonious discussions with a staff committee on salaries had ended; for the time being we had successfully resisted a proposal to use arbitration and to bring in an outside negotiator. The discussions on the recommendations of the Commission on University Government, hung up for a month on faculty ultimata, were now more relaxed and promising. Student politics had taken a conservative turn. Early in the year, the student body, by an overwhelming majority, had decided to withdraw from the militant Canadian Union of Students, and recent SAC elections had returned a moderate slate of officers. *The Varsity* had morosely subsided for the year, and the publication of examination timetables had wonderfully concentrated the student mind. I had cleared up a personal dilemma. I had worked out an agreement with the Board of Governors whereby I would leave office at the end of the next academic year, the announcement to take place well in advance of the event. The dismal Ontario March had finally been broken and the first warm breath of spring could be felt. On the whole, a time for relaxation and for dealing with pleasant and important subjects, like discussing with Robert Finch his appointment as writer-in-residence, and talking to Archie Hallett, who had agreed to be principal of University College, about the nature of his new job.

When I came into my office on the morning of March 25, I was told of a phone call from a group of students saying that a deputation for the day care centre would be calling on me at 1 pm. Margaret Donovan, my secretary, had replied that I had a luncheon engagement at that hour (which was correct), and would not be available. I did not quarrel with her reply; the day care centre was a minor administrative problem that was being handled by the officer in charge of property acquisition. I had not concerned myself with the details, although I knew the general situation. We had given an unofficial student-faculty group use of an old house as a centre where they could share co-operatively the care of their pre-school children. The house was on the site where the new building for Innis College was to go up and thus was destined for demolition. Under the circumstances we did not want to spend money renovating it, and there was no place in our plans, and consequently in our budget, to replace it. The immediate issue was money for minor but immediately necessary renovations, optimistically estimated to amount to two or three thousand dollars. I was in agreement with the refusal to spend money from the university budget on this project, but I saw no reason why I could not draw upon a special fund contributed by the alumni if the alumni agreed. It was important to maintain the principle that the university could not spend money for non-academic purposes unless it was authorized to do so by the board; but it was also important to avoid an emotional confrontation on a non-issue, and the Varsity Fund could provide the answer.

Within an hour or so a minor procedural problem had been swollen into flaming absolutes. *The Varsity*, revived, published a special issue devoted exclusively to the subject. Its highlight was the reproduction of the administrative letter that had turned down the request for renovation – for *The Varsity*'s purpose a splendid example of cold bureaucratese. The paper's general line was that the administration was insensitive to its social responsibilities. At 12.30, as I waited in my office confident that I could quickly answer the complaints, the deputation unexpectedly appeared. It turned out to be mass meeting that had become mobile and was moving down the road towards Simcoe Hall. The crowd assembled below my windows, and a few minutes later a group of men and women came into my office. Several of the women had infants harnessed on their backs. Balloons were attached to the harnesses, a sickly carnival touch in the generally censorious atmosphere. I recognized only one of the group, a member of the department of philosophy, Lorrene Smith, and began to speak to her. She replied that the group was authorized only to ask me to come down to address the rally. I replied that I would not address the rally. I was prepared to talk to an accredited deputation immediately, or to go to the day care centre for a general discussion on the first evening I had free, which was a week away. If I were to join the crowd outside, I would be snared, in a few minutes, in a simple 'yes' or 'no' proposition, and simple answers could not resolve complex questions.

The deputation filed out of my office. Their message to the crowd below was received with shouts of anger. The shouts became louder and shriller; the crowd surged through the front doors and filled the staircase and the hallway outside my office. I could make out the basic chant, 'We want Bissell now.' I was to all intents and purposes confined to my office, and was to remain so for several hours. The crowd outside was too large to be dispersed except by the use of concentrated force; and our polite, friendly, university constables were not able to play this role. They had quickly yielded to the vanguard of the crowd, mothers with infants on their backs, striding forward like heavily armoured tanks in advance of the infantry. There were the usual reports of police brutality (I could hear the ritual shout of 'pigs' from time to time), but the only scent of real brutality was the carrying of small children into a dangerous situation.

I decided to pursue the matter of the use of the special alumni funds for the day care centre renovations. The alumni gave me great latitude in the use of these funds, but for any new project I asked for the approval of a board of directors. I talked to two or three of the directors by telephone and they responded positively. It was all a little absurd, since I said not a word about the immediate crisis and made my suggestion as if I had just been politely approached for help. Later in the afternoon I met a delegation of students and reported to them that I had talked to the alumni and was sanguine about success. (I left my office by a back passageway, unknown to the students, used only a few times before to escape from difficult, persistent visitors, and met the delegation in Convocation Hall, feeling a little like a beleaguered general, in a secret rendezvous, bargaining for peace terms.) My declaration of good intent was taken back to the crowd outside my office. I could hear a spirited debate going on. Steven Langdon, I was told, had urged the crowd to accept my offer and disperse. But the decision was to insist upon a personal guaranty from me; and there was renewed shouting and an ominous bulging of the outer door as the crowd surged forward. Margaret Donovan and I hurriedly stuffed the papers on my desk into locked files and awaited the confrontation. However, another shift had taken place. The crowd had decided to occupy the Senate chamber just down the hall from my office – an obvious symbol of university authority, and much more comfortable than the barren hall with its cold stone floor and vacant walls. This was a relief, for I knew that all my belligerence would be aroused by an invasion of my personal quarters, whereas I could contemplate the occupation of the Senate chamber with a degree of equanimity.

Around 5.30, Robin Ross came to my office, now that the siege was lifted, and suggested that I go down the hall and talk to the crowd. I agreed. The Senate chamber was crowded. I had a general impression of a mass of bodies, like several casts of *Hair* resting between acts. There was a debate in progress, but it ceased on my entrance. I was handed a bull horn, an electronic amplifying device that briefly deifies those who use it. I talked about the general theoretical problem of the extent to which the university was responsible for the general welfare of students and staff and the need for a representative committee to examine the larger question. (This was greeted with derisory laughter, in which I joined, since for the past three years I had been wandering through a thicket of committees.) I then told them about my confidence in getting alumni money for renovations. Then, suddenly sick of the whole solemn farce, resentful of the blighted day that was to have been used for a dozen positive acts, I said that I was now going home to have a double Scotch, an action that I recommended to them. I urged them (suddenly shifting to paternal adjuration) to leave the Senate chamber immediately. It was not a happy intervention. There was resentment of the facetious touch (the double Scotch suggested steely tycoons); the final remark followed by an abrupt departure was interpreted as a refusal to debate the problem. But one does not create a mood for cheerful dialogue by steadily thumping one's interlocutor on the head; and at the time my only desire was to withdraw.

That evening I summoned a council of advisers to my home – Robin Ross, Ernest Sirluck, and three faculty members of the President's Council. For some time now the house had been under constant guard, not as a result of any incident but as a general precautionary measure. That night there were reinforcements patrolling the grounds, and keeping watch on the kitchen door under the eye of our motherly housekeeper, Alice. It all seemed pretentious and exaggerated, but we knew that the vanguard groups had been increasingly vocal and influential, doing their best to prolong and harden the protest; and in their revolutionary euphoria, fiction could become reality and the absurd slip into the tragic. As my colleagues and I talked, we got periodic reports from Don Forster, who had remained behind in Simcoe Hall: 'They are bringing in mattresses'; 'Some are leaving but the number in the Senate chamber is still very large'; 'The sac has voted five hundred dollars for food for the sit-iners'; 'The chamber is heavy with the sweet smell of pot'. Discussions made little progress. Ernest Sirluck greatly admired the president of Chicago, Edward H. Levi, and suggested we use his deliberate and devastating technique: to wait out the sit-in as long as there was no threat to essential services (and for Ernest, essential services meant the library), then use tough academic sanctions against the hard core. Our legal adviser, who was present, was sceptical of this procedure; he thought that he could make mincemeat of any charges that might be brought by the university. Robin Ross was even more sceptical: he said bluntly that we had a bad cause and had acted ineptly in our initial response. In the midst of the whirling and elusive discussion, I left to go to the bathroom and returned relieved in mind and body with a proposed statement that everybody cheerfully agreed to. It was a simple reaffirmation of what I'd already said, phrased more positively: that the university had an interest in day care centres and that, provided the occupation ceased, I would solemnly pledge to get the money for immediate renovations from the alumni fund. As Ernest and Robin left they said, a little doubtfully, that 'we were going to win'. I was doubtful too, and went off to a sleepless bed.

In my office the following morning, having cancelled all appointments for the day, I polished my statement. My general plan was to make the statement (without much hope of its acceptance), deliver a warning, and, if the chamber were not then evacuated, call in the police. As a prelude I had called a meeting of the President's Council. Five members of the board were present; this was the first time in the series of confrontations that board members had participated in any of the preliminary discussions. At the outset, a faculty member of the President's Council, who had gone to the Senate chamber after the meeting at my home the previous night and was concerned about the drift of initiative to the vanguard groups, asked if Mrs Smith and a fellow faculty member, Natalie Davis, could have permission to speak to the council. The council unenthusiastically agreed. The ladies came in and each delivered a speech on the need in the university for day care centres; Mrs Davis, who taught medieval history, made an emotional appeal based on the need to rescue the female intellectual from the consequences of childbearing. All this was the overture to the wrong opera. Board members disliked appeals made on high moral principles; besides, we had met to resolve a political and disciplinary problem and not to discuss women's liberation. Arthur Kelly, an Ontario Supreme Court judge and a member of the board, whose integrity was as staunch as his conservatism, led off by reading the Criminal Code on trespassing; he then added that if we failed to recognize that we were dealing with a criminal act he would not find it possible to continue as a member of the board or the council. Sydney Hermant, another governor, made remarks in a similar vein. Ernest Sirluck thought that this was being needlessly catastrophic; we should distinguish between actions that did not interfere with the academic program and actions that contained an immediate threat to the essential life of the university. All the time we were receiving messages from the front. Chandler Davis, Natalie Davis's husband, a faculty member of widely advertised radical views, was reported to be issuing white arm bands to his associates in the expectation that negotiations would break down. In a happier vein, word came that my statement was being discussed and that there seemed to be considerable chance of its acceptance. Shortly after, Mrs Smith returned with a compromise statement, the key distinction to the protesters being a request for my personal guaranty of renovation. To me, the key point was that, under the compromise, the protesters admitted the need to look at the long-term responsibilities of the university, and this seemed more important to me than yielding on a practical point (particularly since the particular point had already been resolved). The council agreed to accept the compromise, although the board members gave only a silent acquiescence. I returned to the Senate chamber accompanied by Mrs Smith and Mrs Davis, Mrs Smith, calm and maternal befitting an expectant mother, and Mrs Davis, small and animated, bubbling over with happy excitement. I made my statement without garnishing. When I came to the phrase 'personal guaranty,' there were bursts of jubilation reaching crescendo in chants of, 'We won' and 'Power to the people.' (I caught a glimpse of Bob Barkwell, the vice-president of the Students' Administrative Council, looking like an evangelist receiving a sinner at the mercy seat.) I felt a little sick about the response, but at the same time immensely relieved. In a few minutes the Senate chamber was empty except for a few students who were industriously sweeping up the debris of pamphlets and food cartons.

The public response to my handling of the affair was cool. The Toronto *Star* was in its best bluff, no-nonsense mood and spoke sharply of my surrender to irresponsible elements. The *Globe and Mail* damned me with faint praise, and published a cartoon in which a long-nosed figure in full academic regalia dangled at the end of a branch, clutching a watering can with which he was trying to nourish the roots of the University of Toronto tree.

IV

During my final academic year in office, from July 1970 to June 1971, there were no big dramatic events that caught the attention of the public. The year seethed with unresolved questions – the constitution of the committee that would select my successor (which was amicably settled after six months of proposals and counter-proposals), the protest of some graduate students living in new high-rise apartments on the fringe of the campus against what they considered excessive rents, and, most continuously and seriously, student agitation in the Faculty of Arts and Science for the adoption of a simple parity principle – equal staff and student representation – in the reconstruction of the faculty council. But the students' leadership now lacked the single-minded militancy of the preceding two years. The chief unifying figures had left the university and were pursuing advanced studies in other universities, like revolutionary statesmen seeking a haven in which they could meditate on past events and analyse the nature of things. The new student leaders turned to me for support and encouragement in a curious reversion to the old paternalism. On the issue of parity I was to put an obdurate staff in its place, and, in the matter of rents, to proclaim the friendly solicitude of the university for the welfare of students in opposition to the rapaciousness of the Ontario Housing Commission. I refused to be drawn in. My obsessive concern was the discussions – invisible to the academic community – going on with the board and the government about the new Act, and I was anxious to blunt other issues, or to have them resolved without any interference from above. I felt like a prize fighter entering the final round confident that he was ahead on points and determined not to run into a wild knockout blow from a desperate and dangerous opponent.

The parity issue was the dominating issue of the year. In simplest form, parity was a doctrine that students and teaching staff should have equal representation in university bodies. It was pure doctrine, since it had no inherent logic of its own. It was part symbol – a declaration of the joint interest of students and staff in the learning process – and part psychological – an assurance to students that their ideas would be taken seriously. The doctrine had nothing to do with democracy – pure democracy would have turned the university over permanently to the vast student majority – nor, as even the students pointed out, did it proclaim a basic intellectual equality. It was simply a technique for debate and discussion. I insisted on an important distinction between 'simple' and 'complex' parity. 'Simple' prevailed when the body was made up exclusively of students and staff, and there would then be two equal groups; 'complex' prevailed when other representation was introduced from administrators, laymen, or alumni, and the equal representation of students and staff was thereby placed in a more complex situation, cushioned against confrontation.

I had signed the report of the Commission on University Government, which is discussed further in the next chapter, and which the students declared to be a firm parity document. The commission's recommendations for a top body embodied the principle of complex parity, and although the principle was not enjoined at lower levels, it was commended. I believed that parity, although only in its complex form, was a principle that could work, provided that staff and students were willing to accept it. But the staff, although sympathetic two years earlier to the setting up of a simple parity body for the commission, was now bitterly opposed to the principle. Obviously parity could not just be proclaimed; rather than providing a firm base for discussion, such a move would fix positions for extended warfare. We would have to fall back on the general principle of having substantial staff and student representation, and then let the nature of the specific body determine the numbers.

The student radicals had managed to bring the parity issue, which was largely confined as an issue to the Faculty of Arts and Science, to the level of a broad university confrontation and had marshalled the wide support that existed for the cause. They might have created a basic division that would have postponed indefinitely any university reform. Philosophically, they had the best issue they had ever had; politically, they were in a strong position since the Faculty of Arts and Science council, in general session, had not only turned down a recommendation for a parity committee to examine the structure of the council, but had, with schoolmasterly tartness, voted for a committee in which student representation would be only one-quarter of the total. Yet the issue never gathered an intense emotional charge. Even the student leaders treated it a little lightly. They organized a festival in the foyer of Sidney Smith Hall and decorated the walls with slogans, including Robin Ross's biblical emendation, 'And now abideth faith, hope, parity, these three; but the greatest of these is parity.' Finally, they decided on a strike or, as they explained a brief boycott of classes if a majority of the 13,000 students in the Faculty of Arts and Science gave their approval. A strike committee worked zealously, and I fully expected a small total vote with a sweeping majority in favour of calling the strike. But the students turned out in unusually large numbers – around 8,000 – and there was, to my amazement, a slight majority against the strike proposal. The students' strike committee was dismayed. Mass action was now out of the question and the parity issue became the property of the persistent ideologues.

One final test remained. It came in the year after I left office during Jack Sword's second period as acting president. (His first had been when I was at Harvard.) I was still at the university, beginning a year's leave of absence, and I found myself emotionally involved. In a sense I felt responsible, since the new library was at the heart of the problem, and I gladly accepted major responsibility for it. The ostensible issue was the question of who could use the library, and who could have access to its stacks – a complex and technical question. It could be resolved only by patient analysis of the varying needs of readers and the physical structure of the new building. But the technical issue was simplified by the students as a conflict between elitism and egalitarianism, and it was imbedded in other issues. The library, which a decade or so ago would have been hailed as a triumphant realization of a true university, was now suspect. Here, the argument went, was a huge concrete embodiment of the knowledge industry – information assembled in one place to be processed in isolated cells by scholars concerned only with the extension of their own specialities. Here in this electronic, tribalized, acoustic age was a vast monument to linear, self-contained, visual man. Thus, serious philosophical considerations coalesced with the repugnance to books felt by some members of the academic community and with the great cost of the building, which had pre-empted all available capital funds.

Again there was a sit-in, which went through the usual stages of hard core protest, sympathetic expansion, tense confrontation (during which the city police were called in), compromise, discussion, and resolution. I was unsympathetic to the students' actions, not disposed to criticize the bringing in of the police, and unhappy about discussion of library policy outside the official representative bodies created for the purpose. Still, one could not help taking some satisfaction in the placing of the library in the forefront of student concerns. Students, despite their often-stated dislike of the new building, were still keen to be full participators in it.

v

It is generally agreed that the period of militant student action came to an end with the end of the sixties. Students, it is said, are returning to their somnambulistic ways while the universities follow their old course, self-satisfied, defensively self-contained, tolerating a few violent extremists, who persist like a disease in a sound but sluggish body. Some have called it revolution that turned out to be no revolution, in the words of Sir Lewis Namier about the revolution of 1848: 'a turning point at which history failed to turn.'

This could not be said about the late sixties at Toronto. There, despite the crises that caught the headlines, there were solid changes, contemporary with the organized expression of student dissent, to some extent springing out of that dissent, certainly influenced by it. It was not a quiet revolution but it was an inner revolution, so vital and central that at the time it was not seriously noted.

In political associations and impacts the student movement at Toronto was less visible than it was at a dozen American universities. Lewis Feuer has observed that all major student uprisings have attached themselves to a 'carrier' movement, that is, to a large important social cause, and have been carried forward on its momentum. That was certainly true of the student movement in the United States. It grew out of the civil rights cause among the blacks and was sustained by opposition to the Vietnam war. Its ideology came from progressivist thought in education and from a variety of attacks on the ordered, corporate world of business; and it picked up some of the more romantic concepts of Marxism, particularly the idea of the alienation of the worker from the means of production. But the ideology was too eclectic to have any effect, certainly to provide any sustaining and directing force. It was the political side that provided the dynamism; when all else failed one could emphasize a close association of a large complex university and the war machine.

In Canada there was no 'carrier' movement. There was a halfhearted attempt to follow the American pattern, and protests against on-campus recruitment of graduates by the manufacturers of war materials continued throughout the entire period. The argument used in such instances was a simple and effective one: Canada was part of the American war machine by reason of the defence-sharing agreement between the two countries; and the universities in Canada as in the United States were a vital part of that machine. But in the absence of 'body count' headlines, and without the constant hazard of the draft, it was hard to make the war issue real. Nor was there any distinctive Canadian issue to which the student movement could attach itself. One read occasionally about the plight of minority groups; and in Quebec there were tough ties between separatism and student dissent, but that issue grew steadily weaker as it crossed the border and moved into the southern heartland of Ontario.

The revolutionary student groups at Toronto had firm political connections with obscure parties in the far left that were not even visible on the national political scene. Among the radicals, no doubt the closest and most effective ties were with the New Democratic Party, not in the sense that there were any directives from outside, but simply by reason of the political sympathies of the student leaders. The NDP knows a good deal about the reality of power, and the student radicals followed a shrewd, pragmatic policy. They knew that if they were to exert real power in the university they must deal with issues that were close to the academic community. The very absence of the great emotional national issues (which in the United States could bring about a sordid tragedy, like that at Kent State, without having any deep, lasting effect on the institution concerned) led to a concentration on specific academic issues and eventually to fundamental changes. The student radical movement at its strongest and best was concerned with the way in which decisions were made within the university, and in this concern it coalesced, without being aware of it, with similar concerns held by the faculty and administration.

Staff members had long been concerned about playing a part in the making of final decisions, especially those decisions that changed the emphasis within the university and committed it to a course of future development.

They had also become aware, although slowly, of the dangers of outside pressure as governments became at once more bountiful and more demanding. To these concerns, which I shared, I added administrative impatience with the byzantine methods that were bound up with the division into the two worlds of the academic and the financial. I had long argued, with little effect, that the vice-president for business affairs should report directly to the president, and should not be able, except on routine matters, to go independently to the chairman of the board. Fortunately, the new vice-president for business affairs, Alex Rankin, who had come back to the university in 1967 after a long absence in the business world, fully agreed with this principle, and the board, anxious to get his services, had not clung to the old ways. Student radicals were unaware of these issues. They were indifferent to organizational problems – indeed, they were suspicious of any steps that would strengthen the university as an institution. And they did not see government as a threat; it was, on the contrary, a force that could be employed to put the proud university in its place. The problem, then, was to keep the powerful forces in relationship: the need to widen the internal basis for decision-making; the need to rationalize the structure of organization; the need to establish a firm and clear relationship of the institution to the government.

The debate and the resolution of these varying or conflicting ideas was the real revolution at the University of Toronto. It stretched over a period of three years and found expression not in the sensational protests that made the headlines, but in the prolonged, intensive, and often tedious discussions of duly appointed bodies.

9 / The Real Revolution

The first meeting of the Commission on University Government took place on December 10, 1968. The committee met in the Senate chamber, sitting around four tables arranged to form a hollow square, at the north end of the large chamber just below the dais with its three formal university crest-embossed chairs. There was a nervous embarrassed sense of the historical importance of the moment. We were in direct succession to the commission of 1906 that had enunciated the structure of the modern University of Toronto and greatly influenced the structure of all Canadian universities subsequently founded. But the intervening years had erased all resemblances, except in the name – and even that, particularly the use of the word 'commission', was hotly disputed as appearing to confer too much dignity and insinuate too much power. The commissioners of 1906 represented the intellectual, social, and financial elite of Ontario. In the official declaration of their appointment King Edward VII had declared that in them 'we have and repose full confidence.' The commission of 1968, on the other hand, was unheralded and unproclaimed. Its initial meeting brought back the memory of another incident, in 1856, when Sir Daniel Wilson, president of University College, and a few associates, fearful of sectarian protests against the 'godless' college, met at night to lay the cornerstone of the new building which would be the nucleus of the university.

The final form of the Commission on University Government represented a victory for the radical students. It existed outside the formal structure of university government. Certainly the Board of Governors had no interest in sponsorship. The board's original proposal, a complex parity committee, with equal representation from board, students, staff, and administration, had been rejected; and the board felt justifiably aggrieved, like a suitor from an old wealthy family who had adopted an easy democratic manner to win the hand of a popular beauty, and even then had been turned down. The acting chairman, O.D. Vaughan, said that the board could no longer take any direct responsibility for the committee, but was prepared to send two representatives as observers and to provide accommodation and a moderate budget. The board, moreover, steadfastly refused to refer to the committee as a 'commission,' since it had had its origins in no official action either by the government or by the university. Some of the governors thought that the board should set up a parallel committee, but wiser counsels prevailed. Such a move would have initiated a public conflict and might have blocked any reform. The original appointees of the board, Vacy Ash and Wallace McCutcheon, agreed to attend the meetings of the commission, but their decisions to do so were reached separately, slowly, and painfully; they represented an attitude of wise tolerance and forbearance all the more admirable since in the atmosphere of the time the board and its members could expect little understanding and no praise.

The teaching staff were officially responsible for the form the commission took, although 'staff' here meant only a small group. Most of the staff, I believe, would never have agreed that such an important body should be constituted in accordance with the principle of simple parity – staff and students in equal numbers, on the assumption that these were the only estates that were entitled to determine the future of the university and that each had an equal share in making the final decisions. The simple parity principle was slightly shadowed by the inclusion of the president as a voting member, but he was thought of essentially as a resource person who would not disturb the essential nature of the commission.

The student and staff members of the commission were elected. This was a crucial decision arising out of the resolution of the Association of the Teaching Staff at its meeting of October 3, 1968. All previous discussion of methods for appointment had fixed on selection by the appropriate senior bodies. The Association of the Teaching Staff had already nominated its two representatives for the original commission as proposed by the Board of Governors. But there had been dissatisfaction with this closed procedure; and the resolution of October 3 prescribed election by ballot of the entire staff. The radical students were less enthusiastic about such elections, which they considered as overzealously democratic. They would argue that since the Students' Administrative Council was already democratically elected (albeit by a small minority of the student body) it should have the right to make appointments. But having won their main point, the students agreed to elections. They refused, however, to accept the faculty prescription of dividing the university into four constituencies along lines of academic disciplines, and insisted on one all-university election for student representatives. This procedure, they knew, would have the probable effect of eliminating students in professional faculties, since such students did not seem deeply enough interested in the problems of government to run for election, and if they did, it was fairly certain that they would be overwhelmed by the larger and more radical Arts vote.

The election was run successfully. More than a thousand staff, about sixty per cent of the ATS membership, voted. The student voters numbered a little under 5,000, about sixteen per cent of the eligible population, statistically a poor showing, although much better than the usual student performance. The faculty constituencies made it inevitable that there would be at least two representatives from the professional faculties, and this prevented the commission from losing its credibility at the very outset.

I awaited the results of the election with concern. Would we have a hopeless hodgepodge of far-out radicals and far-out reactionaries, a staff determined to put students in their proper place, and students sworn to humiliate administration and governors? One cheerful sign was that the Toronto Student Movement had decided to boycott the elections, and in one of the rare glints in those days of undergraduate humour (grotesque teutonic branch) had entered a tape recorder, 'Twitchy,' as a candidate. The elected students (three undergraduates in Arts and one graduate) were all radicals who, however, believed that the present system could be reformed. A declared 'moderate,' actually a member of the extreme right-wing Edmund Burke Society (hideously misnamed), was edged out for the fourth seat by a few votes, and the commission was thus saved from being a battleground. The elected staff were all scholars known and respected within and outside the university with, as far as I knew, liberal and flexible views. Nobody at that time observed that there was no woman on the commission; but democracy is cautious and slow moving, and in 1968 did not consort with the Women's Liberation Movement.

The student who received the highest vote was Bob Rae, by now firmly established in the student mind as its most eloquent and effective spokesman. In the subsequent deliberations of the commission he thoroughly justified the role: he pursued his ideas with unceasing and inventive devotion, and he was tireless and unshakeable in argument, unless he had previously decided on a retreat. He had just turned twenty, was in his final year in modern history, and within a few months was to be chosen one of the two Ontario Rhodes Scholars. D'Arcy Martin, a third-year student in Latin-American studies, had come next to Rae in the popular vote. He was older than Rae, had taken a year off to travel in South America, and had a considered and mature approach toward the work of the commission. The third undergraduate was Stephen Grant, a second-year student in general Arts, diffident, reluctant to speak before his more self-confident, articulate fellows; but he was thoughtful and intelligent and played his share in the writing of the final report. The fourth student member was Gary Webster, a graduate student in political science, who had taken his first degree at Williams College, in Massachusetts, and had taught for two years in Nigeria before coming to Toronto. Of the student representatives, he was the one with the most hardened views, shaped, one gathered, by his experience of colonialism in Africa. His American experience was rarely introduced, never, certainly, by way of admonition and guide. He belonged to the group of anti-American Americans who were more influential in university life than the imperialists who were constantly arousing the indignation of the national critics.

The four faculty representatives were all senior professors with administrative experience. J.E. Hodgetts was principal of Victoria College. Ben Etkin was chairman of the department of engineering science and a professor in the Institute of Aerospace Studies. James S. Thompson was the chairman of the department of anatomy. Lawrence E. Lynch, professor of philosophy at St Michael's College, had long been interested in university government. He had made some of the early proposals in the President's Council about methods of analysis and evaluation, and at the time of the October 3 crisis he had written a long letter to me analysing the various conflicts in the university: between concepts of the university, as a service agent for society, as a tool of social change, or as an independent institution for research and instruction; between attitudes towards the board, as a legal entity representing the public, as a centre of power for vested interests, or as an advisory group on the edge of the academic community; between concepts of the president, as chief executive officer in a chain of command, as the negative pole of a dialectical tension, or as first among academics. It was a brilliant and incisive summary of the tangled web of assumptions that lay behind attempts to fix upon a common policy; and Larry Lynch, more than any of his academic colleagues, knew the work that lay ahead if any degree of agreement was to be reached.

All the staff members were, fortunately, endowed with reserves of patience. They were good at keeping a cheerful face when confronted with extreme statements. On the whole, the students did not use the shock tactics of the far left – inflamed rhetoric, or raw, abrasive language. But they would occasionally hover on the edge, and a violent response from the staff might have toppled them over and the commission with them. None of the faculty was patriarchal and condescending in manner. They were equipped to engage in a sustained skirmish between the generations, to explore the alien tracts that lay between those separated by two or three decades.

Of the two board members, Wallace McCutcheon was the more reluctant participant. Even the first version of the amended proposals, which would have left board representation intact while increasing the total number of students and staff to four each, aroused his suspicions. He wrote to me that he had serious doubts whether anything could be accomplished by the commission and whether he could serve any useful purpose as a member. But he responded warmly to a letter that I wrote to him in reply, and agreed to serve. Then came the humiliation of disfranchisement of the board, and for several weeks he was adamant about not serving. What brought him in finally, I think, was an awareness of the dangerous situation in which the university found itself, with an increasingly hostile and alienated board, and a triumphant and aggressive student movement that had for the time being co-opted the staff. In the 'secret brief' crisis he had been a cool and accommodating intermediary. His loyalty to the university was deep, and he was prepared to make sacrifices for its sake. He came to the commission with little hope that it could lead to anything of value; and he soon won the respect of the students because he was direct and informed in his comments, which were delivered with a disarming, gruff wit. At one session, a visiting member of the staff, a psychiatrist, took him to task for a sweeping rebuttal he had made: 'On what did you base your remarks?' he asked testily. 'On intuition, pure intuition,' McCutcheon replied with a disarming grin. It was the perfect reply. His sudden death, just when the commission was moving beyond preliminary explorations, was a severe blow. He would, no doubt, have become the principal liaison between board and commission, and he might have prevented the board's subsequent drift into confused inactivity.

Vacy Ash, the other board representative, attended almost all of the hundred and forty-odd meetings of the commission, listening patiently while discussion swirled about him—calm reflective passages suddenly broken by brief, intense, eliptic exchanges. Only occasionally would he grow irritated at the repeated left-wing assumptions and plead for some evidence. He was particularly irate at the dismissal of the Board of Governors as a survival from another age, an irrelevance so obvious, it was implied, that it did not even require a cursory demolition.

Following McCutcheon's death, the board appointed William B. Harris as his successor. It was a tribute to the board's capacity for sophisticated ambivalence, since Bill Harris, much younger than most of the board members, knew some of the student leaders and was sympathetic to the new wave. It would be up to him to explain the new ideas to the board and to provide a link with whatever succeeded it.

Alumni representation, spurned by the students, had been restored by the staff. Initially it consisted of a single non-voting member; but in effect four alumni members participated in discussions. Robert Hicks was the official observer, but he had three active alternates: Eva McCutcheon, Ronald McKinlay, and Ruth Peters. As the discussion thickened towards action, the alumni became more assertive and influential.

Administratively, the commission was a remarkable example of the capacity (too often only latent) of the academic community to move swiftly and efficiently. The administrative responsibilities were handled by Robin Ross, and he established a small secretariat from his own office. We were apprehensive about the budget, which had to be authorized by the board: we felt a little like an emancipated son asking his wealthy establishment father to pay for a course in subversion. But the budget was kept under strict control, and only towards the last, with the expense of publication, did it go over fifty thousand dollars. A government commission of the same kind would have absorbed that sum in the first week. Student members received small stipends to compensate them for income lost during the summer; the faculty members worked without any additional compensation, fitting the meetings and the long hours of reading briefs and preparing drafts into their academic schedules.

The commission was conscious that it must generate its own authority. It turned down the idea of an outside chairman and chose co-chairmen from within, Larry Lynch and Gary Webster. It had no official sponsor within the university, since the President's Council had no official status. The university community responded with briefs and presentations, but despite the openness of the meetings, exhibited little sustained interest. The commission had a feeling that it was working in isolation; that the only vital dialogue was between its own members.

At first the dialogue was halting – more polite and formal exchanges than communication. One observer, psychologically trained, thought that the commission should retire to a remote spot and submit itself to the healing effects of group therapy. We instinctively resisted this proposal. By the middle of March, after some two months of meetings, staff members thought that we were making good progress; but suddenly at the end of the meeting of March 4, Stephen Grant read out a carefully prepared indictment of our activities. We were not, he said, reaching each other: staff members were more interested in a structure than they were in general ideas; unless there was a change, the commission might just as well dissolve. We were distressed, especially since Grant was the mildest and least assertive of the student members. We suspected that the move had been carefully planned as part of a shock technique.

This little crisis passed over, and we moved ahead with no sense of impairment. A second crisis came late in June when it seemed that we might be approaching acceptable compromises, and could begin writing our report.

On June 13 Ernest Sirluck delivered the address at one of the annual convocations for the conferring of degrees. Sirluck did not relish the usual convocation oratorical fare – innocuous, high-sounding, remote generalizations. He liked to use every occasion to discuss major university issues, and on this occasion he used the events of the preceding year to demonstrate that the university was committed to reform and was making good progress towards its goal. As I listened to the speech, I admired Sirluck's directness and found the narrative generally accurate. He was critical of student motives and techniques, but also flattering about some student policies – especially the policy of openness that he and his colleagues had once feared but now accepted. At the end of the speech, Steven Langdon, who was then writing for a Toronto paper, arose in the gallery and declared that the speech was false in all its parts. Some of Sirluck's interpretation of events could be questioned, but I wondered at the furiousness of Langdon's response. Perhaps he was simply angered by Sirluck's assignment of a heroic role to the administration; a role that in the mythology of the student movement was reserved for the students alone. Langdon's intervention caused no stir, except for a thin wave of applause from some of the graduating students. In the relaxation of convocation exercises, the audience may have thought that the intervention was all part of the medieval ritual. I thought no more about the incident, beyond congratulating myself that it had passed off harmlessly. A week or so later Bob Rae made an angry, dramatic entrance into the commission meeting and produced copies of letters that he had written to Sirluck, in which he accused Sirluck of making 'a vicious, insulting, and completely inaccurate attack on the student movement as a whole,' and reported that he was 'asking the President for a statement regarding your remarks and their status, a statement that makes clear that your speech in no way represents administration or university policy.' Rae clearly had the support of his fellow students on the commission, and my faculty colleagues and I wondered whether, even at this advanced stage, our discussions might collapse. I refused to issue a statement about Sirluck's speech; what my colleagues said in public was their business, and I had no intention of even hinting at a retrospective censorship. Rae sensed my position; his anger cooled; and, with relief, we turned back to the business.

The commission's discussions on vital questions were usually conducted in a restrained manner with a minimum of *ad hominem* abuse. An exception to this was a paper presented by Gary Webster on 'student involvement' in governance, with particular reference to student membership on the committee concerned with the hiring, dismissing (the students preferred the more jagged word, 'firing'), promotion, and tenure of academic staff. His argument for strong student participation, amounting in this case really to control, was that staff were selfish 'haves' concerned with self-preservation and self-perpetuation, and students were 'sensitive thinking adults whose range of experiences is different than, often more limited in range than, that of a teacher, but is not necessarily less valuable in the academic world for all that.' The staff members concluded that Webster was using the techniques of a tough bargainer: to start in a wildly extreme position in order that any slight retreat to rationality will be received with relief and even greeted with applause.

The one organizational failure was in commissioned research. There were two major errors: the hiring of 'research associates' who proved to be dogmatically committed and interpreted 'research' as systematic exercises in special pleading; and the agreement that they should carry out research in large comprehensive subjects. Since the work of the commission was completed in eight months, there was inadequate time for research on a large scale; two of the reports, one on the process of decision-making in the Faculty of Arts and Science, and one on decision-making in the professional divisions, were completed too late to have any effect on the commissions' final discussions. Reading them later, some of us congratulated ourselves on avoiding in our own report the dizzier abysses of style and thought of the popular radical critique. ('The movement of students for reform of knowledge – for whom and for what –' one report solemnly concluded, 'is linked to a consciousness that the monopolies of knowledge for the guild constitute a small part of social reality and scientific reality and a disproportionate amount of the university curriculum.') A third report on the growth of the college system was completed well in advance of the writing of the report and produced some useful material.

The preparation of the report was, in every sense, a practical exercise in participatory decision-making. A specific general topic would be examined by one student and one staff member together, each preparing a position paper. The papers would then be discussed by the full commission, finally concentrating on areas of disagreement. When satisfactory compromises had been reached, the topic would be left for final treatment and incorporation in the report. The final document justified the quiet boastfulness of the opening sentences of its preface: 'Most reports are written by one person and signed by others. This report, however, involved all the Commission members in each stage of its drafting.'

I was not asked to prepare any of the drafts and my formal contributions were brief papers on the organization of the central governing body: these were not solicited, but were my responses to proposals actively being considered. I thought that the report was a remarkable distillation of our discussions, whether oral or written, with an easy movement, and a unified, interrelated presentation of a great deal of material. The most cogent sections were the opening discussion of general principles – a continuous argument punctuated by only one recommendation – and the final section on the governing structure, which clearly and cogently related the principal recommendations to past history and present developments. In between lay less appealing areas of detailed discussion, where the numerous recommendations, typographically set off on the pages in boldface, frequently squeezed the commentary into narrow boxes. The general tone of the report was optimistic, reflecting a sense of triumph in the final resolution within the commission of apparently irreconcilable oppositions.

These oppositions were not primarily ideological. Both students and staff favoured a critical university – a university that guarded its right to criticize social practice and institutions and, if need be, to work actively for reform. Any differences would have come over the degree of responsibility that the university should be prepared to take in supporting a given social idea – the students coming down on the side of imposed specific direction, the faculty clinging to a free market on ideas. Nor were students and staff at loggerheads on the question of the 'democratic' university. There was never any question of democracy in its ordinary sense, one-man/one-vote, for this would have turned teaching staff into employees tied to popular whims. All members of the commission accepted the idea of the university as made up of several estates, of which students and teaching staff were the most important; but this idea had nothing to do with popular democratic theory. Also, from the very beginning, both students and staff assumed that the partition between the academic and the financial was wrong, and that the Board of Governors and Senate were incapable of responding adequately to the problems of the university. We all took for granted the necessity of a single, authoritative body on which there would be representation from all the estates. And there was no fundamental difference of opinion about the university as an intellectual centre, although staff were inclined to think in this connection chiefly of learned books written by academics, while students thought of the learning process in which they, in association with staff, played an important role. The real opposition was psychological and emotional – the inevitable differences between middle age and youth, between experience and exuberance, between ordered discipline and individual intuition, between the weight of the past and the breath of the future. In practical terms the opposition narrowed down to differences of opinion about the participation of students in decisions that shaped the university.

The commission had to choose among a variety of opinions, ranging from extreme to moderate, each level having a faculty or student version. The most extreme faculty version, held by only a few diehards, was that students should have no part whatsoever at any level in university decisions. The extreme student version was as far to the left as that faculty version was to the right. It was known as parallel decision-making, and called for initial decisions to be made by staff and students meeting separately in assemblies with each group having the veto over the other. This was the version favoured by the Students' Administrative Council and solemnly propounded to the commission. It was ultimately derived, an American colleague told me once, from theories put forward during the English Puritan Revolution of the seventeenth century; whether this was true or not, it aroused associations appropriate to the young student radicals who espoused it, since in manner and spirit they resembled Cromwellian zealots. The central position between these extremes also had two versions. The staff version welcomed student participation at the highest levels, in the top governing bodies and in the appointment of senior academic officials with administrative responsibilities, but ruled out student participation in decision-making on purely academic appointments. The student version called for participation by students at all levels of decision, preferably through committees in which staff and students had equal representation. A cautious variant was very similar whether held by students or staff: student advice should be actively sought for, but student membership on decision-making committees should be granted only when student interests were actively involved, e.g., in the planning of residential accommodation, or the setting up of a counselling office.

It was evident to the commission that the only source from which an acceptable compromise could come was the central position. The extreme positions, whether wildly to the right or wildly to the left, would immobilize the university; and the cautious position belonged to the fumbling meliorism of the fifties. But at the centre there was little room for manoeuvre.

The crucial question was the manner of making academic appointments, promotions, and dismissals, and of determining tenure. The very nature of the university could turn upon the decision here. Staff were apprehensive on two grounds. First, direct student participation would leave the way open for political intimidation. This opinion was firmly riveted by what the staff saw of the students who pressed for participation most militantly: they came from the social sciences; they measured academic worth in terms of adherence or non-adherence to a political norm – clearly a social science virus that might spread elsewhere. Second, and even more telling in staff eyes, was the need to defend the professional competence of the university's teachers by having them judged only by their peers. If this was disregarded, the way was open for the rapid decline of academic standards, and the eventual quarantine of the University of Toronto by the academic world. The university could end up with a faculty dominated by lucid squares or untroubled dogmatists. The faculty members of the commission were sympathetic to this point of view. They had won the confidence of their colleagues by their scholarly qualities, and they knew the penalty that a university pays if it appears to slight scholarly criteria. But they also felt that the faculty attitude was often based on fear, and that there was no absolute reason why students could not demonstrate tolerance and discretion. They finally agreed to a compromise that seemed to have inherent restraints. Students would be eligible for committees on staff appointments, but must first demonstrate a major academic commitment to the department concerned; assessment of staff members would be made separately by staff and students, and, what was most important, the final decision on promotion, dismissal, or tenure would be the sole responsibility of the chairman of the academic department.

The demand for parity proved to be another stumbling block in the way of compromise. There is a crucial distinction, as I have pointed out, between simple parity – where staff and students in equal numbers face each other alone – and complex parity – where this state is modified by the presence of other representatives. The commission elected for the latter and usually (depending on the nature of any specific body) in such a way as to give the faculty a clear majority through the presence of academic administrators, who technically are not teaching staff but in fact are staff temporarily serving in other capacities. Such an interpretation of parity did not, it seemed to me, threaten the traditional dominance of staff. In addition to the sense of commitment, the knowledge, and the experience that staff members would take to discussions (*prima facie* superior on all scores to the students') they would have an actual majority, or would be in a position to form and direct a commanding alliance.

The writing of the report was finished in the early fall of 1970. I now faced the question of whether I should sign it. I knew that the commission's compromise on appointments was not acceptable to the staff, and I doubted that it could ever actually work. The report's attitude to parity was defensible, especially if it were confined to the new Governing Council (which would replace both Board of Governors and Senate) and to committees for the appointment of senior academic administrators. But both questions were for the time being subsidiary to the main question of the composition of the Governing Council – a council on which all the estates of the university would be represented. This was a recommendation that I hoped would be given priority and whose implementation would spell the beginning of a new era. If I abstained from signing the report, or if I put in a minority report on the basis of my doubts about appointment procedures and parity, I would then highlight these issues and postpone indefinitely debate on the nature of the Governing Council.

As the discussions in the commission had moved towards the forming of specific recommendations, there had been increasing interest in the strategy for discussing and implementing the report. At the beginning, the students had thought in terms of a grand leap from recommendation to implementation. They assumed that this was possible first on the departmental level where, they contended, the real issues lay. In a section of the report that was drafted but not approved, these statements were made: 'At the department level we would urge that faculty and students settle the question of constituency and composition of departmental councils and their committees, including the admittedly difficult problem of personnel, as soon as possible. Where there is agreement at this level we see no reason why these changes could not be implemented right away.' Such a policy, I was sure, spelled disaster. It would turn an already suspicious staff irrevocably against the report. I hastily wrote an alternative section on implementation, pointing out that the top body in our recommendations had an unusual concentration of power and that it would delegate some of that power to constituent parts of the university only by its own action: in short, that only the top governing body could authorize appointment procedures and departmental and divisional organization. We had rightly emphasized decentralization as a principle of governance, but decentralization must not become a tolerance of anarchy. The students were unhappy about my comments; they had assumed that they had a licence to legitimize revolution. But the primacy of the question of the Governing Council could not be denied. The final report did not mention implementation. It concluded with a simple, unequivocal request for the debate to concentrate on the Governing Council. With this emphasis, I felt that I could sign the report.

The commission addressed itself with systematic enthusiasm to the wide dissemination of the report so that no one in the whole community could complain that he had been kept in ignorance. Some thirty-five thousand copies in newspaper tabloid form were printed and distributed. For a few days the report blanketed the campus; soon the inevitable detritus of printed matter appeared – abandoned and torn sheets, huddles of neglected copies. But the commission had completed the last act of its concentrated drama. Now was the time for commentary and assessment, from which eventually a few clear actions might result.

It soon became evident that the commission was only a first step in a movement towards change; and such a jolting step that it might well induce a permanent immobility. An overwhelming majority of the Board of Governors was strongly opposed to the concept of one central representative body, with the reduction in the lay power that this involved. Vacy Ash had not been converted by the hours he had spent listening to discussions and steadfastly clung to a modified version of the old system. Bill Harris was at first the only member of the board who was prepared to accept some version of the commission's proposals; he was eventually joined by Malim Harding, who had taken a liberal and flexible view throughout the discussions.

For the time being, the board was inclined to wait patiently, perhaps in the expectation that the academic community would consume itself in fruitless debate and would return with relief to the old familiar ways. And for the first two post-commission months there was a considerable likelihood of that. The teaching staff concentrated obsessively and combatively on the recommendations for methods of staff appointments, promotion, tenure, and dismissal, and those for staff-student parity in departmental and faculty governance. A motion was placed before the Council of the Faculty of Arts and Science, 'That the Council withhold judgment in matters relating to the top governing structure of the University until these two matters have been satisfactorily resolved.' The adoption of this resolution would, I thought, undo the work of the year. Discussion of the two issues would go on endlessly and acrimoniously, and the possibility of a reconstituted central body would recede rapidly. But, by the middle of December, the fervour of the staff supporters of the resolution had abated, the resolution was withdrawn – to my intense relief – and we were able to address ourselves to the central issue.

The commission had recommended the appointment of a programming committee to organize the university discussions. As eventually constituted, this committee consisted of three students and three staff with Professor Marty Friedland of the Faculty of Law as its chairman. By late January the committee had decided that the time had come for the university to attempt the formulation of a consensus. How was this to be done in a community of thirty thousand and on questions that seemed abstract and remote to the majority? The answer, both simple and bold, was to form a constitutional assembly, a broad and generous representation of the whole university, which would debate and vote on a series of specific resolutions that had emerged from the discussions of the preceding few months. Technically, as I explained to an apprehensive board, the constitutional assembly was to be simply another advisory body to me; actually I hoped that it would, in effect, become the voice of the university, in so far as one voice could rise above the clamour of a community, fractious and articulate.

The University-wide Committee, as this body was called, was to consist of one hundred and sixty people in four broad groups – forty students, forty faculty, forty administrators (both academic and non-academic) and forty other delegates, chiefly alumni (twenty) and members of the board (ten), with the balance representing other university interests. Since there was some scepticism as to whether such a large body could be launched and even more scepticism as to whether it could function in an orderly manner, the programming committee decided to ask for general comments about the support it might command and, at the same time, make enquiries about fundamental attitudes to university government. A questionnaire was worked out under the guidance of the department of sociology, and its results were analysed by a member of that department. The questionnaire was, as such documents go, direct and simple, and anybody who had followed the argument for the previous two years (or, for that matter, the previous two months) could have responded quickly and confidently. The proportion of full-time staff who responded – forty-two per cent – was not a cause for despondency, but the proportion of undergraduate students – eight per cent – was disappointing. For some it confirmed doubts about the student indifference to general university problems; for others it emphasized the difficulties of bringing students effectively into the process of decision-making. Within its limits the questionnaire, as analysed, gave reasonably clear answers to a few basic questions: that the University-wide Committee envisaged was acceptable to a majority of the campus and should meet towards the end of the academic year; and that the governing structure should be revised so as to provide a single body consisting of no more than sixty members.

In the meantime the Association of the Teaching Staff had addressed itself to the determination of firm proposals on the top governing body. Its university government committee drew up what seems to me, in retrospect, the most compelling statement on the subject and, given the temper of the general discussions, the best specific proposal. The ATS committee succinctly summarized the historical process by which both Board of Governors and Senate had withered away to ineffectiveness under the pressure of new provincial problems so that 'only the president and the committees responsible to him have retained vitality.' They reviewed a new kind of bicameralism emerging in several other Ontario universities whereby the senates had increasingly taken over the responsibility for the allotment of resources and the boards had become simply a means by which the public interest could be protected in the event of academic impetuosity. They decided against such a structure 'on the grounds that the essential unity of the university's social, academic and financial requirements point strongly to a single body.' As to the size and composition of a single body, they came down on the side of an 'internal majority,' i.e., a majority of members from within the academic community; a more substantial representation from academic administration than recommended by the Commission on University Government, on the grounds that this would provide executive talent; and a significant student component, smaller, however, than the faculty component 'on the grounds of faculty experience in the university and sense of institutional responsibility.' The eventual formal ATS recommendation was for a Governing Council of sixty: twenty lay members, twenty staff, ten students, and ten administrators, including the president. The ATS also emphasized the need to give the president strong executive powers: it recommended retaining the provision of the old University of Toronto Act whereby no 'person shall be appointed, or promoted, or removed from office as a Dean of any Faculty, as Chairman of any Department, or as a member of the teaching staff of the University unless he has first been nominated by the President.'

About the same time I worked out my own version of the Governing Council. I favoured a reduction of the sixty recommended by the staff to fifty, to be accomplished by a reduction of five in the number of laymen and a similar reduction in the number of staff. This would reduce the disparity in the representation of students and staff while preserving the principle of the internal majority. I made two other proposals. The first was that there should be an honorarium to lay members – this would encourage the appointment of younger men and women, and of those with special competence and interests who might otherwise be unable to give time to the university (those who were comfortably secure could always direct their honoraria to a favourite university activity) – and that along the same principle, following the practice adopted for the Commission on University Government, provision should be made for student members to postpone their academic work to the summer, with an appropriate stipend to compensate for forgone earnings. My second proposal gained few supporters, but I still think it makes strenuous good sense. It was that no election should be valid unless thirty per cent (I had originally suggested forty) of the eligible voters participated. (I had in mind here the slim electoral responses of students, which constantly undermined their leaders' contention that student power was based on widespread concern.)

The University-wide Committee met on June 1, 2, and 3, 1970. It had before it a clearly enunciated faculty position. The only divisive issue was likely to be the composition of the Governing Council, and especially the relative weight of student and staff representatives. The proposal that received final endorsation, by a comfortable majority of 86 to 46, was a modified version of the faculty proposal – a council of seventy-two, with student representation increased from ten to fourteen (two-thirds of the faculty, which was set at twenty-one), and lay representation increased from twenty to twenty-four (with ten places assigned to alumni). The remaining thirteen places were assigned as follows: the president, three presidential appointees, three administrators, and six representatives of the support staff. By prior agreement the groups of students and teaching staff could defer for further consideration in the fall of 1970 specific resolutions, if the majority of either group sought this. I assumed that the students would claim this privilege, but they did not do so. Despite the tensions and occasional bitterness during a series of ballots on the composition of the Governing Council, there was a sense of immense relief, even a note of jubilation at the outcome. When the chairman of the Association of the Teaching Staff, Professor J.M. Rist, wrote me a few days later he conveyed a refreshing sense of faculty optimism: ' I do not believe that you will ever have a proposal which will command as wide support on the campus as that which is now miraculously available. In particular in carrying the proposals to Queen's Park *quickly* you will have stronger and more widespread backing from the faculty with more shades of political opinion than could possibly have been foreseen.'

I was present as an observer at all the sessions of the University-wide Committee. The meetings were held (except for one in the concert hall of the Faculty of Music Building) in a new block of the Ontario Parliament Buildings. The exterior of the building is massively monotonous, but it has space and facilities not available in the university. Registrants were seated at tables generously spaced; and the physical setting contributed to the success of the discussions. At the university such large meetings would have been held in an auditorium and they would rapidly have taken on the dark colouring of a general political rally, with like-minded members crowded together in tight phalanxes, and speakers, conscious of their constituencies, pitching their voices to the tastes of their allies. But in the Ontario Room of the Macdonald Building an easy parliamentary camaraderie descended.

The success of the meeting was not all a matter of technology. There had been numerous meetings of the constituency groups before June 1, and a program committee had carefully prepared a set of resolutions, each to be introduced by one of its members. The resolutions were arranged so as to move progressively to the climactic debate on the composition of the Governing Council. Most of the resolutions incorporating general principles were passed with overwhelming majorities. The most important of these were that the top governing structure should be unicameral (passed by 115 to 13) and that 'all faculty and academic administrative appointments, promotions, and dismissals should be made by the top governing structure upon the recommendation of the president' (passed unanimously). A crucial factor in the success of the meeting was the tone established by the chairman and his handling of difficult questions in such a diverse body. Archie Hallett, as chairman, responded coolly and confidently to the occasion. He was informed, sensitive, unflappable, and tough.

If the recommendations of the University-wide Committee had gone directly without delay to the provincial government, a new University of Toronto Act would have been launched on a note of buoyant consensus. But another year was to pass before action was taken, and during that time the old divisions reappeared. The board had very carefully avoided any association with the University-wide Committee, and now asserted its right to make an independent approach. It did not respond to a request from the President's Council for a joint committee of the board and council to work out ways of implementing the recommendations of the University-wide Committee. The summer drifted by without any action, and in the fall the board sent forward to the province its own proposals. These proposals were never made public. But they were, in general terms, a re-working of the old system with intensification of the lay control by the appointment of a full-time chairman and the effective reduction of the president to a ceremonial and limited academic role. The government, more finely tuned to the desires of the whole academic community than to the desires of the board, ignored the proposals. At the end of November the board finally issued a statement on the question of university government. This statement had gone through a succession of versions, and its final form was characterized by an uneasy stridency of tone and a fumbling search for a compromise in the face of what looked like inevitable disaster. It made clear the board's opposition to the unicameral idea; then it proceeded to list the actions that might restore confidence, even if unicameralism were adopted: reduction in size of the governing body to about thirty-five; the appointment of a full-time lay chairman; an effective majority of government appointees.

By the spring of 1971 the government had made up its mind to proceed with a new Act on the basis of the recommendations of the University-wide Committee. It made only one major demand: that the number of outside members (those who were neither students at the university nor on the university staff) should be equal to those coming from within. This, of course, made it necessary to revise radically the composition of the Governing Council as recommended by the University-wide Committee, if the relative proportion of the students and staff was to be retained.

How was the government, in particular the minister of university affairs, John White, to work out the details of a new Act with the university? The board was the corporate embodiment of the university; and the majority of the board (including the chairman) was strongly opposed to the very idea of the Act. A strong contingent made this clear to Bill Davis, who had now succeeded John Robarts as premier, at a tense meeting where emotions seethed beneath the frosty exchanges. Davis was not to be moved from his reformist position; it was a question of doing something radical or doing nothing at all, he said, and he was clearly inclined towards the former course. He knew that the university question might be an issue in the election that was fast approaching but he was, he said, first of all concerned with the welfare of the university. It was his university, it was a great university, and it could absorb radical change. I was pleased by the attitude and his words. He had convictions and he was not prepared to bargain them away.

The Act that emerged for first reading on June 3 was the result of discussions between White, his deputy minister, E.E. Stewart, Malim Harding, Bill Harris, and me. We retained the relative proportions of the University-wide Committee, but reduced it to fifty, following here (but less severely) the preference of the board. I was generally satisfied. The composition was as follows: sixteen laymen appointed by the government; twelve elected staff members; eight elected alumni; eight elected students (four undergraduates, two graduates, two part-time); two academic officers appointed by the president; two elected representatives of the administrative staff; and the chancellor and president, members *ex officio*. Since the alumni were likely to have close university associations, the outside fifty per cent was more technicality than actuality. The Act preserved the principles endorsed by the University-wide Committee: a single body, and one representative of all groups in the university.

There remained one final skirmish before peace could descend. After first reading the Act was passed on to the human resources committee of the legislature for consideration; there the student radicals saw the chance to revive the old battle about parity. The compromise of last June had faded in memory, along with the spirit of accommodation that had prevailed at the time. Politicians with an election in the offing were sensitive to the youthful vote, (recently greatly enlarged with the reduction of the voting age to eighteen) and conviction waited easily on political expediency. The strong rumour was that the committee would favour student parity with staff, and that the government would incorporate the recommendation in the bill. I knew that the staff would never accept this and would petition the members of the legislature to keep the old system rather than adopt such a compromise.

The discussions dragged on into July. As of July 1 I was no longer in office and my disposition was to keep out of the discussions. But the minister asked me to attend and I agreed, reluctantly, to do so. At the hearing I listened impatiently to hours of wrangling about petty detail, and then left, half-relieved that the big issues were not coming up. James Conacher of the history department, a moderate reformer whom I greatly respected, came out in some distress. 'You aren't going?' he said. 'The students have been misquot-

ing you constantly about parity. We can arrange for you to speak.' I returned
and was immediately asked to speak. The burden of my remarks was as follows: 'I have had a long interest in university-government reform going back
at least to the launching of the Duff-Berdahl commission in 1962. The Act
before you is a good one; it embodies the two basic principles of reform – the
creation of a single centre of authority, and the representation in that centre
of all the principal estates. The differences of opinion you have heard arise out
of the distribution of seats, particularly as between faculty and students.
This should be left to the evolution of opinion in the university. In the meantime, accept the distribution as determined by the University-wide Committee. The key to a successful Act is faculty response – this is the group by
which the university either lives or dies. The university is a teaching and
scholarly enterprise or it is nothing at all. The centrality of the staff must be
recognized in any new Act. This the proposed Act does, although less
significantly than the University-wide Committee report. Student participation is needed: to keep the university sensitive to new developments; to re-
mind us that the time-scale for students is different from the time-scale for
faculty and administration. But we do not know yet how students will function in the tough business of decision-making. So far they have elected to
stay out of central bodies when invited to do so. We need proof of their commitment and ability before we increase their representation. You must remember that the Act before you is the most radical proposed by an English-
speaking university. At the University of Toronto it stands a good chance of
success because behind it lie five years of intense, widespread debate.'

My words had some effect. There were strong voices raised elsewhere
against student parity – from the provincial faculty association, from members of the legislature, and, in particular, from the Toronto newspapers who
were generally enthusiastic about the proposed reforms but unsympathetic
to student demands.

John White abandoned a compromise whereby the students and the staff
would as a body have elected four additional members (bound to be students
and therefore a covert form of parity). The Act was unchanged in fundamen-
tals when it emerged shortly afterwards as legislation.

We now had the kind of government I had talked and written about five
years ago with no thought that it would come in my time. But there were
sobering reflections. No system contained within itself the guarantee of success; that depended on the attitude and qualities of those who were responsible for its implementation. The main responsibility would be on those who
came from within – on staff and students. If either of these groups were
weak, unconcerned, or factious, then the Governing Council would not be
able to govern.

10 / Final Reckonings

When I left office on June 30, 1971, I had no feeling of triumph. In a solemn obituary notice that my old student antagonist, Steven Langdon, wrote for a national magazine, he observed, with the icy brutality of youth, that on my retirement 'no one mourned very much, and no one celebrated very much.' I took some satisfaction in mere survival at a time when university presidents fled for cover or were shot down in the open. If I had become a radical, it had been in the light of a Butlerian observation: 'Reforms and discoveries are like offences; they must needs come, but woe unto that man through whom they come.' And our 'reforms and discoveries' had brought in their train a number of unpleasant developments.

One development of mixed benefit was the heavy emphasis within the university on political discussions. I recalled my own distaste for politics during my undergraduate days and sympathized with students and staff who cried 'enough.' The most painful outcome of this intense political atmosphere was the decline in the old easy relationship between students and administrators and, increasingly, between students and staff. One could, I realized, easily exaggerate the extent and seriousness of the change. In thousands of classes the old entente remained, as I knew from my year of teaching at Harvard. But an administrator, and the president in particular, had to deal with the young student politicians. He could not appeal over their heads to the great silent majority, for the majority was too often not only silent but apathetic and inclined, when finally cajoled into expressing an opinion, to side with youthful friends rather than with remote administrators.

As the president of a large university, my association with students inevitably was generally remote, deadened by numbers and distance. For a number of years I gave a speech in the early fall designed, traditionally, to welcome incoming students, but broadened in my day into a general commentary on the times and an anticipation of basic problems. In the early spring I went to two or three graduation banquets where I would be asked to reply to the toast to the university briefly and lightly. But the day-to-day associations tended to be with the officers of the Students' Administrative Council and other politically oriented students.

In the early years we had retained a tradition developed by Sidney Smith of inviting the Students' Administrative Council each year to the president's house for a buffet supper, followed by a game of charades in which the students opposed the invited administrators and staff. The students were inventive and imaginative; their charades were often big productions in several scenes, with the phrase to be guessed artfully concealed in the foliage of mime and drama. These were evenings of relaxation and pure enjoyment; Christine and I enjoyed them far more than the receptions and buffet suppers for new staff that struggled to break out from stiff formality. Suddenly, around the middle sixties, the Students' Administrative Council party began to lose its charm. The first sign was a request from the students that they have an informal seminar instead of the charades. Christine could not conceal her sense of outrage. It was a blow to her Highland upbringing – pleasure and work should be kept apart, but each should be pursued with single-minded devotion. She thought it incredible for guests to request that a party be turned into a town meeting. I agreed with her. But there was to be no chance to try charades again. By the time we returned from Harvard the Students' Administrative Council had become a tight political party dedicated to the confounding of the administration. A general social evening was out of the question. 'It would be like the mayor of the city,' said Christine, who took a simpler view of student politicians than I, 'inviting the Mafia to a supper dance.'

I abandoned the opening speech in the fall term. I had enjoyed this more than any other public appearance. Convocation Hall would usually be filled, often with a number of the audience seated around me on the stage. We had gradually stripped away all the formalities that had once clung to the occasion, and the mini-procession of deans and directors on to the platform had been abolished. This was entirely the president's half-hour, a chance to talk informally and directly to students. In the first five or six years it was a pleasantly relaxing event – a celebration of youth and hope at the beginning of a new cycle. Then before I left for Harvard some sterner notes began to appear. *The Varsity* complained that I was too complacent and self-congratulatory about what was going on in the university and was missing a great chance to point out the problems and to arouse critical thought. I was a little indignant about these comments, but concluded that *The Varsity* had a point. In the fall of 1968, after the year at Harvard and the rise of student power, I used the occasion to talk as directly as I could about the nature of student radicalism; and despite some half-hearted student attempts at guerilla theatre, succeeded in keeping the audience with me.

That was the last of the opening addresses. I wrote a speech for the fall of 1969, but with the discipline crisis swirling around me, decided not to give it. In part it was a dread of concerted interruption; I recalled the Clark Kerr incident and the terror that arises when the conventions of a public meeting are shattered, when the contract between speaker and audience is violated. In part, it was fear of being the victim of some wild drug-sustained fling.

Unlike the party for the Students' Administrative Council and the opening address, my attendance at graduation banquets continued uninterruptedly. In my final year I went to two – one for graduating students in the Faculty of Applied Science and Engineering, and one for those of University College. The engineers still preserved the old traditions; students in white ties (on the wearing of which they had been formally briefed); favours delivered to the tables – a beer mug for the men and bath salts for the women; toasts carefully prepared and delivered, the staff reading from prepared manuscripts, salting their serious comments with comic references. I reflected that I might be seeing one of the last survivals of the old, genteel, self-confident university. I felt this even more deeply when I went to the University College dinner. uc was my college, and it was fitting that I should go there at the end of my administrative career. I had been asked to speak; to have given a formal address would have been regarded as paternalistic and pompous, so I put together a few reminiscences, part serious, part facetious. When I arrived at the hotel the atmosphere was feebly unpleasant – a general desire to show that nobody felt the affair was important and, in particular, that my presence was of no significance. One of the leaders of the parity group that had been disrupting meetings of the Faculty of Arts and Science, dressed with elaborate sloppiness, his long hair held back by a headband, wandered about distributing marshmallows. The preliminary comments were dispatched quickly; the students made their way through toasts and responses as if they were taking part in a crude anti-masque. I came on unintroduced, raced through my remarks, eliminating pages of manuscript as I proceeded to the accompaniment of laughter and giggling, most of it nervous reaction of those determined not to be impressed. As soon as I had finished, an intense, unscheduled young man took over the microphone, gave the ritual speech about the faceless and impersonal university, and spoke more in sorrow than in anger about my refusal to intervene in the parity battle on the side of justice. 'After all,' he concluded, on an elegiac note, 'he has been fighting the faculty for thirteen years and he is tired.' I was glad to escape.

What I had seen and heard left me with a faint sense of nausea. There was no association with the university and students of my teaching days and I could not see the faintest glimmer of anything that could take its place.

Christine had not accompanied me to this dinner, as she usually did on such occasions. If she had, the black comedy would have confirmed her deepening distaste for the student world. The Clark Kerr incident remained with her indelibly; and she wondered at the endless hours that went into discussion and negotiation with students while more important matters were untouched. That the board had decided to post a permanent guard on our house – no doubt a wise and thoughtful precaution at the time – did not induce a mood of tranquility, even though the guard was usually an elderly man who patrolled the grounds as if he were taking an untroubled stroll in the public gardens.

Towards the end of the academic year, another incident occurred that aroused Clark Kerr associations. The university had charged an undergraduate with breaking down a door during a protest against the suspension of an employee. The accused young man elected to conduct his own defence and released a swarm of subpoenas to senior administrators – a mischievous action in itself since none of us, as the judge quickly pointed out, was a material witness. The student came to our front door to serve the subpoena. I was away and Christine answered; she refused to accept the paper. The student shouted menacingly that she would be in contempt of court if she refused. With the assistance of Bob Young – a genial but muscular member of the university police force assigned to the president's office – she managed to close the door. Again, as in the Clark Kerr incident, there was the same combination of arrogance, self-righteousness, and contempt for others.

In the summer, relaxing in Cape Breton, the burden of the institution lifted, I wrote these lines on Christine's birthday on August 13. Much of the last few years had been painful to her and the lines were written in acknowledgement of her courage and wise patience:

> Tens and twelves are good, round ways of measurement,
> Handy for storekeepers and earnest schoolboys;
> Easily multiplied and divided; round and bland,
> Smooth working parts of the safe, sound system.
> But thirteen is spare and individual; resists the crowd;
> Is looked at askance, even nervously avoided
> By those whose home is the commonplace.
> The thirteen is yours by right of birth
> And by the spirit's choice; for you are maker;
> Thirteen for you is not mere eccentricity,
> But the sign-post of the imagination.

It's thirteen years too, since together
We took up the task, (the 'challenge' in the cheerful jargon),
Pleasant at first, then twisted with anxiety.
You were always gaily for change, but you hated
The bitterness, the cynical betrayals,
The continuous mocking of grace and manners.
Now on this thirteenth, in blessed Sugar Loaf,
Where the eye is stretched by the surrounding sea,
And by the steady, rolling march of the friendly hills,
We unshoulder the burden, raise a glass to the past,
And set out on another thirteen, or two.

The unpleasant student encounters were, one reflected at such times, un-representative experiences. The mass of students were – as they always had been – sceptical of the university, a little resentful of its demands, but basically relaxed and friendly. Moreover, they could, as in the discipline crisis, discover a basic loyalty to the institution and sweep aside factiousness. But it was not easy for the president of a large university to reach the students, and I was always conscious of my remoteness.

II

It was different with the staff. During my years with Sidney Smith I had developed a network of friends and associates and was at home in any academic gathering. In the late sixties, admittedly, when we were acquiring new staff in numbers never dreamt of before, I felt I was losing this sense of easy citizenship in the academic world. Friends and colleagues became the 'Old Guard' and the new young staff were as anonymous and puzzling as the students – they didn't know about the Toronto traditions and they had no sense of loyalty to the institution. Their services had been requested and they gave them on their own terms. I was, however, known as a 'faculty man,' and except on the one occasion in October 1968 I never lost the sense of staff support.

There were, it is true, grumblings from both the left and the right among the faculty. When the University of Toronto Press published a selection of my speeches, Abraham Rotstein of the department of political economy, apostle of radical nationalism, wrote a review – 'The makings of a President' – in which he suggested that I was an attitudinizer with some gift for phrase-making, and dismissed my reform attempts as both feeble and impractical. The faculty in general were, moreover, not pleased by the recommendations of the Commission on University Government on student participation in appointments, and the 'High and Dry' Party – those who shuddered at the very thought of a student coming near to a teacher's dossier – were incensed. But there was no concerted attack, possibly because the faculty realized that they had been partially responsible for making the Commission on University Government into a simple parity committee and thereby had constricted the area in which compromises could be found.

During the long, intense discussions of university government, the staff had responded vigorously. They had sustained the momentum of the argument and had carried it to a conclusion. Yet they were aware, as was I, that there were other issues that were possibly even more important to them; and some of the malaise of the early seventies arose from a feeling that these issues had been given insufficient attention. First among them was the issue of the curriculum, which had been placed starkly before the university in the report of the Presidential Advisory Committee on Undergraduate Instruction in the Faculty of Arts and Science.

I had been responsible for the setting up of that committee, for the choice of its chairman, Professor Brough Macpherson, for the emphasis in its make-up on young faculty without vested interests in the present curriculum structure, and for the inclusion of a student member. I had also emphasized the wide range of the committee's task; it was to go beyond the curriculum and look at the values and assumptions of the Faculty of Arts and Science. But, having established the committee, I withdrew; and during the year when the report was under discussion, I was absent at Harvard. By the time I returned the report had been filtered down through another committee into a number of specific recommendations, and I was lost in the dense undergrowth of departmental politics that surrounded its implementation.

The report was a revolutionary document, more revolutionary in many ways than the report of the Commission on University Government which it preceded by over a year. Its principal recommendation was that the system of honours courses should be abolished. That system consisted of thirty specialized programs linked closely to individual academic departments. It formed a world of its own; students entered an honours course with special qualifications and were made the peculiar concern of the department involved, spending four years for the BA as opposed to the three required of students in the general course. The indictment of the system was that it created two academic classes – one specially favoured, the other undernourished. Moreover, even for those students admitted to an honours course, there were grievous penalties: a high failure rate during the first year arising in part from too early specialization; great difficulty in transferring to other programs; and a degree of specialization which amounted frequently to a form of professionalism.

The case against the system was strong and it was made with calm, irresis-

tible logic. It was a logic that many of the staff refused to accept. I felt great
sympathy for them. I shared the traditional belief that the peculiar distinction of Toronto was its honours system. It attracted superior students and
gave our best graduates an automatic primacy in any senior graduate school.
I did not believe that the courses were over-specialized, particularly in the
humanities; and, at any rate, specialization was a catch-word of derogation
for a thorough mastery of a major discipline. Graduates of honours courses
had not been inhibited from entering professions or following careers that
had no connection with their former work.

Nevertheless, I sadly concluded that the days of the honours course were
numbered. In the current anti-elitist atmosphere, we couldn't continue a policy based on the slighting of half the student population in our largest faculty. Was it possible to abolish the old qualitative distinctions and still retain standards? The Macpherson report thought so and argued about the
need to level up rather than level down. There were doubts about this –
doubts buttressed by regrets about the disappearance of old ways and the
crumbling of vested interests. Thus, I was emotionally committed to the old
ways but intellectually convinced that they must change. I had always believed that the president should be chary of interfering in curricular disputes,
since he could rarely speak from immediate experience. In addition, I had always been indifferent to curricular detail. No amount of ingenious manipu-
lation of courses, I thought, could produce the educated person. It might be
that after an initial period of strain and confusion, the new, unrestricted
proposals would lead to programs of greater depth and certainly of less rigidity than we had known before. In the meantime, among some of the best of
the staff there was bitterness and resentment, and freely expressed fears of
an academic disaster of unexampled scope and intensity.

Another source of faculty disquiet was the attention directed towards the
university by the resurgent nationalism of the late sixties. Toronto was not
so vulnerable as the new universities, which during the period of rapid expansion had been compelled to turn to the United States for a high proportion
of their staff. But from the nationalist point of view we were at fault in the
social sciences where, in such subjects as anthropology, psychology, and
sociology, American citizens either made up the majority or formed a dominant group of the departmental staff. Toronto was deficient too, the
nationalists held, in courses devoted to Canadian literature and culture and I,
as a student of literature, was held by some responsible.

The nationalistic attack was, however, only a minor irritant. The direction
of the university, both in the central office and in almost all the divisions,
was firmly in the hands of Canadians who had received their first degree in
Canada; and the intellectual leadership of the university – I thought of

Northrop Frye, Marshall McLuhan, Charles Best, Harry Welsh, Don Creighton, Tuzo Wilson, Brough Macpherson, Douglas LePan, Robertson Davies – was predominantly Canadian. Now that our graduate schools were properly supported, an increasing number of staff would in the future have both first and advanced degrees from Canadian institutions. Canadians were finally learning that they could be their own guardians of quality. There would always be a proportion of scholars whose roots were in another country. I was concerned not so much by the slight increase in American citizens on the staff (in the whole of the university it was now fourteen per cent) as by the decline in the staff from the UK (to about nine per cent). Traditionally, staff from the United Kingdom tended to adapt easily to Toronto and they brought with them a concern for standards and a liberal humanism that was part of the Toronto tradition.

Discussions of curriculum and staff qualifications had always been a main academic fare. They furnished the substance for animated talk in common rooms and faculty dining halls. But the sudden change in the financial picture was not a subject for light banter. Suddenly the problem was not that of allotting new money for new ventures, but of using old money to contain inflation and to support the basic, additional needs that a vigorous institution generates.

The university's income was tied to enrolment, and enrolment on the main campus was by my final year as president levelling off; there could be no large annual increase in resources. Staff hiring came to a halt; indeed, the university sought ways of reducing the staff that had been taken on in the years of rapid expansion (a renewed staff emphasis on tenure was related to this economy drive), and the university looked critically at any request for funds not related to a basic curricular need. In this atmosphere of dour economy it was particularly irksome to be told by politicians and newspapers that the university had been profligate and should address itself to stern economies, to greater productivity or, as the minister for university affairs briskly put it, to turning out 'more scholars for the dollar.' Some of the attack on the grounds of financial inefficiency was an overflow from the years of student turmoil, from resentment at the refusal of the university administration 'to throw the young bastards out.' Doubtless there had been some inefficiency in the manner by which we had in the sixties met demands that far exceeded expectations, although, by comparison with government and business, the university way was a tough one, where expense accounts were rare, senior administrators assumed that evenings and weekends were part of the normal work week, and new buildings rarely departed from a norm of strict utility. The charge of inefficiency was usually bound up with vague stories of 'costly duplication' of courses and resources among institutions. With the introduction of the formula financing system, which was based on student numbers, and the sudden, unexpected decline in the rate of enrolment, there was, it is true, a lively competition for students, presumably not altogether a bad thing in a society that valued the competitive instinct as a promoter of excellence. But there was a minimum of duplication in the expensive professional areas, and a reluctance to take on any new professional obligations.

The attack on the university for its inefficiency and extravagance came at a time when doubts were rising among economists about the necessary relationship of university education to personal or public prosperity. One could tolerate a touch of extravagance when the profits were thought to be high; but now that the profits were brought into question, one must insist on ruthless reductions. Obviously the university had been exploiting a set of false assumptions and it must be disciplined. The newspapers gravely accepted the task of chastising the improvident upstarts. For a number of years now the press had been generous in its attitude to the university – supporting university campaigns, urging speedy government action to provide facilities for expansion. During the days of student dissent the newspapers had dealt with explosive and emotional problems in a responsible way. (One could not blame them if they sometimes became promotion agencies for student leaders; the students made good copy and were greedy for headlines.) Now little in the universities pleased the newspapers, and the University of Toronto was a conspicuous target.

The sins of the university were many and grievous: professors ignored the little teaching they had to do to pursue private gain, or to establish themselves in their disciplines; every slight physical expansion of a large urban university like Toronto was a threat to a neighbouring area (although ten years earlier expansion on a huge scale was hailed as a great contribution to humane planning); in this frontier country where men had learned to live by bread alone, universities were guilty of wasting public money by putting up big libraries. The mass media, public attitudes, and political expediency moved towards one simple conviction: the universities were rich, powerful, and, in many of their activities, frivolous and wasteful, and they should be curbed and controlled.

The agent for control was obviously the provincial government. All the power was now in provincial hands, since, at the federal-provincial meetings in 1966, the federal government had, in effect, abandoned its direct concern for higher education. Like an estranged husband it had agreed to a large alimony payment on condition that the wife accepted responsibility for a numerous and difficult family. The total amount of money available for higher education was now plainly visible, and it was a sum large enough to arouse the concern of even the most phlegmatic provincial treasurer. The provincial structure, both among the universities and in the government, became more elaborate. The universities tried to work out common policies and to rationalize expansion on a provincial basis, but they drew back from any structure that might be looked on as a move towards a University of Ontario. The government felt no such inhibitions. In university affairs, the advisory committee seemed to merge with the government department. More decisions were made bureaucratically, without prior discussion with the universities; and the official rhetoric shifted from respect for university autonomy to complaint about university intransigence.

All these developments were predictable, given the sudden shift to provincial responsibility and the necessity of finding methods to regulate the development of a system. The dialogue between the government and the universities was not abandoned. The atmosphere, however, changed radically. Principles were consumed by statistics. Institutions were swallowed up in quantitative measurement. Provincial meetings sounded more like a conference of marketing experts than a meeting of educators.

I found this atmosphere increasingly depressing. I liked to think that I had acquired a certain degree of agility in dealing with basic income units, weighted averages, and gross cubic feet, but I shrank from some of the more elaborate formulae as from a poisonous snake. At one of the final provincial meetings I attended, I recorded my sentiments:

> Banish all vanities,
> Down with humanities:
> The Bible's
> Not viable;
> The classics
> Are spastic;
> English Lit's
> A Misfit.
> If you can't measure it
> Don't treasure it.
>
> Here's the suture
> To bind up the future:
> Rationalize;
> Categorize;
> Disaggregate;
> Eliminate.

Confound gentility
Raise productivity;
Sharpen your bent
For the relevant.
If assumptions muddy
Try in-depth study;
If in a mental fog –
Meaningful dialogue.
Hopefully results will be
Stark as the GNP.
Sing not old alma mater
But a firm indicator.

If the system absorbed the institution, if each university became a smooth part of a large machine, Canada would lose a principal line of defence against uniformity and facelessness. With all its defects – its tortured self-doubts, its endless hesitations, its constant cynical juxtaposition of the ideal and the actual – the university remained the institution that reminded man most insistently of the need for the examined life. To the extent that the developments of the last few years had weakened the foundations of the university and had endangered its future as an institution, they had done harm.

III

Had these developments harmed the University of Toronto? In the summer of 1971, there was some cause for taking a dark view, provided one permitted immediate discontents to blot out the past. And this was easy enough to do. For the university, despite its high stake in the past, was a constantly changing society, inclined to immerse itself in the immediate. It was all the more urgent, from time to time, to look back, and to get a perspective on the immediate issues.

The first ten years of my term of office were the final period of the old feudalistic university based upon rigid assumptions that went unquestioned. But they were also years of great achievement – a final triumphant flowering of the old regime. The university may have been feudalistic in its structure, but it was sustained by nineteenth century liberalism: the belief in progress through knowledge, and the striving for objectivity through balanced support from private business and the state. The system had many advantages. Because of the hierarchical structure, initiatives could be strongly exercised at the top, and the period from 1958 to 1968 reverberated with action. The faculty seemed for the most part happy with the compact whereby they handed over power to a lay board in return for safety, security, and the illusion of freedom in a separate, protected kingdom; the students accepted distinctions on the basis of measured intellectual achievement, and student awards were based on these distinctions.

There was, during the period, a mood of optimism, and the sense of a great intellectual ferment. McLuhan's seminars in the fifties prepared the way for his two basic books – *The Gutenberg Galaxy* and *Understanding Media*. Frye, after his two big literary studies in the forties and fifties, *Fearful Symmetry* and *The Anatomy of Criticism*, emerged in the sixties as the twentieth century Matthew Arnold – concerned with culture and society. In the social sciences, Vincent Bladen's two reports, one on university financing and one on the automobile industry, had a wide impact, and the Watkins report on foreign ownership and the structure of Canadian industry gave substance to the nationalist debate. Toronto social scientists played important roles in two other commissions of the sixties, the Carter Commission on Taxation and the Commission on Bilingualism and Biculturalism. The staff were also active abroad: they constituted almost a second civil service when Tanzania was emerging, and supported educational and other development in many other parts of the Third World. This was also the period when the specialized institutes were established, and they thrust themselves with vigour into the hurly burly of the immediate. The Great Lakes Institute fought pollution long before it became a popular rallying cry; the Shade Tree Laboratory in the Faculty of Forestry developed an effective method of combatting the Dutch Elm Tree disease; the Centre for Criminology opened windows in some of the more fetid chambers of law and penology. Finally, and from my point of view most important, all of the major decisions on the expansion of the colleges and of the library system were made before 1968.

This period was also the peaking of the old presidency – the double ambassadorship, from the business to the academic world, and from the academic to the business world. There was a multitude of major decisions to be made about people and policy with the likelihood that the decisions would be accepted and implemented. There was a secure campus so that the president could accept responsibilities away from the campus. I was chairman of the Canada Council from 1960 to 1962, and I found then that the work, although demanding, complemented my presidential duties. I went to China in 1962 for a month, along with Geoffrey Andrew, at that time the deputy to the president of the University of British Columbia. We were the guests of the Chinese government when any visit of westerners constituted a form of ambassadorship. In the springs of 1966 and 1967 I was the only Canadian taking part in seminars in Colombia and Chile at which South American rectors discussed university problems with North American presidents.

The period closed with a remarkable example of community co-operation in the Teach-Ins. At the time we had a sense of confidence and optimism; the university had moved into the heart of the major issues and had done so in a spirit of unity and self-confidence.

After 1968 the basis of the old structure began to crumble: the hierarchical separation was challenged, first by the staff and then by the students; the alliance of the university with business and government was attacked, on the left from staff and students, who saw it as corrupting, and on the right by government, who rejected an alliance of partners and called for a master-servant relationship; the sanctity of knowledge was questioned and new qualities were exalted – sensitivity, involvement, a feeling of community solidarity. University education was thought of not as something to be earned by the sweat of the brow or by the superior performance in examinations; it was a natural right and, therefore, should be subsidized.

The years from 1968 to 1971 were directed almost entirely to attempts to adapt the new ideas to the old concept of the university. These were years of turmoil and long, drawn-out efforts at compromise. The university was starkly visible to society. It became an advanced political seminar in a generally conservative environment. The public saw the 'sit-ins,' the occasional violence, the apparent capitulations to student disorder, but did not see the dialectic of action, response, and synthesis.

The revolution between 1968 and 1971 was, in essence, the opening up of the university. The university lost its rigid hierarchical structure (although the distinction between various estates remained and even sharpened); it lost its protected position in society, with the end of business control and the growth of government suspicions. The university was now, in a sense, on its own. Autonomy was no longer a grace automatically bestowed; it had to be won in the dust and heat of the arena; and a long, tough road lay ahead. Within, dissident elements must be reconciled, and a strong, rational centre created to speak for the whole; outside, the university must greatly expand and intensify its program of explanation, and work out more direct, specific means of relating scholarship to social action.

But the revolution had not disturbed the central academic core of the university. It retained a capacity for electric diversity. It had a bent for exploring the high points on the frontier, whether it was medieval culture, or the mathematics of outer space, or the seismic movement of the earth, or the structure of the creative imagination, or the impact of technological change, or the syntax of the Chinese language, or the metaphysics of Canadian nationhood. Its group of internationally known scholars was constantly being replenished from the ranks of the young. The building of the library was a declaration of our scholarly commitment.

The immediate vexations were not signs of weakness and confusion; they were the by-products of a necessary struggle. I had the feeling that the university had cleared away the debris of the past, and was ready to deal with the besetting problems. And despite the tensions of the last five years, I had never doubted that the complex and mysterious institution could always draw upon resources of wisdom. The great good place of my youth had gone forever, but a new place – more clamorous, but more vital – was emerging.

Index

Lightning Source UK Ltd.
Milton Keynes UK
UKHW030613210722
406167UK00006B/653